RUBÁIYÁT OF OMAR KHAYYÁM

Type of work : Philosophical Poem
Translator : Edward FitzGerald (1809–1883)

Rubai means a poem of four lines called quatrain. Rubaiyat is the plural of Rubai.

Omar Khayyam (1050–1132) was Persian scientist and poet. Khayyam lived in Khurasan as a renowned mathematician, astronomer and philosopher. Omar's Rubaiyat, written in a clear, concise and epigrammatic style and in a meditative vein, reveals his mind as concerned with the perennial questions of life and the universe. He reflects on the frailty of human existence, the cruelty of fate and the ignorance of man.

Finding no solution, he turns to a vivid appreciation of earthly, sensuous beauties and preaches 'eat, drink and be merry' as a panacea.

Edward FitzGerald (1809–1883) was an English poet and translator. His translatiosn from Persian, Spanish and Greek were a poet's recreation, and he is remembered for the Rubaiyat, exotic versian of Victorian pessimism and for the ease and wit of his letters.

Khayyam owes much of his popularity in the west to FitzGerald's ingenious metrical paraphrase of the Rubaiyat.

EDWARD FITZGERALD
1809–1883

RUBÁIYÁT OF
OMAR KHAYYÁM

RENDERED INTO ENGLISH VERSE BY

EDWARD FITZGERALD

followed by
EUPHRANOR
A DIALOGUE ON YOUTH

and

SALÁMÁN AND ABSÁL
AN ALLEGORY TRANSLATED FROM
THE PERSIAN OF JÁMI

Edited by
GEORGE F. MAINE

With an Introduction by
LAURENCE HOUSMAN

RUPA

Published by
Rupa Publications India Pvt. Ltd 2000
7/16, Ansari Road, Daryaganj
New Delhi 110002

Sales centres:
Allahabad Bengaluru Chennai
Hyderabad Jaipur Kathmandu
Kolkata Mumbai

This is a work of fiction. Names, characters, places and incidents are either the product of the author's imagination or are used fictitiously and any resemblance to any actual person, living or dead, events or locales is entirely coincidental.

ISBN: 978-81-716-7439-8

Ninth impression 2019

15 14 13 12 11 10 9

Printed at Yash Printographics, Noida

RUBÁIYÁT OF
OMAR KHAYYÁM

EDWARD FITZGERALD

EDWARD FITZGERALD was born on March 31st 1809 at the White House, between Woodbridge and Bredfield village, about seven miles north-east of Ipswich. He was the seventh of the eight children of John Purcell, a country gentleman, who in 1801 had marrried his own first cousin, Mary Frances FitzGerald, daughter and heir of John Fitz-Gerald, a man of great wealth owning the ancient FitzGerald estate, Little Island in the Waterford River as well as estates in Northamptonshire, Suffolk, Lancashire and Staffordshire. On the death of his father-in-law in 1818, John Purcell assumed the name and arms of FitzGerald.

Both the families of Purcell and FitzGerald were of Anglo-Norman descent. The Purcells had entered England at the time of the Norman conquest and settled in Ireland in the 12th century; the FitzGeralds traced their lineage from Otho Geraldino a trusted commander under William the Conqueror; they were among the most powerful and illustrious families of Ireland, holders since 1316 of the earldom of Kildare which later was merged with the dukedom of Leinster. Edward FitzGerald's parents lived in great style. They owned a town house in London, a manor house at Naseby, Northamptonshire, and several other estates. They travelled and they entertained lavishly. In later years, however, much of their fortune was lost in a coalmining venture.

Edward FitzGerald received his first schooling at a private school in Woodbridge, and in 1816 accompanied his parents to France (St. Germain and Paris) where, during the next two years, he was tutored in French. After the family's return to England, he and his brothers John and Peter were sent to the Edward VI Grammar School at Bury St. Edmunds. There he formed a number of friendships which were to last a lifetime e.g., with W. B. Donne (a descendant of John Donne), James Spedding and J. M. Kemble. In October 1826 he entered Trinity College, Cambridge. He spent three most agreeable years at the University, devoting himself—as was then the custom with wealthier students—with greater zeal to the pleasures of social life than to the pursuit of learning. Among his contemporaries—some of whom later became his close friends—were John Allen, later Archdeacon of Salop, William Hepworth Thompson, afterwards Master of Trinity, Charles Merivale, later Dean of Ely, Richard Trench, later Archbishop of Dublin, the brothers Frederick, Charles and Alfred Tennyson, and W. M. Thackeray.

Having obtained his degree in February 1830, he journeyed to Paris where, in the company of Thackeray, he spent a few interesting and instructive months. After his return to England, he stayed first at Southampton and subsequently in London, Wherstead in Suffolk (which had become his parents' principal country residence), Cambridge and Naseby. At Naseby in 1831, he wrote *The Meadows in Spring*, the first of his works to be published. It appeared in *Hone's Yearbook* in April 1831 and again in the *Athenaeum* in July.

Financially independent and possessed of no special ambitions, he chose to lead the 'good life,' the essence of which, so it seemed to him, was admirably summed up in the

Wordsworthian principle of 'plain living and high thinking. Accordingly, observing frugal habits and cultivating his mind by reflection, leisurely studies, and in the congenial company of like-minded friends, he roamed about England for several years, with no fixed abode except some humble lodgings in London, staying at times in Cambridge or visiting his parents' country home and the homes of friends and relatives in various counties.

Like many young men of his generation he was deeply interested in, and at times greatly disturbed by those implications of modern scientific discoveries and theories which appeared to be in conflict with the dogmas and teachings of the Christian religion. Lively debates on these questions were carried on between him and his friends. Among his most intimate friends of those years were Thackeray, Allen, Spedding and Alfred Tennyson.

In 1837 he took possession of a cottage on the estate of Boulge Hall near Bredfield, which his father had recently acquired. Boulge Cottage became the pivot on which his life was to turn for the next sixteen years. Throughout those years he continued his peregrinations, spending the summers mostly at Geldestone, Norfold, the home of his eldest sister Mrs. Kerrich. He regularly saw his old friends and acquired new ones, notably Bernard Barton, the Quaker poet, George Crabbe, Vicar of Bredfield, Edward Byles Cowell, then a young Oriental scholar who later became Professor of Sanskrit at Cambridge and who induced him to study Spanish and Persian, William Kenworthy Browne, and Thomas Carlyle. When at Boulge Cottage he lived quietly, reading, wrting, and supervising his father's estates.

In 1849 Bernard Barton died. FitzGerald edited his poems and letters and wrote a short biography of his friend which he published the same year as *Memoir of Bernard Barton.*

Two years later he was launched on his literary career with the publication of *Euphranor*, a criticism in dialogue form of the English system of education. Within the next five years he published a longer version of the dialogue and three new works, *Polonius*, an anthology of aphorisms on many topics (1852); *Six Dramas of Calderon* freely translated from the Spanish (1853), and a translation from the Persian of the allegorical poem *Sálámán and Absál* (1856). FitzGerald had taken up the study of Persian at Oxford in 1852 under Cowell's supervision, and as soon as he had mastered the grammar began to study Persian literature, especially the ancient Persian poets. The translation of *Sálámán* was his first 'little monument' to his Persian studies.

In 1848 his father's mining venture ended in a bankruptcy court with the loss of most of his fortune as well as the fortunes of others who had shared in the enterprise. FitzGerald found himself financially reduced for several years until he came into his inheritance on the death of his mother in 1855. In 1853 he gave up his cottage at Boulge, and resumed his migratory existence. In 1856 he married Lucy Barton, the daughter of his late friend. However, he and his wife were in every way totally unsuited to each other, and after six months of discord and ever mounting tension, the ill-conceived marriage ended in permanent separation.

In 1856 Cowell discovered the rubáiyát or quatrains of Omar Khayyám in a Persian manuscript in the Bodleian Library at Oxford, and made a transcript for FitzGerald. In July 1857 the latter began the translation, completing it six months later. *Fraser's Magazine* refused to publish a selection of thirty-five of the stanzas. On April 9th, 1859 the first book edition of 250 copies of the *Rubáiyát of Omar Khayyám*, printed and produced at FitzGerald's expense, was issued at a shilling a copy by the London bookseller Bernard Quaritch. The edition lay on the shelves for almost two years and was finally 'dumped' at a penny a copy. Then suddenly the merit of the work was discovered by Rosetti, Swinburne, Burne-Jones, William Morris, Ruskin and others, and introduced to America by Charles Eliot Norton. Further editions appeared, and by the turn of the century the work had become a mania which swept the world. Edward FitzGerald was not acknowledged as the translator until 1875.

From 1860 to 1873 FitzGerald made his headquarters in lodgings at Woodbridge, Suffolk, spending his summers mostly by the sea at Lowestoft and other places on the East Coast. He loved the company of fishermen and sailors, and sailing became one of his favourite hobbies. He purchased a small yacht which he named *Scandal* and later entered into a herring-fishing partnership with Joseph Fletcher, a Lowestoft fisherman in whose welfare he took a paternal interest.

At the same time he steadily pursued his literary and scholarly interests, reading the Greek and Latin classics, editing, writing, and making translations from the Persian and Spanish, and from Æschylus and Sophocles. In 1874 he moved from his lodgings in Woodbridge to a house in the same town which he had purchased and enlarged some years previously. There, at Little Grange, he spent the remainder of his life.

During his last years he was engaged on three works which he left unfinished. The first was a selection of Dryden's prefaces; the second a dictionary of Madame de Sevigné's Letters which was eventually completed by his great-niece in 1914; the third was a biography of Charles Lamb. In spite of gradually failing health, his mode of life did not change much, and he kept up his numerous friendships by personal contact and by correspondence, to the very end. His claim to a permanent place in English literature rests, perhaps, as much on his letters as on his translation of the *Rubáiyát*.

He died while on a visit to George Crabbe (junior) Rector of Merton, on June 14th 1883, and was buried in the churchyard at Boulge.

H. d. R.

CONTENTS

INTRODUCTION

Laurence Housman

INTRODUCTION

For the great bulk of English readers—if in this connection a 'great bulk' of readers can be predicated—the *Rubáiyát* of Omar Khayyám means the one particular translation done so divinely well by Edward FitzGerald, when the Victorian era was at its most self-centred and self-sufficient stage of development.

The poem made so little mark on its first appearance—so little mark with the critics and the general public, that is to say—that the original edition, passing out of sight, became presently a delightful rarity for the next generation of second-hand book lovers to unearth, for the high appreciation in two kinds which was then awaiting it—the literary and the monetary. And it remains essentially, like all other translations—even the authorised version of the Bible—a second-hand book.

For the translator of poetry and vision always stands between us and the original. And whatever the beauty, or the exact meaning of the original may have been, in this case we can hardly doubt that, for English minds, the translator has given to it a reconciling beauty and flavour of his own, which make it more acceptable to all but scholars or pedants.

Of this, indeed, we have proof in the very free and pliant variants of the rival versions—the earlier and the later—

which are so fortunately available; and it is only necessary to compare FitzGerald's amended form of the opening stanza with his original, to realise how large a liberty he gave himself when rendering into English the richly-coloured similes of the East.

Wake! For the Sun behind yon Eastern height
Has chased the Session of the Stars from Night;
And, to the field of Heav'n ascending, strikes
The Sultán's Turret with a Shaft of Light.

That is one version; this is the other, and the earlier—:

Awake! for Morning in the Bowl of Night
Has flung the Stone that puts the Stars to Flight:
And Lo! the Hunter of the East has caught
The Sultán's Turret in a Noose of Light.

Both are charming—many, I think, would hold that the earlier is the better; but the existence of variants so widely different informs us definitely that FitzGerald's rendering is an inspired paraphrase rather than a translation. What he began doing—westernising, the better to acclimatise, his importation from Persia in the eleventh to England in the nineteenth century—he went on doing with added touches and second thoughts throughout his elaboration of the whole poem: the strange similes, in the earlier version of the stanza just quoted, are softened and made more graceful in the amended one. And still more strikingly is this shown in the first line of the stanza which follows, where the fantastic imagery of the earlier version—

Dreaming, when Dawn's Left Hand was in the sky—

becomes changed to the more graceful but more ordinary—

Before the phantom of False Morning died.

Probably, in the present day, we could have stood, and even welcomed, a good deal more of the bizarrerie of Eastern fancy, under the smooth and almost perfect diction of FitzGerald's presentation of it, than he allowed to remain in his more finished version. But FitzGerald, though a recluse in his day, was still a Victorian—of an unusual kind; and it was in a Victorian direction that he gave himself a free hand, and introduced, as will presently be shown, arguments which had in them the hectic touch of European theology rather than the bland, imperturbable acquiescence of the East.

And so, as we read it, this fortunate paraphrase, so full of ease and grace, so supple in its diction and its imagery, makes us forget—as we never forget in reading a translation of Homer or Dante, however good—that it is a translation, and that we are listening at a far remove, to a school of thought much more alien in its mode of expression than the skilful artifice of this version allows us to feel. FitzGerald, by his superlative tact, has done us the favour of deceiving us, making either the East seem West, or the West seem East, in a sympathy of thought and feeling which, at that time, had hardly begun to exist.

But for all its suavity and grace, this gospel of flesh versus spirit, coming in the midst of that very church-going Victorian age, should by its content, one might think, have caused a shock almost as great as Darwin's *Origin of Species* or Swinburne's *Poems and Ballads*. Perhaps being only a translation made its challenge less evident; but there the challenge was; and though for the time thrown down into the rubble of the second-hand book box (price one penny) as a thing too insignificant for notice, its significance grew more apparent as time went on; and when it touches its centenary in 1959, it will almost certainly have lasted better than *In Memoriam*, which—its predecessor by ten years—might in a sense be regarded as the rival oracular pronouncement of that day on the problem of life after death.

For these two poems appeared at a time when, while religious convention was still rampant, religious belief was beginning to seek new supports for the faith that was in it, though the outlook which is now called 'modernist' had scarcely begun.

Faith, in the Victorian age (we see it now) was a sort of St. Paul's Cathedral, which—though not perceptibly to the general eye—was beginning to shift on its foundations; and while it still held up an imposing façade, the under-pinning process had already started, and reconstruction was becoming inevitable.

It was at this juncture that these two poems appeared, both of an elegiac character—though it is not as an elegy that the *Rubáiyát* is generally regarded. *In Memoriam*, while incidentally written to commemorate the death of a friend, was in substance an elegy on a disintegrating form of faith, which in Tennyson's estimation could no longer be held by men of open mind, but only by their sisters. And with considerable perturbation of spirit, and not without a certain distrust of that larger hope which he professes, Tennyson lets his weaker sister go to the wall under which she can still find shelter, and builds up for the rest his main thesis that immortality must surely be awaiting us, because it would have been so unfair of God to allow the human race to form false expectations.

The *Rubáiyát*—a more serene, more cheerful, and more contented document—is an elegy on all faiths whatsoever. It states its case with a certain touch of melancholy, but without any cry of distress. Too resigned to be poignant, too philosophical to be bitter about it, it dismisses the dream, and accepts with appetite—almost with gratitude—what is left.

That, at least, seems clearly the thesis of the original. But though FitzGerald keeps up well his western end of it, and makes a brave show of not caring, it is on this very point that, here and there, the influence of his Victorian environment, with its sharpening interrogative, begins to creep in.

The Ball no question makes of Ayes and Noes,
But Right or Left, as strikes the Player, goes.

There is the good, wise example set before us; but immediately, and in the same stanza. FitzGerald himself departs from it, and asserts very emphatically that there is a Somebody outside who—

Knows about it all—He knows—HE knows!

And then, having asserted the existence of the Knowing One, he proceeds to rub in once more the impotence of human destiny:—

With Earth's first Clay They did the Last Man's knead,
And then of the Last Harvest sowed the Seed:
And the first Morning of Creation wrote
What the Last Dawn of Reckoning shall read.

And thus launched on the high seas of Calvinism, he goes on further to adumbrate, for indignant protest, the possibility that divine punishment may be in store for those who enjoy life in their own way.

What! out of senseless Nothing to provoke
A conscious Something to resent the yoke
Of unpermitted Pleasure, under pain
Of Everlasting Penalties, if broke!

And so—leading up in a crescendo of indignation—to that famous final apostrophe:—

Oh, Thou, who Man of baser Earth didst make,
And who with Eden didst devise the Snake;
For all the Sin wherewith the Face of Man
Is blacken'd, Man's forgiveness give—and take!

Now here it is pretty evident that FitzGerald has caused his Omar to stumble against the Deity begotten by the theologians of Geneva; and his voice vibrates with passion, and his war-whoop is the war-whoop of a Victorian letting himself loose, because he has not the far, wise mind which can see ahead for a generation or two, and can afford to be patient and smile over a mirage that has only lasted for a few hundred years.

And so we see that though FitzGerald might be in revolt against the theology of his day, he could not indifferently escape it as though it did not exist. His Persian carpet was not so magic as to waft him away entirely from his 'suburb grange' to the singing rose gardens of Naishápúr.

But for all that he gave to English literature something that was new, beautiful, and permanent. Steadily through changing schools of expression, and changing interest in matters of technique, the form of expression here chosen has commended itself to minds differently trained, differently attuned, and still to its purpose seems perfect.

More than that: it would be difficult to name any single poem—long or short—written during the last hundred years which has so taken hold of the thought of succeeding generations, not necessarily for agreement with its ethical content, but for recognition. To a thesis which, without it, might have seemed soulless—materialism run to seed—it has given a dignity, a grace, and a logical force which 'orthodoxy' must reckon with. It is harder than it was formerly to damn a man theologically for believing that, in this life, life as we see it is the only true guide.

For in the Market-place, one Dusk of Day,
I watch'd the Potter thumping his wet Clay;
And with its all obliterated Tongue
It murmur'd, 'Gently, Brother, gently, pray!'

And has not such a story from of old
Down Man's successive generations rolled
Of such a clod of saturated Earth
Cast by the Maker into Human mould?

The argument is too humanly persuasive for our minds to escape from it. Without believing so much in the Potter —or pretending to know so much about Him as did the theologians of Geneva—here is a writer, a divine, who helps us to think better of Him, and to be sure—if He exists—that He is not so black as the theologians have painted him.

But while he gives us this certificate of the Potter's good character, and His kindly treatment of the clay—as clay, it is but a negative goodness of which he assures us; and that, some are inclined to think, is not enough for the Potter Himself to rest content with.

That is the crucial point where the philosophy of Omar and FitzGerald stops short; they make a guess that the Potter exists, but they don't quite like to guess that He is as good as they are—and as interested in life. And so, while the Ayes and the Noes of this problem of human existence still entangle them more than they are aware, the Noes generally have it; and it is significant, I think, that at the one point in the whole poem where FitzGerald breaks form, and, for the sake of added emphasis, inserts a redundant rhyme, the word he goes out of his way to insert is—'Lies.'

Oh, come with old Khayyám, and leave the Wise
To talk; one thing at least is certain, that Life flies:
One thing is certain and the Rest is Lies;
The Flower that once has blown for ever dies.

There is an honest man overstating his case. Tennyson had a 'larger hope' which he did not call a certainty; but he was not a liar for holding it. I myself am more inclined to share the doubts of FitzGerald and Omar than the hopes of Tennyson, but I am by no means sure about it. Also the Potter may be improving in the manipulation of His material. Who knows? We have the authority of FitzGerald for saying that the Potter Himself knows. If, then, the Potter is really improving in His craft, something more may come of it; we may even come to share His knowledge, without being adjudged 'liars.'

LAURENCE HOUSMAN

EDWARD FITZGERALD

THE MAN AND HIS WORKS

G. F. Maine

THE MAN

EDWARD FITZGERALD, the seventh of a family of eight children, three of whom were boys, was born on March 31st, 1809, at Bredfield House, a late Jacobean building standing in its own park of sixty-five acres, near Woodbridge, Suffolk. His father, John Purcell, was the son of a wealthy Irish doctor. His mother, Mary Frances FitzGerald Purcell, also came of a well-to-do family, and when her father died in 1818 leaving her the whole of his fortune, her husband assumed the name of FitzGerald. They were first cousins. The family lived in great splendour. They had a town house in London, at least four estates in the country, and at the age of seven Edward enjoyed the advantages of spending two years in St. Germain and Paris. When twelve years of age he was sent to King Edward VI Grammar School, Bury St. Edmunds, and in 1826, when he was seventeen, he went up to Trinity College, Cambridge. From 1826 until 1835 the family lived at Wherstead Lodge, which stands on high ground overlooking the river Orwell some two miles south of Ipswich, and during those years Edward was a familiar figure in the town. His favourite haunt was the second-hand book shop kept by James Read, who supplied him with fuel for the mind and the imagination and became his lifelong friend.

FitzGerald had an engaging personality which found

expression in the tastes of the patrician, the way of life of the scholar and the habits of the bohemian. He was too much the individualist ever to become blighted by respectability, but a delicate fastidiousness kept him aloof from undergraduate dissipation. He had all the money one could wish for, but would seem to have spent little on himself. One pictures him during those four years at Cambridge in the serenity and beauty of an environment in which he could indulge his tastes as the spirit moved him, for, being well provided for, he had neither ambition nor goal. He read discursively but extensively, wrote some poetry, played the piano, painted in water colours, or just lazed. He was habitually untidy, shaved as seldom as possible, dressed as he pleased, and his rooms were constantly littered with clothes, books, music, pictures, pipes and what not. But he was a delightful companion and had a wide circle of friends among whom were W. M. Thackeray, F. D. Morris, John Kemble, W. B. Donne, Richard Monckton Milnes (later Lord Houghton) and James Spedding. Later he was to write of Alfred Tennyson: 'I remember him well —a sort of Hyperion': that they did not meet when undergraduates was probably due to FitzGerald's shyness and indifference. His enthusiasm for Tennyson's poetry, at first impersonal, grew with their friendship. Some years later he wrote to John Allen: 'I will say no more of Tennyson than that the more I have seen of him, the more cause I have to think him great.'

He took his degree with modest competence in January 1830, and left the University to spend the springtime of the year in Paris, where, on the arrival of the truant Thackeray, the threat of boredom gave place to the carefree and unselfconscious exhilaration of kindred spirits enthralled by the delights of novel experiences perfectly shared together. On his return to England he spent most of the summer at Southampton and the remainder of the year in London, Suffolk and elsewhere, and in the years that followed he was again and again irresistibly drawn to Cambridge.

When the family took up residence at Boulge Hall in 1835 Edward chose, from 1837 onwards, to live during the summer months in the thatched cottage of two rooms standing just outside the park gates. Spring, summer, autumn, winter---sixteen years advanced and dwindled in long, untragic crescendos and diminuendos. But FitzGerald was not wholly idle. He interested himself in the management of his father's estates, read widely and omnivorously of whatever his mind craved for, bought pictures, wrote for his own pleasure, entertained, and was entertained by, his friends. And if he could remark to Frederick Tennyson: 'Here I sit, read, smoke, and become very wise, and am already quite beyond earthly needs,' it should be remembered to his credit that in an age when the social conscience was little stirred by the poverty of the masses, he was deeply concerned about the penury and suffering he saw about him and did what he could to assuage such evils.

On his father's death in 1853 the Hall passed to his elder brother John, who suffered from religious mania. He is said to have roamed about the country, preaching wherever he could find an audience. When listening to a sermon he would remove his shoes and stockings, empty his pockets of their contents and give vent to his emotion by emitting shrill whistles. 'We FitzGeralds are all mad,' Edward used to say, 'but John is the maddest for he does not know it,' and this may explain his decision to leave the cottage and lodge with his friend Job Smith in the picturesque farmhouse of Farlingay on the outskirts of Woodbridge. Farlingay

Hall was his home until 1860—it was here that Carlyle paid him a visit in 1855—but his was a restless spirit, and although he never travelled abroad, he could not abide to remain in one place for any length of time. During those years he made frequent visits to London, to his brother Peter at Twickenham, his sister Andalusia at Bath and his mother at Richmond, until her death in Brighton in 1855. He went on visits to friends for months at a time, preferring their warm hospitality to the more forbidding atmosphere of hotels or the purlieus of the family. He detested the pomp and circumstance of courts and officialdom and the spurious glamour of the social scene. For him, such activities were unsubstantial and alien to the spirit, and he had no need of them. What he required was freedom to express his many-sided personality with genuine bonhomie and spontaneity, and he was probably happiest of all when lodged in friendly detachment nearby simple country people.

Among his close friends in Woodbridge was the banker and Quaker poet Bernard Barton who was some twenty-five years his senior. In the course of Barton's last illness in 1849 FitzGerald had given an assurance that he would make provision for his daughter Lucy, and a death-bed incident in which her father joined his daughter's and FitzGerald's hands and gave the pair his blessing would seem to have been interpreted by FitzGerald as an unformulated but unambiguous directive. It is probable that his original intention was simply to make Lucy an allowance to supplement her slender income, but this her sense of propriety forbade her to accept. As time went on FitzGerald became increasingly conscious of his 'obligation,' but his father's bankruptcy involved him in financial difficulties which for a time made marriage inadvisable. These ended on the death of his mother and, disregarding the protestations of his friends, Lucy and he were married on November 4th, 1856—seven years after her father's death.

As the twig is bent, so is the tree inclined, and that the marriage was a failure was soon apparent in ever growing unhappiness and incompatibility. In a letter to Spring Rice, FitzGerald had described his forthcoming marriage as 'a very doubtful experiment', and to Crabbe he wrote: 'George, I am going to be married—don't congratulate me.' The plain truth is that FitzGerald was not the marrying kind; no two mortals could have been more unsuited to each other. He was too ascetic in temperament, too eccentric in his habits, too settled in his bachelor ways ever to accommodate himself to such a loveless union. His wife was too precise, too normal, too confirmed in her determination to reform her husband's manners and way of life. In the words of F. R. Barton: 'the more she tried in her fond, tactless way to win his regard, the more she repelled him.' On the other hand, she could hardly have been expected to conform to the pact which FitzGerald made before they were married: 'to see no company, to keep no establishment, and to live very quietly.' As everyone had foreseen, the situation was irremediable, but there was no divorce. In August 1857 they agreed to separate permanently and FitzGerald made Lucy a generous settlement.

'You know well enough,' he wrote to a friend, 'that *I* am very much to blame, both on the score of stupidity in taking so wrong a step, and want of courageous principle in not making the best of it when taken. She has little to blame herself for, except in fancying that she knew both me and herself better than I had over and over again told her was the truth *before* marriage.' Lucy, who was forty-eight years of age at the time of her marriage, died at Croydon in 1898 at the age of ninety.

In December 1860, FitzGerald removed to lodgings at Berry's, a Gunsmith's shop on the Market Hill, Woodbridge, where he lived until 1873. He must have known that his reputation was that of an eccentric. Furthermore, he had been parted from his wife for three years and it required considerable moral courage thus boldly to face the gossips of the town, to whom she was a well-known and popular figure. He shunned Woodbridge society but made many friends among the townspeople, and although he took little part in civic affairs, he was not unmindful of those in need and found ways and means quietly to distribute his benefactions. It required something more than mere eccentricity to burn the bond for £500 which Frederick Spalding's father and a friend had signed so that the son might establish a business. That was the act of a generous and big-hearted man.

FitzGerald loved the sea. Tentative beginnings with river boats and a passage to Berwick-on-Tweed in a smack during the summer of 1861 led him to experiment with larger craft and, in 1863, to the building of his yacht *Shamrock*, the which, however, was soon rechristened *Scandal*, that being 'the staple product of Woodbridge.' How exhilarating he must have found those summer coastal cruises from Lowestoft during the ensuing eight years. A friend or two with whom to read poetry and share the wisdom of great minds; a cold pasty and a bottle of sherry, or the more humble bread and cheese and stout, for the needs of the body: 'the flung spray and the blown spume, and the sea-gulls crying.' What more, short of paradise, could one of his temperament have wished for?

In the spring of 1864 FitzGerald made the acquaintance of Joseph Fletcher a Lowestoft fisherman, for whom he soon had a great affection. Tall and strong and native to the sea, 'Posh' was a bearded giant of sturdy independence and simplicity of character and, as is so often the case in men endowed with great physical strength, his gentleness and guileless humour were quite disarming. 'The Greatest Man I have known,' wrote FitzGerald, and they became firm friends. Indeed for a time (1867–1873) they were partners in a fishing lugger, the *Meum et Tuum*, and if this venture brought FitzGerald no monetary gain, it earned him dividends infinitely more precious in the coin of human values and experience.

As was inevitable in such a relationship there were disappointments, misunderstandings brought about by interfering busybodies, recriminations and estrangements, but nothing could quite sever the bond between them. Even when their business relationship had foundered, FitzGerald commissioned Lawrence to paint 'Posh's' portrait 'to hang up by old Thackeray and Tennyson, all three having a stamp of grandeur about them in their several ways, and occupying great places in my Soul.' 'Posh's' opinion of FitzGerald can be summed up in a single sentence: 'Ah! he was a master rum un, was my ole guv'nor!'

In 1864 he bought the Little Grange, an estate of about six acres on the outskirts of Woodbridge. A year later he had the house enlarged and refurnished, but although he loaned it occasionally to his Kerrich nieces and to some of his friends, he himself did not move in until the spring of 1874. This was his last home. He was, as always, stubborn in his resolve to have nothing to do with 'the County,' but he continued to be a jovial and voluminous correspondent, and the visits of Sir Frederick Pollock, Frederick Tennyson and many others of his friends, the English summers at Lowestoft and elsewhere, and his brief visits to London, all brought him keen enjoyment.

In 1876 he was surprised and delighted to receive a visit from Alfred Tennyson and his son Hallam. The Tennysons had been touring in Norfolk and were on their way back to London. Little Grange was in the hands of the painters and his guests were lodged in the Bull Hotel on the Market Hill. Twenty years had elapsed since their last meeting, and now, during this brief interlude of two days, they yarned about old friends and re-lived experiences they had shared together. There were times when he found the great man a little overpowering, but nothing could suppress FitzGerald's native buoyancy—'Tennyson's little humours and grumpiness were so droll that I was always laughing'—and both felt in parting the pangs of their last farewell.

The remaining years of FitzGerald's life were filled with quiet melancholy. He was much saddened by the death of friends and relatives but, stooping a little, he carried his years with stubborn and ungraceful vigour. His mind was as lively as ever, and he was constantly occupied with one project and another, including a third edition of *Euphranor*. That he left unfinished at least three books on which he had been working off and on prior to his death, belies his self-accusation that he was lacking in industry.

Even death was kind to him, for he passed quietly in sleep at Merton Rectory on June 14th, 1883, while on his annual visit to his friend the Rev. George Crabbe, grandson of the poet. He was seventy-four. His body was interred on June 19th in the little churchyard in Boulge Park, and there grows the famous rose tree the hips for which were picked by William Simpson from rose bushes on the grave of Omar Khayyám in Náishapur in 1884, and raised at Kew Gardens before being planted at Boulge in 1893.

But of what avail is it to garner and patch and seam, for not thus shall we recapture the soul of the poet. His whimsical and eccentric personality, that part of him which was incorrigibly fond of mimicry and drollery, is perhaps best revealed in his letters, but Francis Hindes Groome has brought to life the figure which was so familiar to the village gossips: 'I can see him now walking down to Woodbridge with an old Inverness cape, double-breasted flowered satin waistcoat, slippers on feet and a handkerchief, very likely, tied over his hat. Yet one always recognised in him the Hidalgo.' But life does not consist of outward acts and is little affected by them: it is an inward and subjective experience. The real FitzGerald, the creative artist who abridged, concentrated and distilled the work of the Persian master, escapes us, save what we glimpse of him in the *Rubáiyát* of our own perception and awareness.

THE WORKS OF FITZGERALD

I

Earlier Ventures in Publishing

THE first printed work by FitzGerald, *Euphranor, A Dialogue on Youth* in the Platonic manner, was published in 1851 when he was forty-two. It mirrors in the somewhat thin disguise of classical nomenclature the author's collegiate life and associations during his undergraduate sojourn at Cambridge, and while its serious purpose is to criticise the English system of education of that day, its whimsical and kindly philosophy is spun from a mind to which old ties of custom and friendship were both hallowed and enduring. In 1852 there appeared *Polonius, A Collection of Wise Saws and Modern Instances*. This consisted of short moral aphorisms and larger excerpts arranged under abstract headings, some original, the rest derived from English, French and German classical sources, and even from the Persian of the *Masnavi*, evidence of the beginning of FitzGerald's interest in this field of literature. In general the book reflects the wide range of his reading, and that it contains a disproportionate number of quotations from Carlyle is testimony to still another of his close friendships. This book (in common with *Euphranor*) was published at his own expense and met with small success. Turning his attention to Spain, he published in the following year a translation in free blank verse of *Six Dramas of Calderon* (1600–1681) whom he thought to be 'one of the Great Men of the World,' a volume which, in spite of its considerable merit, had so unfavourable a reception that he felt obliged to withdraw it from circulation. This was the first and indeed the only book to bear his name, for he would never again consent to use it.

In the course of his pilgrimages to Cambridge in middle life, FitzGerald became friendly with Edward Byles Cowell, an oriental scholar of distinction and a man of great personal charm and modesty. Cowell was then at Oxford, but he left England in 1856 to become Professor of History at the new Presidency College, and soon after Principal of the Sanskrit College, Calcutta, and did not return until 1867 when he was elected Professor of Sanskrit at Cambridge. Cowell quickened and fostered FitzGerald's interest in his Persian studies, which began with Háfiz 'whose best is untranslatable because he is the best Musician of Words,' and in a letter to Frederick Tennyson in 1853 is found this sentence: 'I amuse myself with poking out some Persian, which E. Cowell would inaugurate me with; I go on with it because it is a point in common with him and enables us to study a little together.' Thus it came about that in 1856 there appeared anonymously FitzGerald's version of the Sufi allegorical work *Salámán and Absál* by Jámi, which, in spite of certain weaknesses in translation, deserved a better reception than was accorded to it. This literary exercise he was to find invaluable for his work on Omar.

In 1876 he produced a version of the *Agamemnon* of Æschylus in which, too, he strove to capture the spirit of the original rather than to give a too literal rendering. In 1880–81 he issued for private circulation translations of the two Œdipus tragedies, which are full of poetic beauty. His last publication, *Readings in Crabbe* (which had been privately distributed in 1879) appeared in 1882 and is interesting primarily as a gesture of friendship to the poet's grandson.

2

The Rubáiyát of Omar Khayyám

The original manuscript by Omar Khayyám is thought to have comprised at least seven hundred and fifty and possibly many more quatrains. These were never intended to represent a continuous work or story. Each quatrain is a separate poem, the epigrammatic expression of a single thought about such subjects as would occur to the mind of a Persian poet-philosopher, and, moreover, one skilled in mathematics and astronomy. The *Rubáiyát* are the expression of Omar's own life, the fruits of his own experience, and they were not written for publication.

Of this large and varied collection, the Ouseley manuscript discovered by Cowell among a mass of uncatalogued material in the Bodleian Library, Oxford, in 1856 contains 158 quatrains written in purple ink on yellow paper and powdered in gold. It dates from 865, i.e. A.D. 1460–61, some 338 years after the death of Omar. From the transcript which he made from Cowell's copy of the original, Fitz-Gerald selected and compounded for his first edition of the *Rubáiyát* seventy-five quatrains, on which he worked for several years. By the middle of 1857 he had finished his 'first Physiognomy' and the following year he wrote to Cowell: 'My translation will interest you from its form, and also in many respects in its detail, very unliteral as it is. Many quatrains are mashed together, and something lost, I doubt, of Omar's simplicity, which is such a virtue in him. But there it is, such as it is.'

The 'less wicked' of the quatrains FitzGerald sent to Parker of *Fraser's Magazine* in January 1858, but when a year had elapsed and nothing had been published, he recalled the manuscript, replaced the 'wicked' stanzas and resolved to print it for private circulation. Thus there appeared in the early summer of 1859 the quarto pamphlet of twenty-four pages in its unassuming brown paper cover, 'Beggarly disguise as to paper and print, but magnificent vesture of verse.'

A comparative examination of translations from the Persian original, and especially that of the Teheran manuscript dated 604, i.e. A.D. 1207, which was acquired by Cambridge University Library in 1950, translated by Professor Arthur J. Arberry and published in 1952, makes clear that FitzGerald did not so much translate Omar as make a poetic transfusion of the quatrains to suit his own fancy. This he did with such skill and beauty that some have thought his work incomparably better than the original, but he took great liberties with the text. About half of the quatrains are faithful paraphrases of the Persian. The remainder are built up of ideas taken from this quatrain and that, of figures which have no prototypes in the original but come from numerous kindred sources such as Háfiz and the *Mantiq al-Tayr (The Discourse of the Birds)* of Attár. However the whole underwent so singular a poetic metamorphosis that FitzGerald's rendering is justly considered the apotheosis of craftsmanship—but it is not Omar.

In a letter to Cowell, dated 27th April, 1859, he wrote: 'I hardly know why I print any of these things, which nobody buys; and I scarce now see the few I gave them to. But when one has done one's best, and is sure that the best is better than so many will take pains to do, though far from the best that might be done, one likes to make an end of the matter by print. I suppose very few people have ever taken such pains in translation as I have, though certainly not to be literal.' And again: 'It is a desperate sort of thing, unfortunately at the bottom of all thinking men's minds, but made music of.' It is this music, coupled with the seemingly dark philosophy of the *Rubáiyát*, that continues to enthral the western world.

3

Exoteric or Esoteric?

There are two schools of thought about the *Rubáiyát*. The first contends that FitzGerald recaptured and expressed with admirable restraint and superb poetic imagery the thoughts of Omar on love and wine, and life and death, and this notwithstanding that he destroyed the verisimilitude of the work by too many borrowings, too free renderings, and by giving it a continuity that does not exist in the original.

Omar's, say the adherents of this school, was a materialist philosophy which could be summed up in a single epigram: 'Eat, drink and be merry, for to-morrow we die.' It is hard indeed to fit this interpretation to many of the quatrains even in FitzGerald's renderings, but it is fair to say that this was his own opinion, that it is Professor Arberry's opinion and that it is the opinion of the majority. It does not follow, of course, that it is the right one. How, for example, shall we attribute other than a mystical interpretation to Quatrain 34 in FitzGerald's fifth edition of the *Rubáiyát?*

Then of the THEE IN ME who works behind
The Veil, I lifted up my hands to find
A lamp amid the Darkness; and I heard,
As from Without—'THE ME WITHIN THEE BLIND!'

No corresponding quatrain is found in the Cambridge codex, and it must be admitted that of its 252 quatrains hardly any can be said to bear evidence of mystical teaching; but that Omar was not unaware of such is hinted at in the quatrains which Professor Arberry translates as follows:

The secrets of the world, as we
Succinctly on our tablets write,
Are not expedient to recite:
A plague to heart and head they be.

Since there is none, as I can find
Of those brave wizards of today
Worthy to hear, I cannot say
The wondrous thoughts I have in mind.

Or again:

Lord, I am weary unto death
Of this mean being that is mine:
The fetters that my heart confine,
My muddy hands, my narrow breath.

Yet Thou hast power to transmute
The naughted unto entity:
O raise me to the sanctuary
Of Thine own Being Absolute.

The other school which began with the Moslem mystics and was revived by M. Nicolas, Omar's French translator, claims that Omar was a philosopher who was concerned primarily with spiritual values, a man going his own way in solitude, appealed to by others but independent of their thought; moreover, a man passionate in revolt against the fixed ideas of his age. For them the *Rubáiyát*, in translations which were formerly thought to be more faithful to the original, must be given a spiritual interpretation. In other words, they have an allegorical significance.

This would seem to have been the opinion of Sharastani (A.D. 1074–1153) a dogmatic theologian of the Asharite sect and a distinguished doctor of law who lived for a time in Naishápúr, and paid tribute to Omar as the greatest scholar of his time, one versed in the philosophy and political theory of the Greeks, and who exhorted men to seek the One Author of all by the purification of the senses and the sanctification of the soul. He confirms the modern view that Omar found in the orthodox Sufism of his day much that was repugnant to him and hints plainly that the *Rubái* have an esoteric significance. 'The later Sufis,' he wrote. 'have caught at the apparent sense of parts of his poems and accommodated them to their own canon, making them a subject of discussion in their assemblies and conventicles, but the esoteric sense consists in axioms of natural religion and principles of universal obligation. When the men of his time anathematised his doctrines, and drew forth his opinions from the concealment in which he had veiled them, he went in fear of his life and placed some check on the sallies of his tongue and pen.' We are asked, then, to distinguish between Omar's own high philosophy and the spurious and decadent Sufism of his day, and to regard him as a great Satirist, to be ranked with Lucian and Carlyle. If we probe behind the symbol or metaphor, we shall discover a noble philosophy which will guide us through the mysteries of life and destiny.

The Tavern or Caravanserai is symbolic of Pilgrimage, the Sufi way of Life with its five stages of Repentance, Renunciation, Poverty, Patience and Acquiescence to the Will of God. The Temple is a thing of Time which, when it has served its purpose, will pass away; not so the Temple of the Dweller in the Heart. Wine is symbolic of the Spirit: the Cup the receptacle of the Spiritual powers poured out in Service: Bread the Divine Mind or Food from Heaven; the Bulbul or Persian Nightingale the Symbol of the Soul, singing in the darkness or hidden depths of man's own being. And so on.

It is evident that, be the quatrains secular or mystical, their form and significance in English must depend upon the wisdom and skill of the translator. It would be foolish to suppose that *all* have a mystical significance. The correct verdict on the evidence is probably that, in so large and varied an anthology, some reflect in symbolic language the inner philosophy of the spirit, while others are epigrammatic expressions of the mundane.

The reader who is interested may pursue his investigations and sift the evidences to form his own judgment by examining versions such as those of Professor Arthur J. Arberry, John Leslie Garner, E. H. Whinfield and the French of M. Nicolas, or he may decide to rest satisfied with the FitzGerald rendering. This is so felicitous, so Schubert-like in the excellence of its poetry, that it will always find a readier response among English-speaking peoples than the more literal, though excellent, prose translations of Justin Huntly McCarthy and Edward Heron-Allan.

4

Comparative Translations

It is interesting to compare one of the FitzGerald quatrains with that of other translators, and I have chosen for this purpose Quatrain 77 from the fifth edition of the *Rubáiyát*; which reads:

And this I know: whether the one True Light
Kindle to Love, or Wrath-consume me quite,
One flash of It within the Tavern caught
Better than in the Temple lost outright.

In the metrical version by E. H. Whinfield this quatrain reads:

In taverns better far commune with Thee,
Than pray in mosques and fail Thy face to see!
O first and last of all Thy creatures Thou;
'Tis Thine to burn, and Thine to cherish me!'

That by Brigadier-General E. H. Rodwell, C.B., reads:

In some low Inn I'd rather seek Thy face
Than pray without Thee toward the Niche's place.
O First and Last of all! As Thou dost will,
Burn me in Hell—or save me by Thy grace!

That by Professor A. J. Arberry (in his translation of the Cambridge manuscript) reads:

Better at tavern, and with wine,
To lay Thee all my secrets bare,
Than to intone the parrot prayer
And Thou not with me, in the shrine.

Thy Name is last and first to tell;
Whatever is, save Thee, is nil;
Then cherish me, if so Thy Will
Be done—or burn my soul in hell!

Compare the literal prose version of the same quatrain by Justin Huntly McCarthy:

I would rather in the tavern with Thee pour out all the thoughts of my heart, than without Thee go and make my prayer unto Heaven. This, truly, O creator of all things present and to come, is my religion; whether Thou castest me into the flames, or makest me glad with the light of Thy countenance.

There follows the version of Edward Heron-Allen:

If I tell Thee my secret thoughts in a tavern,
it is better than if I make my devotions before
the Mihráb without Thee.
O Thou, the first and last of all created beings!
burn me an Thou wilt, or cherish me an Thou wilt.

No quatrain has caused more controversy than that numbered 68 in FitzGerald's fifth edition of the *Rubáiyát:*

We are no other than a moving row
Of Magic Shadow-shapes that come and go
Round with the Sun-illumined Lantern held
In Midnight by the Master of the Show;

According to Dr. Richard Ettinghausen, writing in the bulletin of the American Institute for Persian Art and Archaeology, 'The poet speaks of a lamp with a revolving shade on which figures are painted, for him a symbol of human life, the purposeless movement of men and the all-moving power. . . . Such a lantern is made of paper in the form and size of a bucket; on its surface strange comical looking figures are painted. Inside the lanterns, which are hung up before the shops, are wax candles which, by the heat of their flames, cause the shade to move round incessantly so that new figures appear.'

The Heron-Allen rendering of the same rubái reads:

This vault of heaven, beneath which we stand bewildered,
We know to be a sort of magic-lantern:
Know thou that the sun is the lamp-flame and
the universe is the lamp,
We are like figures that revolve round it.

Did Omar know that the earth revolves in space and travels round the sun, and that the solar system describes a still greater orbit? The ancient Egyptians possessed this knowledge. May not the wise men of the east have been similarly enlightened?

5

The Five FitzGerald Transcriptions

Until the end of his life FitzGerald kept working on the *Rubáiyát*, adding or reducing the number of quatrains, changing their order, their phrasing, striving for a perfection that for ever eluded him. Four versions were published anonymously during his lifetime. The first, to which I have referred, containing seventy-five quatrains, appeared in 1859. The second edition, that of 1868, contained one hundred and ten, but in the third and fourth editions which appeared in 1872 and 1879 respectively, the number of quatrains was reduced to one hundred and one. On his death, his friend William Aldous Wright found in a tin box a printed copy of the 1879 text in which FitzGerald had marked some further changes. This, the fifth and last revision, was incorporated in *Letters and Literary Remains of Edward FitzGerald* (3 vols.) published in 1889, when for the first time his name appeared as the author of the *Rubáiyát*. The present volume gives the first, second and fifth editions of the *Rubáiyát* in full, together with the variations in the texts of the third and fourth editions.

The work aroused as little enthusiasm in the country of its adoption as it had done in the country of its origin in the eleventh century. It is a sobering reflection that, thanks to Thomas Sergeant Perry, a distinguished critic, editor and teacher, it was widely read and appreciated in the United States of America long before it became popular fare in this country, largely because of the reactionary mode of thought which followed upon the Civil War. When, however, in 1885 Tennyson dedicated *Tiresias and other Poems* to the memory of FitzGerald, there began in Great Britain an awakening of interest in the *Rubáiyát* which has grown to such proportions that it is now known and quoted wherever English is spoken.

6

Advent in English

The manner of its advent is not without interest. In the year 1861 the more perceptive among those who are for ever drawn to second-hand book stalls as the magnetic needle to the pole, bought at a penny a piece a pamphlet which bore the title: *Rubáiyát of Omar Khayyám the Astronomer-Poet of Persia, Translated into English Verse.* The name of the translator was not disclosed. In 1859 Bernard Quaritch the bookseller had had printed for the author two hundred and fifty copies, of which FitzGerald retained forty for his friends. The majority of these were never distributed, but he gave copies to Cowell, who 'was naturally alarmed at it, he being a very religious man,' to George Borrow and to Donne. The remainder he gifted to his publisher. These were advertised in Quaritch's Catalogue No. 158, dated March 15th 1860, at 1*s*., with a notice from the *Literary Gazette* of October 1859, but the work aroused little interest, and as none could foresee that it was destined to become a best-seller, it was gradually reduced in price until it found its way into 'the penny box.' Indeed had not Rossetti and Swinburne got wind of this singular second-hand bargain, the bulk of the first edition would probably have been disposed of as waste paper. Soon this 'remainder' was being sold at ever-increasing prices, until a guinea and more was paid for single copies. To-day its value to the collector is such that a copy sold in the U.S.A. in 1929 fetched eight thousand dollars, and another was sold by Hodgson's in London on June 12th the same year for £1410.

It has been said that happiness consists of having something to love, something to do, and something to hope for. FitzGerald loved his friends by whom he was held in warm affection as an amiable and kindly spirit, an affection which, overcoming time and circumstance, has attained immortality. That he enjoyed his literary work, and in particular that on the *Rubáiyát*, is plain from the fact that he returned to it again and again. Did he hope that this, the best-loved of his creations, would one day achieve the world-wide popularity which it now enjoys? Surely the answer must be that one who was so modest as to choose the cloak of anonymity had no such mundane hope, and that the *Rubáiyát* was the offspring of labours that gave wings to his soul.

In a letter to his friend Cowell he wrote: 'June over! a thing I think of with Omar-like sorrow, and the roses here are blooming—and going—as abundantly as even in Persia. I am still at Geldestone, and still looking at Omar by an open window, which gives over a greener landscape than yours.'

Rain, sun and Rain! and the free blossom blows:
Sun, rain and Sun! and where is he who knows?
From the great deep to the great deep he goes.

G. F. MAINE

OMAR KHAYYÁM

Edward FitzGerald

OMAR KHAYYÁM

Omar Khayyám was born at Naishápúr in Khorásán in the latter half of our Eleventh, and died within the First Quarter of our Twelfth Century. The slender Story of his Life is curiously twined about that of two other very considerable Figures in their Time and Country: one of whom tells the Story of all Three. This was Nizám-ul-Mulk, Vizier to Alp Arslan the Son, and Malik Shah the Grandson, of Toghrul Beg the Tartar, who had wrested Persia from the feeble Successor of Mahmud the Great, and founded that Seljukian Dynasty which finally roused Europe into the Crusades. This Nizám-ul-Mulk, in his *Wasiyat*—or *Testament*—which he wrote and left as a Memorial for future Statesmen—relates the following, as quoted in the *Calcutta Review*, No. 59, from Mirkhond's *History of the Assassins*.

'One of the greatest of the wise men of Khorásán was the Imám Mowaffak of Naishápúr, a man highly honoured and reverenced,—may God rejoice his soul; his illustrious years exceeded eighty-five, and it was the universal belief that every boy who read the Koran or studied the traditions in his presence, would assuredly attain to honour and happiness. For this cause did my father send me from Tús to Naishápúr with Abd-us-samad, the doctor of law, that I might employ myself in study and learning under the guidance of that illustrious teacher. Towards me he ever turned an eye of favour and kindness, and as his pupil I felt for him extreme affection and devotion, so that I passed four years in his service. When I first came there, I found two other pupils of mine own age newly arrived, Hakim Omar Khayyám, and the ill-fated Ben Sabbáh. Both were endowed with sharpness of wit and the highest natural powers; and we three formed a close friendship together. When the Imám rose from his lectures, they used to join me, and we repeated to each other the lessons we had heard. Now Omar was a native of Naishápúr, while Hasan Ben Sabbáh's father was one Ali, a man of austere life and practice, but heretical in his creed and doctrine. One day Hasan said to me and to Khayyám, "It is a universal belief that the pupils of the Imám Mowaffak will attain to fortune. Now, even if we *all* do not attain thereto, without doubt one of us will; what then shall be our mutual pledge and bond?" We answered, "Be it what you please." "Well," he said, "let us make a vow, that to whomsoever this fortune falls, he shall share it equally with the rest, and reserve no pre-eminence for himself." "Be it so," we both replied, and on those terms we mutually pledged our words. Years rolled on, and I went from Khorásán to Transoxiana, and wandered to Ghazni and Cabul; and when I returned. I was invested with office, and rose to be administrator of affairs during the Sultanate of Sultán Alp Arslan.

'He goes on to state, that years passed by, and both his old schoolfriends found him out, and came and claimed a share in his good fortune, according to the school-day vow. The Vizier was generous and kept his word. Hasan demanded a place in the government, which the Sultán granted at the Vizier's request; but discontented with a gradual rise, he plunged into the maze of intrigue of an oriental court, and, failing in a base attempt to supplant his benefactor, he was disgraced and fell. After many mishaps and wanderings, Hasan became the head of the Persian sect of the *Ismailians*, —a party of fanatics who had long murmured in obscurity, but rose to an evil eminence under the guidance of his strong and evil will. In A.D. 1090, he seized the castle of Alamút, in the province of Rúdbar, which lies in the mountainous tract south of the Caspian Sea; and it was from this mountain home he obtained that evil celebrity among the Crusaders as the OLD MAN OF THE MOUNTAINS, and spread terror through the Mohammedan world; and it is yet disputed whether the word *Assassin*, which they have left in the language of modern Europe as their dark memorial, is derived from the *hashish*, or opiate of hemp-leaves (the Indian *bhang*), with which they maddened themselves to the sullen pitch of oriental desperation, or from the name of the founder of the dynasty, whom we have seen in his quiet collegiate days, at Naishápúr. One of the countless victims of the Assassin's dagger was Nizám-ul-Mulk himself, the old school-boy friend. *

'Omar Khayyám also came to the Vizier to claim his share; but not to ask for title or office. "The greatest boon you can confer on me," he said, "is to let me live in a corner under the shadow of your fortune, to spread wide the advantages of Science, and pray for your long life and prosperity." The Vizier tells us, that, when he found Omar was really sincere in his refusal, he pressed him no further,

* Some of Omar's *Rubáiyát* warn us of the danger of Greatness, the instability of Fortune, and while advocating Charity to all Men, recommending us to be too intimate with none. Attár makes Nizám-ul-Mulk use the very words of his friend Omar [*Rub*. xxviii], 'When Nizám-ul-Mulk was in the Agony (of Death) he said, "Oh God! I am passing away in the hand of the wind." '

but granted him a yearly pension of 1200 *mithkáls* of gold, from the treasury of Naishápúr.

'At Naishápúr thus lived and died Omar Khayyám, "busied," adds the Vizier, "in winning knowledge of every kind, and especially in Astronomy, wherein he attained to a very high pre-eminence. Under the Sultanate of Malik Shah, he came to Merv, and obtained great praise for his proficiency in science, and the Sultán showered favours upon him."

'When Malik Shah determined to reform the calendar, Omar was one of the eight learned men employed to do it; the result was the *Jaláli* era (so called from *Jalál-ud-din*, one of the king's names)—"a computation of time," says Gibbon, "which surpasses the Julian, and approaches the accuracy of the Gregorian style." He is also the author of some astronomical tables, entitled Zíji-Malikshâhí,' and the French have lately republished and translated an Arabic Treatise of his on Algebra.

'His Takhallus or poetical name (Khayyám) signifies a Tentmaker, and he is said to have at one time exercised that trade, perhaps before Nizám-ul-Mulk's generosity raised him to independence. Many Persian poets similarly derive their names from their occupations; thus we have Attár, "a druggist," Assár, "an oil presser," etc. * Omar himself alludes to his name in the following whimsical lines:—

Khayyám, who stitched the tents of science,
Has fallen in grief's furnace and been suddenly burned;
The shears of Fate have cut the tent ropes of his life,
And the broker of Hope has sold him for nothing!

'We have only one more anecdote to give of his Life, and

* Though all these, like our Smiths, Archers, Millers, Fletchers, etc., may simply retain the Surname of an hereditary calling.

that relates to the close; it is told in the anonymous preface which is sometimes prefixed to his poems; it has been printed in the Persian in the Appendix to Hyde's *Veterum Persarum Religio*, p. 499; and D'Herbelot alludes to it in his Bibliothèque, under *Khiam*.— *

'"It is written in the chronicles of the ancients that this King of the Wise, Omar Khayyám, died at Naishápúr in the year of the Hegira, 517 (A.D. 1123); in science he was unrivalled,—the very paragon of his age. Khwájah Nizámi of Samarcand, who was one of his pupils, relates the following story: 'I often used to hold conversations with my teacher, Omar Khayyám, in a garden; and one day he said to me, "My tomb shall be in a spot where the north wind may scatter roses over it." I wondered at the words he spake, but I knew that his were no idle words. † Years after, when I chanced to revisit Naishápúr, I went to his final resting-place, and lo! it was just outside a garden, and trees

* '*Philosophe Musulman qui a vécu en Odeur de Sainteté dans sa Religion, vers la Fin du premier et le Commencement du second Siècle*,' no part of which, except the *Philosophe*, can apply to our Khayyám.

† The Rashness of the Words, according to D'Herbelot, consisted in being so opposed to those in the Koran: 'No Man knows where he shall die.'—This story of Omar reminds me of another so naturally—and when one remembers how wide of his humble mark the noble sailor aimed—so pathetically told by Captain Cook—not by Doctor Hawkesworth—in his Second Voyage (i. 374). When leaving Ulietea, 'Oreo's last request was for me to return. When he saw he could not obtain that promise, he asked the name of my *Marai* (burying-place). As strange a question as this was, I hesitated not a moment to tell him "Stepney;" the parish in which I live when in London. I was made to repeat it several times over till they could pronounce it; and then "Stepney Marai no Toote" was echoed through an hundred mouths at once. I afterwards found the same question had been put to Mr. Forster by a man on shore; but he gave a different, and indeed more proper answer, by saying, "No man who used the sea could say where he should be buried."'

laden with fruit stretched their boughs over the garden wall, and dropped their flowers upon his tomb, so that the stone was hidden under them.'"'

Thus far—without fear of Trespass—from the *Calcutta Review*. The writer of it, on reading in India this story of Omar's Grave, was reminded, he says, of Cicero's Account of finding Archimedes' Tomb at Syracuse, buried in grass and weeds. I think Thorwaldsen desired to have roses grow over him; a wish religiously fulfilled for him to the present day, I believe. However, to return to Omar.

Though the Sultán 'shower'd Favours upon hin,' Omar's Epicurean Audacity of Thought and Speech caused him to be regarded askance in his own Time and Country. He is said to have been especially hated and dreaded by the Sufis, whose Practice he ridiculed, and whose Faith amounted to little more than his own, when stript of the Mysticism and formal recognition of Islamism under which Omar would not hide. Their Poets, including Háfiz, who are (with the exception of Firdausi) the most considerable in Persia, borrowed largely, indeed, of Omar's material, but turning it to a mystical Use more convenient to Themselves and the People they addressed; a People quite as quick of Doubt as of Belief; as keen of Bodily Sense as of Intellectual; and delighting in a cloudy composition of both, in which they could float luxuriously between Heaven and Earth, and this World and the Next, on the wings of a poetical expression, that might serve indifferently for either. Omar was too honest of Heart as well as of Head for this. Having failed (however mistakenly) of finding any Providence but Destiny, and any World but This, he set about making the most of it; preferring rather to soothe the Soul through the Senses into Acquiescence with Things as he saw them, than to perplex it with vain disquietude after what they *might* be. It has been seen, however, that his Worldly Ambition was not exorbitant; and he very likely takes a humorous or perverse pleasure in exalting the gratification of Sense above that of the Intellect, in which he must have taken great delight, although it failed to answer the Questions in which he, in common with all men, was most vitally interested.

For whatever reason, however, Omar, as before said, has never been popular in his own Country, and therefore has been but scantily transmitted abroad. The MSS. of his Poems, mutilated beyond the average Casualties of Oriental Transcription, are so rare in the East as scarce to have reacht Westward at all, in spite of all the acquisitions of Arms and Science. There is no copy at the India House, none at the Bibliothèque Nationale of Paris. We know but of one in England: No. 140 of the Ouseley MSS. at the Bodleian, written at Shiráz, A.D. 1460. This contains but 158 *Rubáiyát*. One in the Asiatic Society's Library at Calcutta (of which we have a copy), contains (and yet incomplete) 516, though swelled to that by all kinds of Repetition and Corruption. So Von Hammer speaks of *his* Copy as containing about 200, while Dr. Sprenger catalogues the Lucknow MS. at double that number. * The Scribes, too, of the Oxford and Calcutta MSS. seem to do their Work under a sort of Protest; each beginning with a Tetrastich (whether genuine or not), taken out of its alphabetical order; the Oxford with one of Apology; the Calcutta with one of Expostulation, supposed (says a Notice prefixed to the MS.) to have arisen

* 'Since this paper was written' (adds the Reviewer in a note), 'we have met with a Copy of a very rare Edition, printed at Calcutta in 1836. This contains 438 Tetrastichs, with an Appendix containing 54 others not found in some MSS.'

from a Dream, in which Omar's mother asked about his future fate. It may be rendered thus:—

Oh, Thou who burn'st in Heart for those who burn
In Hell, whose fires thyself shall feed in turn;
How long be crying, 'Mercy on them, God!'
Why, who art Thou to teach, and He to learn?

The Bodleian Quatrain pleads Pantheism by way of Justification.

If I myself upon a looser Creed
Have loosely strung the Jewel of Good deed,
Let this one thing for my Atonement plead:
That One for Two I never did mis-read.

The Reviewer, * to whom I owe the Particulars of Omar's Life, concludes his Review by comparing him with Lucretius, both as to natural Temper and Genius, and as acted upon by the Circumstances in which he lived. Both indeed were men of subtle, strong, and cultivated Intellect, fine Imagination, and Hearts passionate for Truth and Justice; who justly revolted from their Country's false Religion, and false, or foolish, Devotion to it; but who fell short of replacing what they subverted by such better *Hope* as others, with no better Revelation to guide them, had yet made a Law to themselves. Lucretius, indeed, with such material as Epicurus furnished, satisfied himself with the theory of a vast machine fortuitously constructed, and acting by a Law that implied no Legislator; and so composing himself into a Stoical rather than Epicurean severity of Attitude, sat down to contemplate the mechanical Drama of the Universe which he was part Actor in; himself and all about him (as in his own sublime description of the Roman Theatre) discoloured with the lurid reflex of the Curtain

* Professor Cowell.

suspended between the Spectator and the Sun. Omar, more desperate, or more careless of any so complicated System as resulted in nothing but hopeless Necessity, flung his own Genius and Learning with a bitter or humorous jest into the general Ruin which their insufficient glimpses only served to reveal; and, pretending sensual pleasure as the serious purpose of Life, only *diverted* himself with speculative problems of Deity, Destiny, Matter and Spirit, Good and Evil, and other such questions, easier to start than to run down, and the pursuit of which becomes a very weary sport at last!

With regard to the present Translation. The original *Rubáiyát* (as, missing an Arabic Guttural, these *Tetrastichs* are more musically called) are independent Stanzas, consisting each of four Lines of equal, though varied, Prosody; sometimes *all* rhyming, but oftener (as here imitated) the third line a blank. Somewhat as in the Greek Alcaic, where the penultimate line seems to lift and suspend the Wave that falls over in the last. As usual with such kind of Oriental Verse, the *Rubáiyát* follow one another according to Alphabetic Rhyme—a strange succession of Grave and Gay. Those here selected are strung into something of an Eclogue, with perhaps a less than equal proportion of the 'Drink and make-merry,' which (genuine or not), recurs over-frequently in the Original. Either way, the Result is sad enough: saddest perhaps when most ostentatiously merry; more apt to move Sorrow than Anger toward the old Tent-maker, who, after vainly endeavouring to unshackle his Steps from Destiny, and to catch some authentic Glimpse of TO-MORROW, fell back upon TO-DAY (which has outlasted so many To-morrows!) as the only Ground he had got to stand upon, however momentarily slipping from under his Feet.

INTRODUCTION TO THIRD EDITION

WHILE the second Edition of this version of Omar was preparing, Monsieur Nicolas, French Consul at Resht, published a very careful and very good Edition of the Text, from a lithograph copy at Teheran, comprising 464 *Rubáiyát*, with translation and notes of his own.

Mons. Nicolas, whose Edition has reminded me of several things, and instructed me in others, does not consider Omar to be the material Epicurean that I have literally taken him for, but a Mystic, shadowing the Deity under the figure of Wine, Wine-bearer, &c., as Háfiz is supposed to do; in short, a Sufi poet like Háfiz and the rest.

I cannot see reason to alter my opinion, formed as it was more than a dozen years ago (1868) when Omar was first shown me by one to whom I am indebted for all I know of Oriental, and very much of other, literature. He admired Omar's Genius so much, that he would gladly have adopted any such Interpretation of his meaning as Mons. Nicolas' if he could. * That he could not, appears by his Paper in the *Calcutta Review* already so largely quoted; in which he argues from the Poems themselves, as well as from what records remain of the Poet's Life. And if more were needed

* Perhaps would have edited the Poems himself some years ago. He may now as little approve of my Version on one side, as of Mons. Nicolas' Theory on the other.

to disprove Mons. Nicolas' Theory, there is the Biographical Notice which he himself has drawn up in direct contradiction to the Interpretation of the Poems given in his Notes. (See pp. xiii-xiv of his Preface.) Indeed I hardly knew poor Omar was so far gone till his Apologist informed me. For here we see that whatever were the Wine that Háfiz drank and sang, the veritable Juice of the Grape it was which Omar used, not only when carousing with his friends, but (says Mons. Nicolas) in order to excite himself to that pitch of Devotion which others reached by cries and '*hurlemens.*' And yet, whenever Wine, Winebearer, &c., occur in the text—which is often enough—Mons. Nicolas carefully annotates '*Dieu,*' '*La Divinité,*' &c.: so carefully indeed that one is tempted to think that he was indoctrinated by the Sufi with whom he read the Poems. (Note to Rub. ii. p. 8.) A Persian would naturally wish to vindicate a distinguished Countryman; and a Sufi to enrol him in his own sect, which already comprises all the chief Poets of Persia.

What historical Authority has Mons. Nicolas to show that Omar gave himself up '*avec passion à l'étude de la philosophie des Soufis?*' (Preface, p. xiii.) The Doctrines of Pantheism, Materialism, Necessity, &c., were not peculiar to the Sufi; nor to Lucretius before them; nor to Epicurus before him; probably the very original Irreligion of Thinking men from the first; and very likely to be the spontaneous growth of a Philosopher living in an Age of social and political barbarism, under shadow of one of the Two and Seventy Religions supposed to divide the world. Von Hammer (according to Sprenger's Oriental Catalogue) speaks of Omar as 'a Free-thinker, and *a great opponent of Sufism;*' perhaps because, while holding much of their Doctrine, he would not pretend to any inconsistent severity of morals. Sir W. Ouseley has written a note to something of the same effect on the fly-leaf of the Bodleian MS. And in two *Rubáiyát* of Mons. Nicolas' own Edition Suf and Sufi are both disparagingly named.

No doubt many of these Quatrains seem unaccountable unless mystically interpreted; but many more as unaccountable unless literally. Were the Wine spiritual, for instance, how wash the Body with it when dead? Why make cups of the dead clay to be filled with—'*La Divinité*'—by some succeeding Mystic? Mons. Nicolas himself is puzzled by some '*bizarres*' and '*trop Orientales*' allusions and images—'*d'une sensualité quelquefois révoltante*' indeed—which '*les convenances*' do not permit him to translate; but still which the reader cannot but refer to '*La Divinité*.' * No doubt also many of the Quatrains in the Teheran, as in the Calcutta, Copies, are spurious; such *Rubáiyát* being the common form of Epigram in Persia. But this, at best, tells as much one way as another; nay, the Sufi, who may be considered the Scholar and Man of Letters in Persia, would be far more likely than the careless Epicure to interpolate what favours his own view of the Poet. I observe that very few of the more mystical Quatrains are in the Bodleian MS. which must be one of the oldest, as dated at Shiraz, A.H. 865, A.D. 1460. And this, I think, especially distinguishes Omar (I cannot help calling him by his—no, not Christian—

* A Note to Quatrain 234 admits that, however clear the mystical meaning of such Images must be to Europeans, they are not quoted without '*rougissant*' even by laymen in Persia—'*Quant aux termes de tendresse qui commencent ce quatrain, comme tant d'autres dans ce recueil, nos lecteurs, habitués maintenant à l'étrangeté des expressions si souvent employées par Khéyam pour rendre ses pensées sur l'amour divin, et à la singularité de ses images trop orientales, d'une sensualité quelquefois révoltante, n'auront pas de peine à se persuader qu'il s'agit de la Divinité, bien que cette conviction soit vivement discutée par les moullahs musulmans et même par beaucoup de laïques, qui rougissent véritablement d'une pareille licence de leur compatriote à l'égard des choses spirituelles.*'

familiar name) from all other Persian Poets: That, whereas with them the Poet is lost in his Song, the Man in Allegory and Abstraction; we seem to have the Man—the *Bonhomme*—Omar himself, with all his Humours and Passions, as frankly before us as if we were really at Table with him, after the Wine had gone round. I must say that I, for one, never wholly believed in the Mysticism of Háfiz. It does not appear there was any danger in holding and singing Sufi Pantheism, so long as the Poet made his Salaam to Mohammed at the beginning and end of his Song. Under such conditions Jeláluddín, Jámi, Attár, and others sang; using Wine and Beauty indeed as Images to illustrate, not as a Mask to hide, the Divinity they were celebrating. Perhaps some Allegory less liable to mistake or abuse had been better among so inflammable a People: much more so when, as some think with Háfiz and Omar, the abstract is not only likened to, but identified with, the sensual Image; hazardous, if not to the Devotee himself, yet to his weaker Brethren; and worse for the Profane in proportion as the Devotion of the Initiated grew warmer. And all for what? To be tantalised with Images of sensual enjoyment which must be renounced if one would approximate a God, who according to the Doctrine, *is* Sensual Matter as well as Spirit, and into whose Universe one expects unconsciously to merge after Death, without hope of any posthumous Beatitude in another world to compensate for all one's self-denial in this. Lucretius' blind Divinity certainly merited, and probably got, as much self-sacrifice as this of the Sufi; and the burden of Omar's Song—if not 'Let us eat'—is assuredly—'Let us drink, for To-morrow we die!' And if Háfiz meant quite otherwise by a similar language, he surely miscalculated when he devoted his Life and Genius to so equivocal a Psalmody as, from his Day to this, has been said and sung by any rather than Spiritual Worshippers.

However, as there is some traditional presumption, and certainly the opinion of some learned men, in favour of Omar's being a Sufi—and even something of a Saint—those who please may so interpret his Wine and Cup-bearer. On the other hand, as there is far more historical certainty of his being a Philosopher, of scientific Insight and Ability far beyond that of the Age and Country he lived in; of such moderate worldly Ambition as becomes a Philosopher, and such moderate wants as rarely satisfy a Debauchee; other readers may be content to believe with me that, while the Wine Omar celebrates is simply the Juice of the Grape, he bragged more than he drank of it, in very defiance perhaps of that Spiritual Wine which left its Votaries sunk in Hypocrisy or Disgust.

EDWARD FITZGERALD

RUBÁIYÁT OF OMAR KHAYYÁM

The First Edition, 1859

I

AWAKE! for Morning in the Bowl of Night
Has flung the Stone that puts the Stars to Flight:
And Lo! the Hunter of the East has caught
The Sultán's Turret in a Noose of Light.

2

Dreaming when Dawn's Left Hand was in the Sky
I heard a voice within the Tavern cry,
'Awake, my Little ones, and fill the Cup
Before Life's Liquor in its Cup be dry.'

3

And, as the Cock crew, those who stood before
The Tavern shouted—'Open then the Door!
You know how little while we have to stay,
And, once departed, may return no more.'

4

Now the New Year reviving old Desires,
The thoughtful Soul to Solitude retires,
Where the WHITE HAND OF MOSES on the Bough
Puts out, and Jesus from the Ground suspires.

5

Iram indeed is gone with all its Rose,
And Jamshýd's Sev'n-ring'd Cup where no one knows;
But still the Vine her ancient ruby yields,
And still a Garden by the Water blows.

6

And David's Lips are lock't; but in divine
High piping Pehleví, with 'Wine! Wine! Wine!
Red Wine!'—the Nightingale cries to the Rose
That yellow Cheek of her's to'incarnadine.

7

Come, fill the Cup, and in the Fire of Spring
The Winter Garment of Repentance fling:
The Bird of Time has but a little way
To fly—and Lo! the Bird is on the Wing.

8

And look—a thousand Blossoms with the Day
Woke—and a thousand scatter'd into Clay:
And this first Summer Month that brings the Rose
Shall take Jamshýd and Kaikobád away.

9

But come with old Khayyám, and leave the Lot
Of Kaikobád and Kaikhosrú forgot:
Let Rustum lay about him as he will,
Or Hátim Tai cry Supper—heed them not.

10

With me along some Strip of Herbage strown
That just divides the desert from the sown,
 Where name of Slave and Sultán scarce is known,
And pity Sultán Mahmud on his Throne.

11

Here with a Loaf of Bread beneath the Bough,
A Flask of Wine, a Book of Verse—and Thou
 Beside me singing in the Wilderness—
And Wilderness is Paradise enow.

12

'How sweet is mortal Sovranty!'—think some:
Others—'How blest the Paradise to come!'
 Ah, take the Cash in hand and waive the Rest;
Oh, the brave Music of a *distant* Drum!

13

Look to the Rose that blows about us—'Lo,
Laughing,' she says, 'into the World I blow:
 At once the silken Tassel of my Purse
Tear, and its Treasure on the Garden throw.'

14

The Worldly Hope men set their Hearts upon
Turns Ashes—or it prospers; and anon,
 Like Snow upon the Desert's dusty Face
Lightning a little Hour or two—is gone.

15

And those who husbanded the Golden Grain,
And those who flung it to the Winds like Rain,
  Alike to no such aureate Earth are turn'd
As, buried once, Men want dug up again.

16

Think, in this batter'd Caravanserai
Whose Doorways are alternate Night and Day,
  How Sultán after Sultán with his Pomp
Abode his Hour or two and went his way.

17

They say the Lion and the Lizard keep
The Courts where Jamshýd gloried and drank deep:
  And Bahrám, that great Hunter—the Wild Ass
Stamps o'er his Head, and he lies fast asleep.

18

I sometimes think that never blows so red
The Rose as where some buried Cæsar bled;
  That every Hyacinth the Garden wears
Dropt in its Lap from some once lovely Head.

19

And this delightful Herb whose tender Green
Fledges the River's Lip on which we lean—
  Ah, lean upon it lightly! for who knows
From what once lovely Lip it springs unseen!

20

Ah, my Belovéd, fill the Cup that clears
TO-DAY of past Regrets and future Fears—
To-morrow?—Why, To-morrow I may be
Myself with Yesterday's Sev'n Thousand Years.

21

Lo! some we loved, the lovliest and best
That Time and Fate of all their Vintage prest,
Have drunk their Cup a Round or two before,
And one by one crept silently to Rest.

22

And we, that now make merry in the Room
They left, and Summer dresses in new Bloom,
Ourselves must we beneath the Couch of Earth
Descend, ourselves to make a Couch—for whom?

23

Ah, make the most of what we yet may spend,
Before we too into the Dust descend;
Dust into Dust, and under Dust, to lie,
Sans Wine, sans Song, sans Singer, and—sans End!

24

Alike for those who for TO-DAY prepare,
And those that after a TO-MORROW stare,
A Muezzin from the Tower of Darkness cries
'Fools! your Reward is neither Here nor There!'

25

Why, all the Saints and Sages who discuss'd
Of the Two Worlds so learnedly, are thrust
 Like foolish Prophets forth; their Words to Scorn
Are scatter'd, and their Mouths are stopt with Dust.

26

Oh, come with old Khayyám, and leave the Wise
To talk; one thing is certain, that Life flies;
 One thing is certain, and the Rest is Lies;
The Flower that once has blown for ever dies.

27

Myself when young did eagerly frequent
Doctor and Saint, and heard great Argument
 About it and about; but evermore
Came out by the same Door as in I went.

28

With them the Seed of Wisdom did I sow,
And with my own hand labour'd it to grow:
 And this was all the Harvest that I reap'd—
'I came like Water and like Wind I go.'

29

Into this Universe, and *why* not knowing,
Nor *whence*, like Water willy-nilly flowing:
 And out of it, as Wind along the Waste,
I know not *whither*, willy-nilly blowing.

30

What, without asking, hither hurried *whence?*
And, without asking, *whither* hurried hence!
  Another and another Cup to drown
The Memory of this Impertinence!

31

Up from Earth's Centre through the Seventh Gate
I rose, and on the Throne of Saturn sate,
  And many Knots unravel'd by the Road;
But not the Knot of Human Death and Fate.

32

There was a Door to which I found no Key:
There was a Veil past which I could not see:
  Some little Talk awhile of ME and THEE
There seemed—and then no more of THEE and ME.

33

Then to the rolling Heav'n itself I cried,
Asking, 'What Lamp had Destiny to guide
  Her little Children stumbling in the Dark?'
And—'A blind Understanding!' Heav'n replied.

34

Then to this earthen Bowl did I adjourn
My Lip the secret Well of Life to learn:
  And Lip to Lip it murmur'd—'While you live
Drink!—for once dead you never shall return.'

35

I think the Vessel, that with fugitive
Articulation answer'd, once did live,
And merry-make; and the cold Lip I kiss'd
How many Kisses might it take—and give!

36

For in the Market-place, one Dusk of Day,
I watch'd the Potter thumping his wet Clay:
And with its all obliterated Tongue
It murmur'd—'Gently, Brother, gently, pray!'

37

Ah, fill the Cup:—what boots it to repeat
How Time is slipping underneath our Feet:
Unborn TO-MORROW, and dead YESTERDAY,
Why fret about them if TO-DAY be sweet!

38

One Moment in Annihilation's Waste,
One Moment, of the Well of Life to taste—
The Stars are setting and the Caravan
Starts for the Dawn of Nothing—Oh, make haste!

39

How long, how long, in infinite Pursuit
Of This and That endeavour and dispute?
Better be merry with the fruitful Grape
Than sadden after none, or bitter, Fruit.

40

You know, my Friends, how long since in my House
For a new Marriage I did make Carouse:
 Divorced old barren Reason from my Bed,
And took the Daughter of the Vine to Spouse.

41

For 'Is' and 'IS-NOT' though *with* Rule and Line,
And 'UP-AND-DOWN' *without* I could define,
 I yet in all I only cared to know,
Was never deep in anything but—Wine.

42

And lately, by the Tavern Door agape,
Came stealing through the Dusk an Angel Shape
 Bearing a Vessel on his Shoulder; and
He bid me taste of it; and 'twas—the Grape!

43

The Grape that can with Logic absolute
The Two-and-Seventy jarring Sects confute:
 The subtle Alchemist that in a Trice
Life's leaden Metal into Gold transmute.

44

The mighty Mahmud, the victorious Lord,
That all the misbelieving and black Horde
 Of Fears and Sorrows that infest the Soul
Scatters and slays with his enchanted Sword.

45

But leave the Wise to wrangle, and with me
The Quarrel of the Universe let be:
 And, in some corner of the Hubbub coucht,
Make Game of that which makes as much of Thee.

46

For in and out, above, about, below,
'Tis nothing but a Magic Shadow-show,
 Play'd in a Box whose Candle is the Sun,
Round which we Phantom Figures come and go.

47

And if the Wine you drink, the Lip you press,
End in the Nothing all Things end in—Yes—
 Then fancy while Thou art, Thou art but what
Thou shalt be—Nothing—Thou shalt not be less.

48

While the Rose blows along the River Brink,
With old Khayyám and Ruby Vintage drink:
 And when the Angel with his darker Draught
Draws up to Thee—take that, and do not shrink.

49

'Tis all a Chequer-board of Nights and Days
Where Destiny with Men for Pieces plays:
 Hither and thither moves, and mates, and slays,
And one by one back in the Closet lays.

50

The Ball no Question makes of Ayes and Noes,
But Right or Left, as strikes the Player goes;
And He that toss'd Thee down into the Field,
He knows about it all—HE knows—HE knows!

51

The Moving Finger writes; and, having writ
Moves on: nor all thy Piety nor Wit
Shall lure it back to cancel half a Line,
Nor all thy Tears wash out a Word of it.

52

And that inverted Bowl we call The Sky,
Whereunder crawling coop't we live and die,
Lift not thy hands to *It* for help—for It
Rolls impotently on as Thou or I.

53

With Earth's first Clay They did the Last Man's knead.
And then of the Last Harvest sow'd the Seed:
Yea, the first Morning of Creation wrote
What the Last Dawn of Reckoning shall read.

54

I tell Thee this—When, starting from the Goal,
Over the shoulders of the flaming Foal
Of Heav'n Parwín and Mushtara they flung,
In my predestin'd Plot of Dust and Soul.

55

The Vine had struck a Fibre; which about
If clings my Being—let the Sufi flout;
Of my Base Metal may be filed a Key,
That shall unlock the Door he howls without.

56

And this I know: whether the one True Light,
Kindle to Love, or Wrath—consume me quite,
One Glimpse of It within the Tavern caught
Better than in the Temple lost outright.

57

Oh, Thou, who didst with Pitfall and with Gin
Beset the Road I was to wander in,
Thou wilt not with Predestination round
Enmesh me, and impute my Fall to Sin?

58

Oh, Thou, who Man of baser Earth didst make,
And who with Eden didst devise the Snake;
For all the Sin wherewith the Face of Man
Is blacken'd, Man's Forgiveness give—and take!

Kuza-Nama

59

Listen again. One Evening at the Close
Of Ramazán, ere the better Moon arose,
In that old Potter's Shop I stood alone
With the clay Population round in Rows.

60

And, strange to tell, among that Earthen Lot
Some could articulate, while others not:
 And suddenly one more impatient cried—
'Who *is* the Potter, pray, and who the Pot?'

61

Then said another—'Surely not in vain
My Substance from the common Earth was ta'en,
 That He who subtly wrought me into Shape
Should stamp me back to common Earth again.'

62

Another said—'Why, ne'er a peevish Boy,
Would break the Bowl from which he drank in Joy;
 Shall He that *made* the Vessel in pure Love
And Fancy, in an after Rage destroy!'

63

None answer'd this; but after Silence spake
A Vessel of a more ungainly Make:
 'They sneer at me for leaning all awry;
What! did the Hand then of the Potter shake?'

64

Said one—'Folks of a surly Tapster tell,
And daub his Visage with the Smoke of Hell;
 They talk of some strict Testing of us—Pish!
He's a Good Fellow, and 'twill all be well.'

65

Then said another with a long-drawn Sigh,
'My Clay with long oblivion is gone dry:
 But, fill me with the old familiar Juice,
Methinks I might recover by-and-bye!'

66

So while the Vessels one by one were speaking,
One spied the little Crescent all were seeking:
 And then they jogg'd each other, 'Brother! Brother!
Hark to the Porter's Shoulder-knot a-creaking!'

67

Ah, with the Grape my fading Life provide,
And wash my Body whence the Life has died,
 And in a Windingsheet of Vine-leaf wrapt,
So bury me by some sweet Garden-side.

68

That ev'n my buried Ashes such a Snare
Of Perfume shall fling up into the Air,
 As not a True Believer passing by
But shall be overtaken unaware.

69

Indeed the Idols I have loved so long
Have done my Credit in Men's Eye much wrong:
 Have drown'd my Honour in a shallow Cup,
And sold my Reputation for a Song.

70

Indeed, indeed, Repentance oft before
I swore—but was I sober when I swore?
 And then and then came Spring, and Rose-in-hand
My thread-bare Penitence apieces tore.

71

And much as Wine has play'd the Infidel,
And robb'd me of my Robe of Honour—well,
 I often wonder what the Vintners buy
One half so precious as the Goods they sell.

72

Alas, that Spring should vanish with the Rose!
That Youth's sweet-scented Manuscript should close!
 The Nightingale that in the Branches sang,
Ah, whence, and whither flown again, who knows!

73

Ah Love! could thou and I with Fate conspire
To grasp this sorry Scheme of Things entire,
 Would not we shatter it to bits—and then
Re-mould it nearer to the Heart's Desire!

74

Ah, Moon of my Delight who know'st no wane,
The Moon of Heav'n is rising once again:
 How oft hereafter rising shall she look
Through this same Garden after me—in vain!

75

And when Thyself with shining Foot shall pass
Among the Guests Star-scatter'd on the Grass,
  And in thy joyous Errand reach the Spot
Where I made one—turn down an empty Glass!

TAMÁM SHUD

RUBÁIYÁT OF OMAR KHAYYÁM

The Second Edition, 1868

I

WAKE! For the Sun behind yon Eastern height
Has chased the Session of the Stars from Night;
 And, to the field of Heav'n ascending, strikes
The Sultán's Turret with a Shaft of Light.

2

Before the phantom of False morning died,
Methought a Voice within the Tavern cried,
 'When all the Temple is prepared within,
Why lags the drowsy Worshipper outside?'

3

And, as the Cock crew, those who stood before
The Tavern shouted—'Open then the door!
 You know how little while we have to stay,
And, once departed, may return no more.'

4

Now the New Year reviving old Desires,
The thoughtful Soul to Solitude retires,
 Where the WHITE HAND OF MOSES on the Bough
Puts out, and Jesus from the ground suspires.

Iram indeed is gone with all his Rose,
And Jamshýd's Sev'n-ring'd Cup where no one knows;
But still a Ruby gushes from the Vine,
And many a Garden by the Water blows.

6

And David's lips are lockt; but in divine
High-piping Pehleví, with 'Wine! Wine! Wine!
Red Wine!'—the Nightingale cries to the Rose
That sallow cheek of her's to incarnadine.

7

Come, fill the Cup, and in the fire of Spring
Your Winter-garment of Repentance fling:
The Bird of Time has but a little way
To flutter—and the Bird is on the Wing.

8

Whether at Naishápúr or Babylon,
Whether the Cup with sweet or bitter run,
The Wine of Life keeps oozing drop by drop,
The Leaves of Life keep falling one by one.

9

Morning a thousand Roses brings, you say;
Yes, but where leaves the Rose of yesterday?
And this first Summer month that brings the Rose
Shall take Jamshýd and Kaikobád away.

10

Well, let it take them! What have we to do
With Kaikobád the Great, or Kaikhosrú?
Let Rustum cry 'To Battle!' as he likes,
Or Hátim Tai 'To Supper!'—heed not you.

11

With me along the strip of Herbage strown
That just divides the desert from the sown,
Where name of Slave and Sultán is forgot—
And Peace to Mahmud on his golden Throne!

12

Here with a little Bread beneath the Bough,
A Flask of Wine, a Book of Verse—and Thou
Beside me singing in the Wilderness—
Oh, Wilderness were Paradise enow!

13

Some for the Glories of This World; and some
Sigh for the Prophet's Paradise to come;
Ah, take the Cash, and let the Promise go,
Nor heed the rumble of a distant Drum!

14

Were it not Folly, Spider-like to spin
The Thread of present Life away to win—
What? for ourselves, who know not if we shall
Breathe out the very Breath we now breathe in!

15

Look to the blowing Rose about us—'Lo,
Laughing,' she says, 'into the world I blow:
 At once the silken tassel of my Purse
Tear, and its Treasure on the Garden throw.'

16

For those who husbanded the Golden grain,
And those who flung it to the winds like Rain,
 Alike to no such aureate Earth are turn'd
As, buried once, Men want dug up again.

17

The Worldly Hope men set their Hearts upon
Turns Ashes—or it prospers; and anon,
 Like Snow upon the Desert's dusty Face,
Lighting a little hour or two—was gone.

18

Think, in this batter'd Caravanserai
Whose Portals are alternate Night and Day,
 How Sultán after Sultán with his Pomp
Abode his destin'd Hour, and went his way.

19

They say the Lion and the Lizard keep
The Courts where Jamshýd gloried and drank deep:
 And Bahrám, that great Hunter—the Wild Ass
Stamps o'er his Head, but cannot break his Sleep.

20

The Palace that to Heav'n his pillars threw,
And Kings the forehead on his threshold drew—
I saw the solitary Ringdove there,
And 'Coo, coo, coo,' she cried; 'Coo, coo, coo.'

21

Ah, my Belovéd, fill the Cup that clears
TO-DAY of past Regrets and future Fears:
To-morrow!—Why, To-morrow I may be
Myself with Yesterday's Sev'n thousand Years

22

For some we loved, the loveliest and the best
That from his Vintage rolling Time has prest,
Have drunk their Cup a Round or two before,
And one by one crept silently to rest.

23

And we, that now make merry in the Room
They left, and Summer dresses in new bloom,
Ourselves must we beneath the Couch of Earth
Descend, ourselves to make a Couch—for whom?

24

I sometimes think that never blows so red
The Rose as where some buried Cæsar bled:
That every Hyacinth the Garden wears
Dropt in her Lap from some once lovely Head.

25

And this delightful Herb whose living Green
Fledges the River's Lip on which we lean—
  Ah, lean upon it lightly! for who knows
From what once lovely Lip it springs unseen!

26

Ah, make the most of what we yet may spend,
Before we too into the Dust descend;
  Dust into Dust, and under Dust, to lie,
Sans Wine, sans Song, sans Singer, and—sans End!

27

Alike for those who for TO-DAY prepare,
And those that after some TO-MORROW stare,
  A Muezzin from the Tower of Darkness cries,
'Fools! your Reward is neither Here nor There!'

28

Another Voice, when I am sleeping, cries,
'The Flower should open with the Morning skies.'
  And a retreating Whisper, as I wake—
'The Flower that once has blown for ever dies.'

29

Why, all the Saints and Sages who discuss'd
Of the Two Worlds so learnedly, are thrust
  Like foolish Prophets forth; their Words to Scorn
Are scatter'd, and their Mouths are stopt with Dust.

30

Myself when young did eagerly frequent
Doctor and Saint, and heard great argument
 About it and about: but evermore
Came out by the same door as in I went.

31

With them the seed of Wisdom did I sow,
And with mine own hand wrought to make it grow:
 And this was all the Harvest that I reap'd—
'I came like Water, and like Wind I go.'

32

Into this Universe, and *Why* not knowing,
Nor *Whence*, like Water willy-nilly flowing:
 And out of it, as Wind along the Waste,
I know not *Whither*, willy-nilly blowing.

33

What, without asking, hither hurried *Whence?*
And, without asking, *Whither* hurried hence!
 Ah, contrite Heav'n endowed us with the Vine
To drug the memory of that insolence!

34

Up from Earth's Centre through the Seventh Gate
I rose, and on the Throne of Saturn sate,
 And many Knots unravel'd by the Road;
But not the Master-Knot of Human Fate.

35

There was the Door to which I found no Key:
There was the Veil through which I could not see
  Some little talk awhile of ME and THEE
There was—and then no more of THEE and ME.

36

Earth could not answer; nor the Seas that mourn
In flowing Purple, of their Lord forlorn;
  Nor Heav'n, with those eternal Signs reveal'd
And hidden by the sleeve of Night and Morn.

37

Then of the THEE IN ME who works behind
The Veil of Universe I cried to find
  A Lamp to guide me through the Darkness; and
Something then said—'An Understanding blind.'

38

Then to the Lip of this poor earthen Urn
I lean'd, the secret Well of Life to learn:
  And Lip to Lip it murmur'd--'While you live,
Drink!—for, once dead, you never shall return.'

39

I think the Vessel, that with fugitive
Articulation answer'd, once did live,
  And drink; and that impassive Lip I kiss'd,
How many Kisses might it take—and give!

40

For I remember stopping by the way
To watch a Potter thumping his wet Clay:
 And with its all-obliterated Tongue
It murmur'd—'Gently, Brother, gently, pray!'

41

For has not such a Story from of Old
Down Man's successive generations roll'd
 Of such a clod of saturated Earth
Cast by the Maker into Human mould?

42

And not a drop that from our Cups we throw
On the parcht herbage but may steal below
 To quench the fire of Anguish in some Eye
There hidden—far beneath, and long ago.

43

As then the Tulip for her wonted sup
Of Heavenly Vintage lifts her chalice up,
 Do you, twin offpsring of the soil, till Heav'n
To Earth invert you like an empty Cup.

44

Do you, within your little hour of Grace,
The waving Cypress in your Arms enlace,
 Before the Mother back into her arms
Fold, and dissolve you in a last embrace.

45

And if the Cup you drink, the Lip you press,
End in what All begins and ends in—Yes;
Imagine then you *are* what heretofore
You *were*—hereafter you shall not be less.

46

So when at last the Angel of the darker drink
Of Darkness finds you by the river-brink,
And, proffering his Cup, invites your Soul
Forth to your Lips to quaff it—do not shrink.

47

And fear not lest Existence closing *your*
Account, should lose, or know the type no more;
The Eternal Sákí from that Bowl has pour'd
Millions of Bubbles like us, and will pour.

48

When You and I behind the Veil are past,
Oh but the long long while the World shall last,
Which of our Coming and Departure heeds
As much as Ocean of a pebble-cast.

49

One Moment in Annihilation's Waste,
One Moment, of the Well of Life to taste—
The Stars are setting, and the Caravan
Draws to the Dawn of Nothing—Oh make haste!

50

Would you that spangle of Existence spend
About THE SECRET—quick about it, Friend!
 A Hair, they say, divides the False and True—
And upon what, prithee, does Life depend?

51

A Hair, they say, divides the False and True;
Yes; and a single Alif were the clue,
 Could you but find it, to the Treasure-house,
And peradventure to THE MASTER too;

52

Whose secret Presence, through Creation's veins
Running, Quicksilver-like eludes your pains:
 Taking all shapes from Máh to Máhi; and
They change and perish all—but He remains;

53

A moment guess'd—then back behind the Fold
Immerst of Darkness round the Drama roll'd
 Which, for the Pastime of Eternity,
He doth Himself contrive, enact, behold.

54

But if in vain, down on the stubborn floor
Of Earth, and up to Heav'n's unopening Door,
 You gaze To-day, while You are You—how then
To-morrow, You when shall be You no more?

55

Oh, plagued no more with Human or Divine,
To-morrow's tangle to itself resign,
And lose your fingers in the tresses of
The Cypress-slender Minister of Wine.

56

Waste not your Hour, nor in the vain pursuit
Of This and That endeavour and dispute;
Better be merry with the fruitful Grape
Than sadden after none, or bitter, Fruit.

57

You know, my Friends, how bravely in my House
For a new Marriage I did make Carouse:
Divorced old barren Reason from my Bed,
And took the Daughter of the Vine to Spouse.

58

For 'Is' and 'Is-not' though with Rule and Line,
And 'Up-and-down' by Logic I define,
Of all that one should care to fathom, I
Was never deep in anything but—Wine.

59

Ah, but my Computations, People say,
Have squared the Year to human compass, eh?
If so, by striking from the Calendar
Unborn To-morrow, and dead Yesterday.

60

And lately, by the Tavern Door agape,
Came shining through the Dusk an Angel Shape
 Bearing a Vessel on his Shoulder; and
He bid me taste of it; and 'twas—the Grape!

61

The Grape that can with Logic absolute
The Two-and-Seventy jarring Sects confute:
 The sovereign Alchemist that in a trice
Life's leaden metal into Gold transmute:

62

The mighty Mahmud, Allah-breathing Lord,
That all the misbelieving and black Horde
 Of Fears and Sorrows that infest the Soul
Scatters before him with his whirlwind Sword.

63

Why, be this Juice the growth of God, who dare
Blaspheme the twisted tendril as a Snare?
 A Blessing, we should use it, should we not?
And if a Curse—why, then, Who set it there?

64

I must abjure the Balm of Life, I must,
Scared by some After-reckoning ta'en on trust,
 Or lured with Hope of some Diviner Drink,
When the frail Cup is crumbled into Dust!

65

If but the Vine and Love-abjuring Band
Are in the Prophet's Paradise to stand,
 Alack, I doubt the Prophet's Paradise
Were empty as the hollow of one's Hand.

66

Oh threats of Hell and Hopes of Paradise!
One thing at least is certain—This Life flies:
 One thing is certain and the rest is lies;
The Flower that once is blown for ever dies.

67

Strange, is it not? that of the myriads who
Before us pass'd the door of Darkness through
 Not one returns to tell us of the Road,
Which to discover we must travel too.

68

The Revelations of Devout and Learn'd
Who rose before us, and as Prophets burn'd,
 Are all but Stories, which, awoke from Sleep
They told their fellows, and to Sleep return'd.

69

Why, if the Soul can fling the Dust aside,
And naked on the Air of Heaven ride,
 Is't not a shame—is't not a shame for him
So long in this Clay suburb to abide?

70

But that is but a Tent wherein may rest
A Sultán to the realm of Death addrest;
 The Sultán rises, and the dark Ferrásh
Strikes, and prepares it for another guest.

71

I sent my Soul through the Invisible,
Some letter of that After-life to spell:
 And after many days my Soul return'd
And said, 'Behold, Myself am Heav'n and Hell:'

72

Heav'n but the Vision of fulfill'd Desire,
And Hell the Shadow of a Soul on fire,
 Cast on the Darkness into which Ourselves,
So late emerg'd from, shall so soon expire.

73

We are no other than a moving row
Of visionary Shapes that come and go
 Round with this Sun-illumin'd Lantern held
In Midnight by the Master of the Show;

74

Impotent Pieces of the Game he plays
Upon this Chequer-board of Nights and Days;
 Hither and thither moves, and checks, and slays;
And one by one back in the Closet lays.

75

The Ball no Question makes of Ayes and Noes,
But Right or Left as strikes the Player goes;
And He that toss'd you down into the Field,
He knows about it all—HE knows—HE knows!

76

The Moving Finger writes; and, having writ,
Moves on: nor all your Piety nor Wit
Shall lure it back to cancel half a Line,
Nor all your Tears wash out a Word of it.

77

For let Philosopher and Doctor preach
Of what they will, and what they will not—each
Is but one Link in an eternal Chain
That none can slip, nor break, nor over-reach.

78

And that inverted Bowl we call The Sky,
Whereunder crawling coop'd we live and die,
Lift not your hands to *It* for help—for It
As impotently rolls as you or I.

79

With Earth's first Clay They did the Last Man knead,
And there of the Last Harvest sow'd the Seed;
And the first Morning of Creation wrote
What the Last Dawn of Reckoning shall read.

80

Yesterday *This* Day's Madness did prepare;
To-morrow's Silence, Triumph, or Despair:
 Drink! for know you not whence you came, nor why:
Drink! for you know not why you go, nor where.

81

I tell you this—When, started from the Goal,
Over the flaming shoulders of the Foal
 Of Heav'n Parwín and Mushtari they flung,
In my predestin'd Plot of Dust and Soul

82

The Vine had struck a fibre: which about
If clings my Being—let the Dervish flout;
 Of my Base metal may be filed a Key,
That shall unlock the Door he howls without.

83

And this I know: whether the one True Light,
Kindle to Love, or Wrath-consume me quite,
 One Flash of It within the Tavern caught
Better than in the Temple lost outright.

84

What! out of senseless Nothing to provoke
A conscious Something to resent the yoke
 Of unpermitted Pleasure, under pain
Of Everlasting Penalties, if broke!

85

What! from his helpless Creature be repaid
Pure Gold for what he lent us dross-allay'd—
  Sue for a Debt we never did contract,
And cannot answer—Oh the sorry trade!

86

Nay, but, for terror of his wrathful Face,
I swear I will not call Injustice Grace;
  Not one Good Fellow of the Tavern but
Would kick so poor a Coward from the place.

87

Oh Thou, who didst with pitfall and with gin
Beset the Road I was to wander in,
  Thou wilt not with Predestin'd Evil round
Enmesh, and then impute my Fall to Sin?

88

Oh Thou, who Man of baser Earth didst make,
And ev'n with Paradise devise the Snake:
  For all the Sin the Face of wretched Man
Is black with—Man's Forgiveness give—and take!

89

As under cover of departing Day
Slunk hunger-stricken Ramazán away,
  Once more within the Potter's house alone
I stood, surrounded by the Shapes of Clay.

90

And once again there gather'd a scarce heard
Whisper among them; as it were, the stirr'd
Ashes of some all but extinguisht Tongue,
Which mine ear kindled into living Word.

91

Said one among them—'Surely not in vain,
My Substance from the common Earth was ta'en,
That He who subtly wrought me into Shape
Should stamp me back to shapeless Earth again?'

92

Another said, 'Why, ne'er a peevish Boy
Would break the Cup from which he drank in Joy;
Shall He that of his own free Fancy made
The Vessel, in an after-rage destroy!'

93

None answer'd this; but after silence spake
Some Vessel of a more ungainly Make;
'They sneer at me for leaning all awry;
What! did the Hand then of the Potter shake?'

94

Thus with the Dead as with the Living, *What?*
And *Why?* so ready, but the *Wherefor* not,
One on a sudden peevishly exclaim'd,
'Which is the Potter, pray, and which the Pot?'

95

Said one—'Folks of a surly Master tell,
And daub his Visage with the Smoke of Hell;
They talk of some sharp Trial of us—Pish!
He's a Good Fellow, and 'twill all be well.'

96

'Well,' said another, 'Whoso will, let try,
My Clay with long oblivion is gone dry:
But, fill me with the old familiar Juice,
Methinks I might recover by-and-bye!'

97

So while the Vessels one by one were speaking,
One spied the little Crescent all were seeking:
And then they jogg'd each other, 'Brother! Brother!
Now for the Porter's shoulder-knot a-creaking!'

98

Ah, with the Grape my fading Life provide,
And wash my Body whence the Life has died,
And lay me, shrouded in the living Leaf,
By some not unfrequented Garden-side.

99

Whither resorting from the vernal Heat
Shall Old Acquaintance Old Acquaintance greet,
Under the Branch that leans above the Wall
To shed his Blossom over head and feet.

100

Then ev'n my buried Ashes such a snare
Of Vintage shall fling up into the Air,
As not a True-believer passing by
But shall be overtaken unaware.

101

Indeed the Idols I have loved so long
Have done my credit in Men's eye much wrong:
Have drown'd my Glory in a shallow Cup,
And sold my Reputation for a Song.

102

Indeed, indeed, Repentance oft before
I swore—but was I sober when I swore?
And then and then came Spring and Rose-in-hand
My thread-bare Penitence apieces tore.

103

And much as Wine has play'd the Infidel,
And robb'd me of my Robe of Honour—Well,
I often wonder what the Vintners buy
One half so precious as the ware they sell.

104

Yet Ah, that Spring should vanish with the Rose!
That Youth's sweet-scented manuscript should close!
The Nightingale that in the branches sang,
Ah whence, and whither flown again, who knows!

105

Would but the Desert of the Fountain yield
One glimpse—if dimly, yet indeed, reveal'd,
Toward which the fainting Traveller might spring,
As springs the trampled herbage of the field!

106

Oh if the World were but to re-create,
That we might catch ere closed the Book of Fate,
And make The Writer on a fairer leaf
Inscribe our names, or quite obliterate!

107

Better, oh better, cancel from the Scroll
Of Universe one luckless Human Soul,
Than drop by drop enlarge the Flood that rolls
Hoarser with Anguish as the Ages roll.

108

Ah Love! could you and I with Fate conspire
To grasp this sorry Scheme of Things entire.
Would not we shatter it to bits—and then
Re-mould it nearer to the Heart's Desire!

109

But see! The rising Moon of Heav'n again
Looks for us, Sweet-heart, through the quivering Plane:
How oft hereafter rising will she look
Among those leaves—for one of us in vain!

110

And when Yourself with silver Foot shall pass
Among the Guests Star-scatter'd on the Grass,
  And in your joyous errand reach the spot
Where I made One—turn down an empty Glass!

TAMÁM

RUBÁIYÁT OF OMAR KHAYYÁM

The Fifth Edition, 1889

1

WAKE! For the Sun, who scatter'd into flight
The Stars before him from the Field of Night,
  Drives Night along with them from Heav'n, and strikes
The Sultán's Turret with a Shaft of Light.

2

Before the phantom of False morning died,
Methought a Voice within the Tavern cried,
  'When all the Temple is prepared within,
Why nods the drowsy Worshipper outside?'

3

And, as the Cock crew, those who stood before
The Tavern shouted—'Open then the Door!
  You know how little while we have to stay,
And, once departed, may return no more.'

4

Now the New Year reviving old Desires,
The thoughtful Soul to Solitude retires,
  Where the WHITE HAND OF MOSES on the Bough
Puts out, and Jesus from the Ground suspires.

5

Iram indeed is gone with all his Rose,
And Jamshýd's Sev'n-ring'd Cup where no one knows;
But still a Ruby kindles in the Vine,
And many a Garden by the Water blows.

6

And David's Lips are lockt; but in divine
High-piping Pehleví, with 'Wine! Wine! Wine!
Red Wine!—the Nightingale cries to the Rose
That sallow cheek of hers to' incarnadine.

7

Come, fill the Cup, and in the fire of Spring
Your Winter-garment of Repentance fling:
The Bird of Time has but a little way
To flutter—and the Bird is on the Wing.

8

Whether at Naishápúr or Babylon,
Whether the Cup with sweet or bitter run,
The Wine of Life keeps oozing drop by drop,
The Leaves of Life keep falling one by one.

9

Each Morn a thousand Roses brings, you say;
Yes, but where leaves the Rose of Yesterday?
And this first Summer month that brings the Rose
Shall take Jamshýd and Kaikobád away.

10

Well, let it take them! What have we to do
With Kaikobád the Great, or Kaikhosrú?
Let Zál and Rustum bluster as they will,
Or Hátim call to Supper—heed not you.

11

With me along the strip of Herbage strown
That just divides the desert from the sown,
Where name of Slave and Sultán is forgot—
And Peace to Mahmud on his golden Throne!

12

A Book of Verses underneath the Bough,
A Jug of Wine, a Loaf of Bread—and Thou
Beside me singing in the Wilderness—
Oh, Wilderness were Paradise enow!

13

Some for the Glories of This World; and some
Sigh for the Prophet's Paradise to come;
Ah, take the Cash, and let the Credit go,
Nor heed the rumble of a distant Drum!

14

Look to the blowing Rose about us—'Lo,
'Laughing,' she says, 'into the world I blow,
At once the silken tassel of my Purse
Tear, and its Treasure on the Garden throw.'

15

And those who husbanded the Golden grain,
And those who flung it to the winds like Rain,
 Alike to no such aureate Earth are turn'd
As, buried once, Men want dug up again.

16

The Worldly Hope men set their Hearts upon
Turns Ashes—or it prospers; and anon,
 Like Snow upon the Desert's dusty Face,
Lighting a little hour or two—is gone.

17

Think, in this batter'd Caravanserai,
Whose Portals are alternate Night and Day,
 How Sultán after Sultán with his Pomp
Abode his destined Hour, and went his way.

18

They say the Lion and the Lizard keep
The Courts where Jamshýd gloried and drank deep:
 And Bahrám, that great Hunter—the Wild Ass
Stamps o'er his Head, but cannot break his Sleep.

19

I sometimes think that never blows so red
The Rose as where some buried Cæsar bled;
 That every Hyacinth the Garden wears
Dropt in her Lap from some once lovely Head.

20

And this reviving Herb whose tender Green
Fledges the River-Lip on which we lean—
  Ah, lean upon it lightly! for who knows
From what once lovely Lip it springs unseen!

21

Ah, my Belovéd, fill the Cup that clears
TO-DAY of past Regrets and future Fears:
  To-morrow!—Why, To-morrow I may be
Myself with Yesterday's Sev'n thousand Years.

22

For some we loved, the loveliest and the best
That from his Vintage rolling Time hath prest,
  Have drunk their Cup a Round or two before,
And one by one crept silently to rest.

23

And we, that now make merry in the Room
They left, and Summer dresses in new bloom,
  Ourselves must we beneath the Couch of Earth
Descend—ourselves to make a Couch—for whom?

24

Ah, make the most of what we yet may spend,
Before we too into the Dust descend;
  Dust into Dust, and under Dust to lie,
Sans Wine, sans Song, sans Singer, and—sans End!

25

Alike for those who for TO-DAY prepare,
And those that after some TO-MORROW stare,
 A Muezzin from the Tower of Darkness cries,
'Fools! your Reward is neither Here nor There.'

26

Why, all the Saints and Sages who discuss'd
Of the TWO Worlds so wisely—they are thrust
 Like foolish Prophets forth; their Words to Scorn
Are scatter'd, and their Mouths are stopt with Dust.

27

Myself when young did eagerly frequent
Doctor and Saint, and heard great argument
 About it and about: but evermore
Came out by the same door where in I went.

28

With them the seed of Wisdom did I sow,
And with mine own hand wrought to make it grow:
 And this was all the Harvest that I reap'd—
'I came like Water, and like Wind I go.'

29

Into this Universe, and *Why* not knowing
Nor *Whence*, like Water willy-nilly flowing;
 And out of it, as Wind along the Waste,
I know not *Whither*, willy-nilly blowing.

30

What, without asking, hither hurried *Whence?*
And, without asking, *Whither* hurried hence!
 Oh, many a Cup of this forbidden Wine
Must drown the memory of that insolence!

31

Up from Earth's Centre through the Seventh Gate
I rose, and on the Throne of Saturn sate,
 And many a Knot unravel'd by the Road;
But not the Master-knot of Human Fate.

32

There was the Door to which I found no Key;
There was the Veil through which I might not see:
 Some little talk awhile of ME and THEE
There was—and then no more of THEE and ME.

33

Earth could not answer; nor the Seas that mourn
In flowing Purple, of their Lord forlorn;
 Nor rolling Heaven, with all his Signs reveal'd
And hidden by the sleeve of Night and Morn.

34

Then of the THEE IN ME who works behind
The Veil, I lifted up my hands to find
 A lamp amid the Darkness; and I heard,
As from Without—'THE ME WITHIN THEE BLIND!'

35

Then to the Lip of this poor earthen Urn
I lean'd, the Secret of my Life to learn:
And Lip to Lip it murmur'd—'While you live,
Drink!—for, once dead, you never shall return.'

36

I think the Vessel, that the fugitive
Articulation answer'd, once did live,
And drink; and Ah! the passive Lip I kiss'd,
How many Kisses might it take and give!

37

For I remember stopping by the way
To watch a Potter thumping his wet Clay:
And with its all-obliterated Tongue
It murmur'd—'Gently, Brother, gently, pray!'

38

And has not such a Story from of Old
Down Man's successive generations roll'd
Of such a clod of saturated Earth
Cast by the Maker into Human mould?

39

And not a drop that from our Cups we throw
For Earth to drink of, but may steal below
To quench the fire of Anguish in some Eye
There hidden—far beneath, and long ago.

40

As then the Tulip for her morning sup
Of Heav'nly Vintage from the soil looks up,
 Do you devoutly do the like, till Heav'n
To Earth invert you—like an empty Cup.

41

Perplext no more with Human or Divine,
To-morrow's tangle to the winds resign,
 And lose your fingers in the tresses of
The Cypress-slender Minister of Wine.

42

And if the Wine you drink, the Lip you press,
End in what All begins and ends in—Yes;
 Think then you are TO-DAY what YESTERDAY
You were—TO-MORROW you shall not be less.

43

So when that Angel of the darker Drink
At last shall find you by the river-brink,
 And, offering his Cup, invite your Soul
Forth to your Lips to quaff—you shall not shrink.

44

Why, if the Soul can fling the Dust aside,
And naked on the Air of Heaven ride,
Were't not a Shame—were't not a Shame for him
In this clay carcase crippled to abide?

45

'Tis but a Tent where takes his one day's rest
A Sultán to the realm of Death addrest;
The Sultán rises, and the dark Ferrásh
Strikes, and prepares it for another Guest.

46

And fear not lest Existence closing your
Account, and mine, should know the like no more;
The Eternal Sákí from that Bowl has pour'd
Millions of Bubbles likes us, and will pour.

47

When you and I behind the Veil are past,
Oh, but the long, long while the World shall last,
Which of our Coming and Departure heeds
As the Sea's self should heed a pebble-cast.

48

A Moment's Halt—a momentary taste
Of BEING from the Well amid the Waste—
And Lo!—the phantom Caravan has reach'd
The NOTHING it set out from—Oh, make haste!

49

Would you that spangle of Existence spend
About THE SECRET—quick about it, Friend!
A Hair perhaps divides the False and True—
And upon what, prithee, may life depend?

50

A Hair perhaps divides the False and True;
Yes; and a single Alif were the clue—
 Could you but find it—to the Treasure-house,
And peradventure to THE MASTER too;

51

Whose secret Presence, through Creation's veins
Running Quicksilver-like eludes your pains;
 Taking all shapes from Máh to Máhi; and
They change and perish all—but He remains;

52

A moment guess'd—then back behind the Fold
Immerst of Darkness round the Drama roll'd
 Which, for the Pastime of Eternity,
He doth Himself contrive, enact, behold.

53

But if in vain, down on the stubborn floor
Of Earth, and up to Heav'n's unopening Door,
 You gaze TO-DAY, while You are You—how then
TO-MORROW, You when shall be You no more?

54

Waste not your Hour, nor in the vain pursuit
Of This and That endeavour and dispute;
 Better be jocund with the fruitful Grape
Than sadden after none, or bitter, Fruit.

55

You know, my Friends, with what a brave Carouse
I made a Second Marriage in my house;
 Divorced old barren Reason from my Bed,
And took the Daughter of the Vine to Spouse.

56

For 'IS' and 'IS-NOT' though with Rule and Line
And 'UP-AND-DOWN' by Logic I define,
 Of all that one should care to fathom, I
Was never deep in anything but—Wine.

57

Ah, but my Computations, People say,
Reduced the Year to better reckoning?—Nay,
 'Twas only striking from the Calendar
Unborn To-morrow, and dead Yesterday.

58

And lately, by the Tavern Door agape,
Came shining through the Dusk an Angel Shape
 Bearing a Vessel on his Shoulder; and
He bid me taste of it; and 'twas—the Grape!

59

The Grape that can with Logic absolute
The Two-and-Seventy jarring Sects confute:
 The sovereign Alchemist that in a trice
Life's leaden metal into Gold transmute:

60

The mighty Mahmud, Allah-breathing Lord,
That all the misbelieving and black Horde
  Of Fears and Sorrows that infest the Soul
Scatters before him with his whirlwind Sword.

61

Why, be this Juice the growth of God, who dare
Blaspheme the twisted tendril as a Snare?
  A Blessing, we should use it, should we not?
And if a Curse—why, then, Who set it there?

62

I must abjure the Balm of Life, I must,
Scared by some After-reckoning ta'en on trust,
  Or lured with Hope of some Diviner Drink,
To fill the Cup—when crumbled into dust!

63

Oh threats of Hell and Hopes of Paradise!
One thing at least is certain—*This* life flies;
  One thing is certain and the rest is Lies;
The Flower that once has blown for ever dies.

64

Strange, is it not? that of the myriads who
Before us pass'd the door of Darkness through,
  Not one returns to tell us of the Road,
Which to discover we must travel too.

65

The Revelations of Devout and Learn'd
Who rose before us, and as Prophets burn'd,
 Are all but Stories, which, awoke from Sleep
They told their comrades, and to Sleep return'd.

66

I sent my Soul through the Invisible,
Some Letter of that After-life to spell:
 And by and by my Soul return'd to me,
And answer'd 'I Myself am Heav'n and Hell:'

67

Heav'n but the Vision of fulfill'd Desire,
And Hell the Shadow from a Soul on fire,
 Cast on the Darkness into which Ourselves,
So late emerged from, shall so soon expire.

68

We are no other than a moving row
Of Magic Shadow-shapes that come and go
 Round with the Sun-illumined Lantern held
In Midnight by the Master of the Show;

69

But helpless Pieces of the Game He plays
Upon this Chequer-board of Nights and Days;
 Hither and thither moves, and checks, and slays,
And one by one back in the Closet lays.

70

The Ball no question makes of Ayes and Noes,
But Here or There as strikes the Player goes;
And He that toss'd you down into the Field,
He knows about it all—HE knows—HE knows!

71

The Moving Finger writes; and, having writ,
Moves on: nor all your Piety nor Wit
Shall lure it back to cancel half a Line,
Nor all your Tears wash out a Word of it.

72

And that inverted Bowl they call the Sky,
Whereunder crawling coop'd we live and die,
Lift not your hands to *It* for help—for It
As impotently moves as you or I.

73

With Earth's first Clay They did the Last Man knead,
And there of the Last Harvest sow'd the Seed:
And the first Morning of Creation wrote
What the Last Dawn of Reckoning shall read.

74

YESTERDAY *This* Day's Madness did prepare;
TO-MORROW's Silence, Triumph, or Despair:
Drink! for you know not whence you came, nor why:
Drink! for you know not why you go, nor where.

75

I tell you this—When, started from the Goal,
Over the flaming shoulders of the Foal
 Of Heav'n Parwín and Mushtari they flung,
In my predestined Plot of Dust and Soul

76

The Vine has struck a fibre: which about
If clings my Being—let the Dervish flout;
 Of my Base metal may be filed a Key,
That shall unlock the Door he howls without.

77

And this I know: whether the one True Light
Kindle to Love, or Wrath-consume me quite,
 Cne Flash of It within the Tavern caught
Better than in the Temple lost outright.

78

What! out of senseless Nothing to provoke
A conscious Something to resent the yoke
 Of unpermitted Pleasure, under pain
Of Everlasting Penalties, if broke!

79

What! from his helpless Creature be repaid
Pure Gold for what he lent him dross-allay'd—
 Sue for a Debt he never did contract,
And cannot answer—Oh the sorry trade!

80

Oh Thou, who didst with pitfall and with gin
Beset the Road I was to wander in,
Thou wilt not with Predestined Evil round
Enmesh, and then impute my Fall to Sin!

81

Oh Thou, who Man of baser Earth didst make,
And ev'n with Paradise devise the Snake:
For all the Sin wherewith the Face of Man
Is blacken'd—Man's forgiveness give—and take

82

As under cover of departing Day
Slunk hunger-stricken Ramazán away,
Once more within the Potter's house alone
I stood, surrounded by the Shapes of Clay.

83

Shapes of all Sorts and Sizes, great and small,
That stood along the floor and by the wall;
And some loquacious Vessels were; and some
Listen'd perhaps, but never talk'd at all.

84

Said one among them—'Surely not in vain
My substance of the common Earth was ta'en
And to this Figure moulded, to be broke,
Or trampled back to shapeless Earth again.'

85

Then said a Second—'Ne'er a peevish Boy
Would break the Bowl from which he drank in joy;
And he that with his hand the Vessel make
Will surely not in after Wrath destroy.'

86

After a momentary silence spake
Some Vessel of a more ungainly Make;
'They sneer at me for leaning all awry:
What! did the Hand then of the Potter shake?'

87

Whereat some one of the loquacious Lot—
I think a Sufi pipkin—waxing hot—
'All this of Pot and Potter—Tell me. then,
Who is the Potter, pray, and who the Pot?'

88

'Why,' said another, 'Some there are who tell
Of one who threatens he will toss to Hell
The luckless Pots he marr'd in making—Pish!
He's a Good Fellow, and 'twill all be well.'

89

'Well,' murmur'd one, 'Let whoso make or buy,
My Clay with long Oblivion is gone dry:
But fill me with the old familiar Juice,
Methinks I might recover by and by.'

90

So while the Vessels one by one were speaking,
The little Moon look'd in that all were seeking:
And then they jogg'd each other, 'Brother! Brother!
Now for the Porter's shoulder-knot a-creaking!'

91

Ah, with the Grape my fading life provide,
And wash the Body whence the Life has died.
And lay me, shrouded in the living Leaf,
By some not unfrequented Garden-side.

92

That ev'n my buried Ashes such a snare
Of Vintage shall fling up into the Air
As not a True-believer passing by
But shall be overtaken unaware.

93

Indeed the Idols I have loved so long
Have done my credit in this World much wrong:
Have drown'd my Glory in a shallow Cup,
And sold my Reputation for a Song.

94

Indeed, Indeed, Repentance oft before
I swore—but was I sober when I swore?
And then and then came Spring, and Rose-in-hand
My thread-bare Penitence apieces tore.

95

And much as Wine has play'd the Infidel,
And robb'd me of my Robe of Honour—Well,
I wonder often what the Vintners buy
One half so precious as the stuff they sell.

96

Yet Ah, that Spring should vanish with the Rose!
That Youth's sweet-scented manuscript should close!
The Nightingale that in the branches sang,
Ah whence, and whither flown again, who knows!

97

Would but the Desert of the Fountain yield
One glimpse—if dimly, yet indeed, reveal'd,
To which the fainting Traveller might spring,
As springs the trampled herbage of the field!

98

Would but some wingéd Angel ere too late
Arrest the yet unfolded Roll of Fate,
And make the stern Recorder otherwise
Enregister, or quite obliterate!

99

Ah Love! could you and I with Him conspire
To grasp this sorry Scheme of Things entire,
Would not we shatter it to bits—and then
Re-mould it nearer to the Heart's Desire!

100

Yon rising Moon that looks for us again—
How oft hereafter will she wax and wane;
How oft hereafter rising look for us
Through this same Garden—and for *one* in vain!

101

And when like her, oh Sákí, you shall pass
Among the Guests Star-scatter'd on the Grass,
And in your joyous errand reach the spot
Where I made One—turn down an empty Glass!

TAMÁM

NOTE BY W. ALDIS WRIGHT

(Added to the Fifth Edition)

It must be admitted that FitzGerald took great liberties with the original in his version of Omar Khayyám. The first stanza is entirely his own, and in stanza 33 of the fourth edition (36 in the second) he has introduced two lines from Attár (see Letters 1,320). In stanza 81 (fourth edition), writes Professor Cowell, 'There is no original for the line about the snake: I have looked for it in vain in Nicholas; but I have always supposed that the last line is FitzGerald's mistaken version of Quatr. 236 in Nicholas's ed. which runs thus:

O thou who knowest the secrets of every one's mind,
Who graspest every one's hand in the hour of weakness,
O God, give me repentance and accept my excuses,
O thou who givest repentance and acceptest the excuses of every one.

FitzGerald mistook the meaning of *giving* and *accepting* as used here, and so invented his last line out of his own mistake. I wrote to him about it when I was in Calcutta; but he never cared to alter it.'

VARIATIONS IN TEXTS

COMPARATIVE TABLE OF QUATRAINS

NOTES

INDEX TO FIRST LINES

GLOSSARY

VARIATIONS IN TEXTS

First Edition (1859)

Quatrain 45 was not included in subsequent editions.

Second Edition (1868)

Quatrains 14, 28, 44, 65, 77, 86, 99 and 107 were not included in subsequent editions. Quatrain 20 was not included in the text in later editions but was quoted in the *note* to Quatrain 18 in the Third and Fourth Editions.

Third Edition (1872)

Quatrain 10, lines 3 and 4 read:

Let Zál and Rustum thunder as they will,
Or Hátim *call* to Supper—heed not you.

Quatrain 12, lines 1 and 2 read:

A Book of Verses underneath the Bough,
A Jug of Wine, a Loaf of Bread—and Thou

Quatrain 13, lines 3 and 4 read:

Ah, take the Cash, and let the *Credit* go,
Nor heed the *rumble* of a distant Drum!

Quatrain 20 (25 in the 2nd Ed.) lines 1 and 2 read:

And this *reviving* Herb whose *tender* Green
Fledges the *River*-Lip on which we lean—

Quatrain 21, line 2 reads:
Today of past *Regret* and future Fears:

Quatrain 27 (30 in the 2nd Ed.) line 4 reads:
Came out by the same door *where* in I went.

Quatrain 30 (33 in the 2nd Ed.) lines 3 and 4 read:
Oh, many a Cup of this forbidden Wine
Must drown the memory of that insolence!

Quatrain 31 (34 in the 2nd Ed.) line 3 reads:
And many *a Knot* unravel'd by the Road;

Quatrain 33 (36 in the 2nd Ed.) line 3 reads:
Nor *rolling Heaven, with all his* Signs reveal'd

Quatrain 34 (37 in the 2nd Ed.) reads:
Then of the Thee in Me who works behind
The Veil, *I lifted up my hands* to find
A Lamp *amid the Darkness; and I heard,*
As from Without—'THE ME WITHIN THEE BLIND!'

Quatrain 35 (38 in the 2nd Ed.) line 2 reads:
I lean'd, the Secret *of my* Life to learn:

Quatrain 36 (39 in the 2nd Ed.) line 3 reads:
And drink; and *Ah! the passive* Lip I kiss'd,

Quatrain 38 in the Third edition (which appears in this edition only) reads:
Listen—a moment listen!—Of the same
Poor Earth from which that Human Whisper came
The luckless Mould in which Mankind was cast
They did compose, and call'd him by the name.

Quatrain 39 (42 in the 2nd Ed.) line 2 reads:
For Earth to drink of, but may steal below

Quatrain 40 (43 in the 2nd Ed.) lines 1, 2 and 3 read:
As then the Tulip for her *morning* sup
Of Heav'nly Vintage *from the soil looks* up,
Do you *devoutly do the like,* till Heav'n

Quatrain 41 (55 in the 2nd Ed.) lines 1 and 2 read:
Perplext no more with Human or Divine,
To-morrow's tangle to *the winds* resign,

Quatrain 42 (45 in the 2nd Ed.) reads:
And if the *Wine* you drink, the Lip you press,
End in what All begins and ends in—Yes;
Think then you are *TO-DAY what YESTERDAY*
YOU were—*TO-MORROW* you shall not be less.

Quatrain 43 (46 in the 2nd Ed.) reads:
So when *the* Angel *of the darker Drink*
At last shall find you by the river-brink,
And, *offering* his Cup, *invite* your Soul
Forth to your Lips to quaff—*you shall* not shrink.

Quatrain 44 (69 in the 2nd Ed.) lines 3 and 4 read:
Wer't not a Shame—*wer't* not a Shame for him
In this clay carcase crippled to abide?

Quatrain 45 (70 in the 2nd Ed.) line 1 reads:
'Tis but a Tent *where takes his one-day's* rest

Quatrain 46 (47 in the 2nd Ed.) line 2 reads:
Account, *and mine, should know the like* no more;

Quatrain 47 (48 in the 2nd Ed.) line 4 reads:
As *the Sev'n Seas should heed* a pebble-cast.

Quatrain 48 (49 in the 2nd Ed.) reads:
A Moment's Halt—a momentary taste
Of BEING from the Well amid the Waste—
And Lo!—the phantom Caravan has reach'd
The NOTHING it set out from—Oh, make haste!

Quatrain 49 (51 in the 2nd Ed.) line 3 reads:
A Hair *perhaps* divides the False and True—

Quatrain 50 (51 in the 2nd Ed.) line 1 reads:
A Hair *perhaps* divides the False and True;

Quatrain 54 (56 in the 2nd Ed.) line 3 reads:
Better be *jocund* with the fruitful Grape

Quatrain 55 (57 in the 2nd Ed.) lines 1 and 2 read:
You know, my Friends, *with what a brave Carouse*
I made a Second Marriage in my house;

Quatrain 57 (59 in the 2nd Ed.) lines 2 and 3 read:
Reduced the Year to better reckoning?—Nay,
'Twas only striking from the Calendar

Quatrain 62 (64 in the 2nd Ed.) line 4 reads:
To fill the Cup—when crumbled into Dust!

Quatrain 66 (71 in the 2nd Ed.) lines 3 and 4 read:
And by and by my Soul return'd to me,
And *answer'd 'I* Myself am Heav'n and Hell.'

Quatrain 81 (88 in the 2nd Ed.) lines 3 and 4 read:
For all the Sin *wherewith the Face of* Man
Is *blacken'd—Man's Forgiveness give*—and take!

Quatrain 84 (91 in the 2nd Ed.) lines 3 and 4 read:
'And to this Figure moulded, to be broke,
Or trampled back to shapeless Earth again.'

Quatrain 85 (92 in the 2nd Ed.) reads:
Then said a Second—'Ne'er a peevish Boy
'Would break the *Bowl* from which he drank in joy;
'And He that with his hand the Vessel made
'Will surely not in after Wrath destroy!'

Quatrain 86 (93 in the 2nd Ed.) line 1 reads:
After a momentary silence spake

Quatrain 87 (94 in the 2nd Ed.) reads:
Whereat some one of the loquacious Lot—
I think a Sufi pipkin—waxing hot—
'All this of Pot and Potter—Tell me, then,
'Who makes—Who sells—Who buys—Who is *the Pot?'*

Quatrain 88 (95 in the 2nd Ed.) lines 1, 2 and 3 read:
'Why,' said another, 'Some there are who tell
'Of one who threatens he will toss to Hell
'The luckless Pots he marr'd in making—Pish!

Quatrain 89 (96 in the 2nd Ed.) line 1 reads:
'Well,' *murmur'd one, 'Let whoso make or buy,*

Quatrain 90 (97 in the 2nd Ed.) line 2 reads:
The little Moon look'd in that all were seeking:

Quatrain 91 (98 in the 2nd Ed.) line 2 reads:
And wash *the* Body whence the Life has died,

Quatrain 95 (103 in the 2nd Ed.) lines 3 and 4 read:
I *wonder often* what the Vintners buy
One half so precious as the *stuff* they sell.

Quatrain 97 (105 in the 2nd Ed.) line 3 reads:
To which the fainting Traveller might spring,

Quatrain 98 (106 in the 2nd Ed.) reads:
Would but some wingèd Angel ere too late
Arrest the yet unfolded Roll of Fate,
And make *the stern Recorder otherwise*
Enregister, or quite obliterate!

Quatrain 99 (108 in the 2nd Ed.) line 1 reads:
Ah Love! could you and I with *Him* conspire

Quatrain 100 (109 in the 2nd Ed.) reads:

Yon rising Moon *that looks for us* again—
How oft hereafter will she wax and wane;
How oft hereafter rising *look for us*
Through this same Garden—and for one in vain!

Quatrain 101 (110 in the 2nd Ed.) lines 1, 2 and 3 read:

And when *like her, Oh Sákí, you* shall pass
Among the Guests Star-scatter'd on the Grass,
And in your *blissful* errand reach the spot

Fourth Edition (1879)

The actual variations between the Fourth and Fifth Editions are slight and consist mainly of literals and punctuation as shown in the following table:

Quatrain	*Fourth Edition*	*Fifth Edition*
1, Line 1	Sun	Sun,
6, „ 4	her's	hers
16, „ 4	was gone	is gone
17, „ 4	Destin'd	destined
21, „ 2	Regret	Regrets
24, „ 3	under Dust,	under Dust
43, „ 1	the Angel	that Angel
44, „ 3	Wer't	Were't
48, „ 3	reacht	reach'd
49, „ 4	does	may
56, „ 1	Line,	Line
67, „ 2	fire	fire,
67, „ 4	emerg'd	emerged
68, „ 3	illumin'd	illumined
74, „ 2	TO-MORROW'S	To-Morrow's
75, „ 4	predestin'd	predestined
79, „ 3	we	he
80, „ 3	Predestin'd	Predestined

COMPARATIVE TABLE OF QUATRAINS IN THE FIVE VERSIONS

First Edition	*Second Edition*	*Third, Fourth and Fifth Editions*
1	1	1
2	2	2
3	3	3
4	4	4
5	5	5
6	6	6
7	7	7
8	9	9
9	10	10
10	11	11
11	12	12
12	13	13
13	15	14
14	17	16
15	16	15
16	18	17
17	19	18
18	24	19
19	25	20
20	21	21
21	22	22
22	23	23
23	26	24

First Edition	Second Edition	Third, Fourth and Fifth Editions
24	27	25
25	29	26
26	66	63
27	30	27
28	31	28
29	32	29
30	33	30
31	34	31
32	35	32
33	37	34
34	38	35
35	39	36
36	40	37
37		
38	49	48
39	56	54
40	57	55
41	58	56
42	60	58
43	61	59
44	62	60
45		
46	73	68
47	45	42
48	46	43
49	74	69
50	75	70
51	76	71
52	78	72
53	79	73
54	81	75
55	82	76
56	82	77

COMPARATIVE TABLE OF QUATRAINS

First Edition	*Second Edition*	*Third, Fourth and Fifth Editions*
57	87	80
58	88	81
59	89	82
60	94	87
61	91	84
62	92	85
63	93	86
64	95	88
65	96	89
66	97	90
67	98	91
68	100	92
69	101	93
70	102	94
71	103	95
72	104	96
73	108	99
74	109	100
75	110	101
	8	8
	14	
	20	
	28	
	36	33
	41	38
	42	39
	43	40
	44	
	47	46
	48	47
	50	49
	51	50
	52	51

First Edition	*Second Edition*	*Third, Fourth and Fifth Editions*
	53	52
	54	53
	55	41
	59	57
	63	61
	64	62
	65	
	67	64
	68	65
	69	44
	70	45
	71	66
	72	67
	77	
	80	74
	84	78
	85	79
	86	
	90	83
	99	
	105	97
	106	98
	107	

NOTES TO SECOND EDITION

The numbers refer to the Quatrains of the Second Edition.

2 The '*False Dawn*'; *Subhi Kázib*, a transient Light on the Horizon about an hour before the *Subhi sádik*, or True Dawn; a well-known Phenomenon in the East.

4 New Year. Beginning with the Vernal Equinox, it must be remembered; and (howsoever the old Solar Year is practically superseded by the clumsy *Lunar* Year that dates from the Mohammedan Hijra) still commemorated by a Festival that is said to have been appointed by the very Jamshýd whom Omar so often talks of, and whose yearly Calendar he helped to rectify.

'The sudden approach and rapid advance of the Spring,' says Mr. Binning [*Two Years' Travel in Persia &c* I.165] 'are very striking. Before the Snow is well off the Ground, the Trees burst into Blossom, and the Flowers start forth from the Soil. At *Now Rooz* [*their* New Year's Day] the Snow was lying in patches on the Hills and in the shaded Vallies, while the Fruit-trees in the Gardens were budding beautifully, and green Plants and Flowers springing up on the Plains on every side—

And on old Hyems' Chin and icy Crown
An odorous Chaplet of sweet Summer buds
Is, as in mockery, set.—

Among the Plants newly appeared I recognised some old Acquaintances I had not seen for many a Year: among these, two varieties of the Thistle—a coarse species of Daisy like the "Horse-gowan"—red and white Clover—the Dock—the blue Cornflower—and that vulgar Herb the Dandelion rearing its yellow crest on the Banks of the Water-courses.' The Nightingale was not yet heard, for the Rose was not yet blown: but an almost identical Blackbird and Woodpecker helped to make up something of a North-country Spring.

4 'The White Hand of Moses.' Exodus iv. 6; where Moses draws forth his Hand—not, according to the Persians, '*leprous as Snow*'—but *white*, as our May-blossom in Spring perhaps. According to them also the Healing Power of Jesus resided in his Breath.

5 Iram, planted by King Shaddád, and now sunk somewhere in the Sands of Arabia. Jamshýd's Seven-ring'd Cup was typical of the 7 Heavens, 7 Planets, 7 Seas, &c., and was a *Divining Cup*.

6 *Pehleví*, the old Heroic *Sanskrit* of Persia. Háfiz also speaks of the Nightingale's *Pehleví*, which did not change with the People's.

6 I am not sure if the fourth line refers to the Red Rose looking sickly, or to the Yellow Rose that ought to be Red; Red, White, and Yellow Roses all common in Persia. I think that Southey, in his Common-Place Book, quotes from some Spanish author about the Rose being White till 10 o'clock; 'Rosa Perfecta' at 2; and 'perfecta incarnada' at 5.

10 Rustum, the 'Hercules' of Persia, and Zál his Father, whose exploits are among the most celebrated in the Shah-nama. Hátim Tai, a well-known type of Oriental Generosity.

13 A Drum—beaten outside a Palace.

15 That is, the Rose's Golden Centre.

19 Persepolis: call'd also *Takht-i-Jamshýd*—THE THRONE OF JAMSHÝD, '*King Splendid*,' of the mythical *Peshdádian* Dynasty, and supposed (according to the Shah-nama) to have been founded and built by him.

19 Others refer it to the Work of the Genie King, Ján Ibn Ján—who also built the Pyramids—before the time of Adam.

19 BAHRÁM GUR—*Bahram of the Wild Ass*—a Sassanian Sovereign—had also his Seven Castles (like the King of Bohemia!) each of a different Colour: each with a Royal Mistress within; each of whom tells him a Story, as told in one of the most famous Poems of Persia, written by Amir Khusraw: all these Sevens also figuring (according to Eastern Mysticism) the Seven Heavens; and perhaps the Book itself that Eighth, into which the mystical Seven transcend, and within which they revolve. The Ruins of Three of those Towers are yet shown by the Peasantry; as also the Swamp in which Bahrám sunk, like the Master of Ravenswood, while pursuing his *Gúr*.

20 *The Palace that to Heav'n his pillars threw,*
And Kings the forehead on his threshold drew—
I saw the solitary Ringdove there,
And 'Coo, coo, coo,' she cried; and 'Coo, coo, coo.'

This Quatrain Mr. Binning found, among several of Háfiz and others, inscribed by some stray hand among the ruins of Persepolis. The Ringdove's ancient *Pehleví Coo, Coo, Coo,* signifies also in Persian '*Where? Where? Where?*' In Attár's 'Bird-parliament' she is reproved by the Leader of the Birds for sitting still, and for ever harping on that one note of lamentation for her lost Yúsuf.

21 A thousand years to each Planet.

24 Apropos of Omar's Red Roses in Stanza 24. I am reminded

of an old English Superstition, that our Anemone Pulsatilla, or purple 'Pasque Flower' (which grows plentifully about the Fleam Dyke, near Cambridge), grows only where Danish Blood has been spilt.

34 Saturn, Lord of the Seventh Heaven.

35 ME-AND-THEE: some dividual Existence or Personality distinct from the Whole.

40 One of the Persian Poets—Attár, I think—has a pretty story about this. A thirsty Traveller dips his hand into a Spring of Water to drink from. By-and-by comes another who draws up and drinks from an earthen Bowl, and then departs, leaving his Bowl behind him. The first Traveller takes it up for another draught; but is surprised to find that the same Water which had tasted sweet from his own hand tastes bitter from the earthen Bowl. But a Voice—from Heaven, I think—tells him the clay from which the Bowl is made was once *Man;* and, into whatever shape renewed, can never lose the bitter flavour of Mortality.

42 The custom of throwing a little Wine on the ground before drinking still continues in Persia, and perhaps generally in the East. Mons. Nicolas considers it 'un signe de libéralité, et en même temps un avertissement que le buveur doit vider sa coupe jusqu'à la dernière goutte.' Is it not more likely an ancient Superstition; a Libation to propitiate Earth, or make her an Accomplice in the illicit Revel? Or, perhaps, to divert the Jealous Eye by some sacrifice of superfluity, as with the Ancients of the West? With Omar we see something more is signified; the precious Liquor is not lost, but sinks into the ground to refresh the dust of some poor Wine-worshipper foregone.

Thus Háfiz, copying Omar in so many ways: 'When thou drinkest Wine pour a draught on the ground. Wherefore fear the Sin which brings to another Gain?'

46 According to one beautiful Oriental Legend, Azräel accomplishes his mission by holding to the nostril an Apple from the Tree of Life.

This and the two following Stanzas would have been withdrawn, as some what *de trop*, from the Text, but for advice which I least like to disregard.

52 From Máh to Máhi: from Fish to Moon.

58 A Jest, of course, at his Studies. A curious mathematical Quatrain of Omar's has been pointed out to me; the more curious because almost exactly parallel'd by some Verses of Doctor Donne's, that are quoted in Izaak Walton's Lives! Here is Omar: 'You and I are the image of a pair of compasses; though we have two heads (sc. our *feet*) we have one body; when we have fixed the centre for our circle, we bring our heads (sc. feet) together at the end.' Dr. Donne:

If we be two, we two are so
As stiff twin-compasses are two;
Thy Soul, the fixt foot, makes no show
To move, but does if the other do.

And though thine in the centre sit,
Yet when my other far does roam,
Thine leans and hearkens after it,
And grows erect as mine comes home.

Such thou must be to me, who must
Like the other foot obliquely run;
Thy firmness makes my circle just,
And me to end where I begun.

61 The Seventy-two Religions supposed to divide the World, *including* Islamism, as some think: but others not.

62 Alluding to Sultán Mahmud's Conquest of India and its dark people.

73 *Fanusi khiyal*, a Magic-lantern still used in India; the cylindrical Interior being painted with various Figures, and so lightly poised and ventilated as to revolve round the lighted Candle within.

75 A very mysterious Line in the Original

O danad O danad O danad O——

breaking off something like our Woodpigeon's Note, which she is said to take up just where she left off.

81 Parwín and Mushtari—The Pleiads and Jupiter.

94 This Relation of Pot and Potter to Man and his Maker figures far and wide in the Literature of the World, from the time of the Hebrew Prophets to the present; when it may finally take the name of 'Pot theism,' by which Mr. Carlyle ridiculed Sterling's 'Pantheism.' *My* Sheikh, whose knowledge flows in from all quarters, writes to me:

'Apropos of old Omar's Pots, did I ever tell you the sentence I found in "Bishop Pearson on the Creed?" "Thus are we wholly at the disposal of His will, and our present and future condition framed and ordered by His free, but wise and just, decrees. *Hath not the potter power over the clay, of the same lump to make one vessel unto honour, and another unto dishonour?* (Rom. ix. 21). And can that earth-artificer have a freer power over his *brother potsherd* (both being made of the same metal), than God hath over him, who, by the strange fecundity of His omnipotent power, first made the clay out of nothing, and then him out of that?"' And again—from a very different quarter—'I had to refer the other day to Aristophanes, and came by chance on a curious Speaking-pot story in the Vespæ (*The Wasps*, lines 1435–40), which I had quite forgotten.

'The Pot calls a bystander to be a witness to his bad treatment. The woman says, "If, by Proserpine, instead of all this 'testifying' (comp. Cuddie and his mother in 'Old Mortality!') you would buy yourself a rivet, it would show more sense in you!" The Scholiast explains *echinus* as any bowl from the potter.'

One more illustration for the oddity's sake from the 'Autobiography of a Cornish Rector,' by the late James Hamley Tregenna, 1871.

'There was one old Fellow in our Company—he was so like a Figure in the "Pilgrim's Progress" that Richard always called him the "ALLEGORY" with a long white beard—a rare Appendage in those days—and a Face the colour of which seemed to have been baked in, like the Faces one used to see on Earthenware Jugs. In our Country-dialect Earthenware is called "*Clome*"; so the Boys of the Village used to shout out after him—"Go back to the Potter, old Clome-face, and get baked over again." For the "Allegory," though shrewd enough in most things, had the reputation of being "*saift-baked*," i.e., of weak intellect.'

7 At the Close of the Fasting Month, Ramazán (which makes the Musulman unhealthy and unamiable), the first Glimpse of the New Moon (who rules their division of the Year), is looked for with the utmost Anxiety, and hailed with Acclamation. Then it is that the Porter's Knot may be heard—toward the *Cellar*. Omar has elsewhere a pretty Quatrain about the same Moon:

Be of Good Cheer—the sullen Month will die,
And a young Moon requite us by and by:
Look how the Old one meagre, bent, and wan
With Age and Fast, is fainting from the Sky!

INDEX TO FIRST LINES OF QUATRAINS

INDEX TO FIRST LINES

INDEX TO FIRST LINES

GLOSSARY

ALIF *[a'-lif]* The first letter in the Persian alphabet.

ALLAH *[al'-lā]* Arabic name for God. The Absolute.

AMIR *[a-meer']* Prince.

ASSÁR *[as'-sār]* Oil pressers.

ATTÁR *[at'-tār]* Druggist.

ATTÁR The persian poet Farrîd-uddîn Attâr, author of *The Mantiq al-Tayr*, i.e., Discourse of the Birds.

BAHRÁM GUR *[bah'-rām goor]* Bahram of the Wild Ass, Persian king and hunter.

CARAVANSERAI *[kar-a-van'-se-ray]* Inn where caravans rest at night.

DANAD He knows, third person singular of *dân*, to know.

FANUSI KHIYAL *[fā-noo'-see khee'-yal]* Magic lantern.

FERRÁSH *[fer-rāsh']* Servant, tent-pitcher.

HÁFIZ *[hā-fiz]*. Persian lyric poet (d. 1389).

HÁTIM TAI *[hā'-tim tye]* A pre-Islamic Arab famed for his generosity.

HIJRA, more commonly HEGIRA *[he-jye-ra]* The migration of Muhammad from Mecca to Medina in A.D. 622 from which Muslims date their era.

IMÁM *[i-mām']* A Muhammadan leader of prayer.

IRAM *[ee'-ram]* A fabulous garden supposed to have been planted in Arabia by Shaddád bin Ad.

JÁMI *[jā'-mi]* Persian poet (d. 1492).

JAMSHÝD *[Jam'-sheed]* Mythical Persian king. According to Firdausî he reigned seven hundred years. His palace was at Persepolis.

JELÁLUDDÍN *[je-lāl'-ud-deen]* Malikshah. A Saljuk sultán (1072-1092)

KAIKHOSRÚ *[Kye'-khos-roo]* Mythical Persian king.

KAIKOBÁD *[kye'-ko-bād]* Mythical king.

KHORÁSÁN *[kho-rā-sān']* The largest of the Persian provinces where Omar was born.

KUZA-NAMA *[koo'-za nā'-ma]* Book of pots, title given to stanzas 59–66 in first edition of the *Rubáiyát.*

MÁH Moon.

MÁHI Fish.

MAHMUD *[mah'-mood]* King of Ghazna, b. 969, d. 1030.

MIHRÁB *[mee-rāb]* The niche in a mosque which indicates the direction of Mecca towards which the Muslim worshipper turns in prayer.

MUEZZIN *[moo-ez'-zin]* Muhammadan crier of the hour of prayer.

MUSHTARI *[mush'-ta-ree]* The planet Jupiter.

NAISHÁPÚR *[nay'-shā-poor]* Nishapur, the city of Khorásán, Iran. where Omar was born.

NOW ROOZ New Year's Day.

NIZÁM UL MULK *[nee-zām' ool moolk']* Vizier to Alp Arslan the Younger.

OMAR KHAYYÁM *[o'-mar khye-yahm']* Persian philosopher, astronomer and poet, author of *The Rubáiyát,* who died in 1132.

PARWÍN *[par'-ween]* The constellation of the Pleiades.

PEHLEVÍ *[peh'-le-vee]* The principal language of the Persians from the third to the ninth centuries A.D.

RAMAZÁN *[ram-a-zān]* Ramadan, the ninth month of the Muhammadan year, devoted to strict fasting.

RUBÁIYÁT *[roo'-bye-yāt]* Plural of the Arabic word *rubáiyáh,* a quatrain or stanza of four lines.

RUSTUM *[rus'-tum]* A mythical Persian hero, son of Zál and father of Sohráb in the *Shah-nama.*

SÁKÍ *[sā-kee]* Cupbearer.

SHAH-NAMA *The Book of Kings* by Abul Kasim Mansur, better known as Firdausî.

SHEIKH *[shaykh]* An Arabian chief; literally, old man.

SUBHI KAZIB *[soob'-hee kā'-zib]* False dawn.

SUBHI SADIK *[soob'-hee sā'-dik]* True dawn.

SUFI *[soo'-fee]* Muhammadan mystic. The elaborate Sufi symbolism was much used by the poets.

SULTÁN *[sul-tān]* King.

TAKHALLUS *[ta-khal-lus]* Pen-name used by Persian poets; for example, Abul Kasim Mansur, author of the *Shah-nama*, called himself Firdausî from Firdaus which means *Paradise*. Omar called himself Khayyám, i.e., Tent-maker.

TAMÁM *[ta-mām]* The end.

TAMÁM SHUD *[ta-mām' shood]* The very end.

VIZIER *[vi-zeer']* A minister or counsellor of state.

ZÁL *[zāl]* The father of Rustum.

EUPHRANOR

A Dialogue on Youth

DURING the time of my pretending to practise Medicine at Cambridge, I was aroused, one fine forenoon of May, by the sound of some one running up my staircase, three or four steps at a time; then, directly, a smart rapping at the door; and, before I could say, 'Come in,' Euphranor had opened it, and, striding up to me, seized my arm with his usual eagerness, and told me I must go out with him —'It was such a day—Sun shining—Breeze blowing—hedges and trees in full leaf. He had been to Chesterton, (he said), and rowed back with a man who now left him in the lurch; I must take his place.' I told him what a poor hand at the Oar I was, and, such walnut-shells as these Cambridge boats were, I was sure a strong fellow like him must rejoice in getting a whole Eight-oar to himself once in a while. He laughed, and said, 'The pace, the pace was the thing—However, that was all nothing, but—in short, I must go out with him, whether for a Row, or a Walk in the fields, or a game of Billiards at Chesterton—whatever I liked—only go I must.' After a little more banter, about my possible Patients, I got up; closed a very heavy Treatise on Magnesia I was reading; on with coat and hat; and in three minutes we had run down-stairs, out into the open air; where both of us calling out together what a glorious day it was, we struck out briskly for the old Wooden Bridge, where Euphranor said his boat was lying.

'By the bye,' said I, as we went along, 'it would be a charity to knock up poor Lexilogus, and carry him along with us.'

Not much of a charity, Euphranor thought—Lexilogus would so much rather be left with his books. Which I declared was the very reason he should be drawn abroad; and Euphranor, who was quite good-humoured, and wished Lexilogus all well, (for we were all three Yorkshiremen, whose families lived no great distance asunder), easily consented. So, without more ado, we turned into Trinity great Gate, and round by the right up a staircase to the Attic where Lexilogus kept.

The door was *sported*, but I knew he must be at home; so, using the privilege of an old friend, I shouted to him through the letter-slit. Presently we heard the sound of books falling, and soon after Lexilogus' thin, pale, and spectacled face appeared at the half-opened door. He was always glad to see me, I believe, howsoever I disturbed him; and he smiled as he laid his hand in mine, rather than returned its pressure.

The tea-things were still on the table, and I asked him (though I knew well enough) if he were so fashionable as only just to have breakfasted?

'Oh—long ago—directly after Morning Chapel.'

I then told him he must put his books away, and come out on the River with Euphranor and myself.

'He could not possibly,' he said;—'not so early, at least—the yearly Examination—'

'Come, come, my good fellow,' said Euphranor, 'that is the very reason, the Doctor says; he will have it so. So make haste.'

I then told him (what I then suddenly remembered) that, beside other reasons, his old Aunt, a Cambridge tradesman's widow whom I attended, and whom Lexilogus helped to support out of his own little funds, wanted to see him directly on business. He should go with us to Chesterton, where she lodged; visit her while Euphranor and I played a game or two of billiards at the Inn; and afterwards (for I knew how little of an Oars-man he was) we would all three take a good stretch into the Fields together.

He supposed he should be back by Hall, of course; about which I would make no conditions; and he then resigned himself to Destiny. While he was busy changing and brushing his clothes, Euphranor, who had walked somewhat impatiently about the room, looking now at the books, and now out of the window at some white pigeons wheeling about in the clear blue sky, went up to the mantel-piece and called out, 'What a fine new pair of screens Lexilogus had got! the present, doubtless, of some fair Lady.'

Lexilogus said they were a present from his sister on his Birth-day; and coming up to me, brush in hand, asked if I recognised the views?

'Quite well, quite well,' I said, and told him to get on with his toilet—'the old Church—the Yew tree,—your Father's house—one cannot mistake them.'

'And were they not beautifully done?' he wanted to know; and I answered without hesitation, they were; for I knew the Girl who had painted them, and that (whatever they might be in point of Art) a still finer spirit than Art had guided her hand.

At last, after a little hesitation as to whether he should wear Cap and Gown, (which I decided he should *not*, for this time only), Lexilogus was ready: and calling out on the staircase to his Bed-maker not to meddle with his books, we ran down-stairs, crossed the great Court—through the Screens thronged with Gyps and Bed-makers, and redolent of perpetual Dinner; thence, after stopping a moment to read some notices, through the cloisters of Neville's Court, and so out upon the open space before the Library. The sun shone broad on the new-shaven expanse of grass, while Holiday-seeming folks sauntered along the River-side, and under the trees, now flourishing in freshest green—the Chesnuts especially in full fan, and bending down their white cones over the sluggish current, which seemed indeed more fitted for the slow merchandise of Coal, than to wash the walls and flow through the groves of Academe.

We now considered we had missed our proper point of Embarkation; but this was righted at a slight expense of college propriety. Euphranor calling out to some one who had his boat in charge with others by the Wooden Bridge, we descended the grassy slope, stepped in, and settled the order of our voyage. Euphranor and I were to pull, and Lexilogus (as I at first proposed) was to steer. But seeing he was averse from meddling in the matter, I agreed to take all the blame of my own awkward rowing on myself.

'And just take care of this, will you, Lexilogus?' said Euphranor, handing him a Book which fell out of his pocket as he took his coat off.

'Oh, Books, Books!' I exclaimed, 'I thought we were to steer clear of them, at all events. Now we shall have Lexilogus reading all the way. What is it—Greek, Algebra, German, or what?'

It was none of these, however, Euphranor said, but only Digby's Godefridus; and then asking me whether I was ready, and I calling out, 'Ay, ay, Sir,' our oars splashed in the water. Threading the main arch of Trinity bridge, we shot past the Library, I exerting myself so strenuously, (as bad rowers sometimes do), that I almost drove the nose of the boat against one of the least ornamental offices of the

College. This danger past, however, we got on better; Euphranor often looking behind him to anticipate our way, and counteracting with his experienced Oar the many misdirections of mine. Amid all this, he had leisure to ask me if I knew those same Digby books?

'Some of them,' I told him—'the Broad Stone of Honour for one; indeed I had got the first Protestant edition of it, now very rare.'

'But not so good as the enlarged Catholic,' said Euphranor, 'of which this Godefridus is part; at least so Hare says.'

'Perhaps not,' I replied; 'but then, on the other hand, *not* so Catholic; which you and Lexilogus will agree with me is a great advantage.'

Which I said slyly, Euphranor being rather taken with the Oxford doctrine just then coming into vogue.

'You cannot forgive him that,' said he.

'Nay nay,' said I, 'one can forgive a true man anything. Digby is a noble Fellow—one of the Few whose Fulness of Soul justifies the venting it in Print."

'If only as a Garden of Quotations,' said Euphranor, 'as plentiful as old Burton, only the Flowers so much richer and rarer.'

'Ay,' said I, 'that one may pilfer at pleasure, and still leave enough to make Midsummer of scores of barren Discourses. And then Euphranor asked me, 'Did I not remember Digby himself at College? perhaps know him?'

'Not that,' I answered, but remembered him very well. And in answer to Euphranor's questions proceeded to give him some personal recollections of his Author.

'And, Hare says, really himself the Knight he drew?'

'At least,' I answered, 'he rowed very vigorously on this river, where I am now labouring so awkwardly.'

In which and other such talk, constantly interrupted by

the little accidents of our voyage, we had threaded our way through the barges congregated at Magdalen; through the Locks; and so for a pull of three or four miles down the river and back again to Cross's; where we surrendered our boat, and footed it over the fields to Chesterton, at whose Church we came just as its quiet chimes were preluding Twelve o'clock. Close by was the humble house whither Lexilogus was bound. I looked in for a moment at the old lady, and left him with her, privately desiring him to join us as soon as he could at the Three Tuns; the Three Tuns, which I preferred to any younger rival, because of the many pleasant hours I had spent there in my own College days.

When Euphranor and I got there, we found all the tables occupied; but one, as usual, would be at our service before long. Meanwhile, ordering some light Ale after us, we went into the Bowling-green, with its Lilac bushes now in full bloom and full odour; and there we found, sitting alone upon a bench, Lycion, with a cigar in his mouth, and rolling the bowls about lazily with his foot.

'What! Lycion! and all alone!' I called out.

He nodded to us both—said he was waiting till some men had finished a pool of billiards up-stairs—'A great bore—for it was only just begun; and one of the fellows a man I particularly detest, so I am obliged to wait here till he is off.'

'Come and console yourself with some Ale, then,' said I. 'Are you ever foolish enough to go pulling on the river, as we have been doing?'

'Not often; he did not see the use,' he said, 'of perspiring to no purpose.'

'Just so,' replied I. 'But here comes our liquor; sweet *is* Pleasure after Pain, at all events.'

We then sat down in one of those little arbours cut into the Lilac bushes round the Bowling-green; and while

Euphranor and I were quaffing each a glass of Home-brewed, Lycion took up the volume of Digby, which Euphranor had laid on the table.

'Ah, Lycion,' said Euphranor, putting down his glass, 'there is one would put you up to a longer and stronger pull than we have had.'

'Chivalry—' said Lycion, glancing carelessly over the pages; 'I thought people had done talking about that sort of thing.'

'What sort of thing?' Euphranor asked him.

'Why, Dragons, Tournaments, old Armour, and so on.'

'Rather a hasty acquaintance to judge of a book in, is it not?' said Euphranor smiling.

Lycion had heard of it before, and laughed at.

'Possibly,' replied Euphranor. 'Nevertheless, I can assure you it is *not* about Tournaments, Dragons, and "that sort of thing" at all—that is, not about them only.'

'Don't you remember,' Lycion said, addressing me, 'what an absurd thing the Eglinton Tournament was? What a complete failure! There was the Queen of Beauty on her throne, and the Heralds, and the Knights in full Armour on their horses—they had been practising for months, I believe—but unluckily, at the very moment of Onset, the rain began, and the Knights threw down their lances and put up umbrellas.'

I laughed, and said I remembered something like it had occurred, though not to umbrella-point, which I thought was an Adelphi or Louis Philippe burlesque on the affair. And I asked Euphranor what he had to say in defence of the Tournament.

'Nothing at all,' he replied. 'It was a silly thing, and fit to be laughed at for the very reason that it *was* only an affair of old armour—As Digby himself emphatically tells us,' he went on, taking the Book and rapidly turning over the leaves.—'Here it is'—and he read—'"The error that leads men to doubt of this first proposition"—that is, you know, that Chivalry is not a thing past, but, like all things of Beauty, eternal—"the error that leads men to doubt of this first proposition consists of their supposing that Tournaments, steel Panoply, and Coat arms, and Aristocratic institutions, are essential to Chivalry; whereas, these are, in fact, only accidental attendants upon it, subject to the influence of Time, which changes all such things."'

'I am told the old Knights were really great Blackguards,' said Lycion, turning his cigar in his mouth, and glancing at his antagonist, 'with all their pretences of fighting for religion, distressed damsels, and so on.'

'Come, Lycion,' said I, 'you must not abuse them; you, whose Pedigree links you through Agincourt and Crecy, almost up to King Arthur.'

'O yes, King Arthur, and his Round Table and Seven Champions; and pray do not forget Don Quixote. He is one of your Heroes, I hope, Euphranor?'

Euphranor declared that Don Quixote was a man of truly Chivalric soul—only—

'Only mad,' interrupted Lycion, 'and mistook Windmills for Giants. And I doubt if King Arthur's Giants were half so substantial.'

'Perhaps Digby would tell us,' said I, who saw Euphranor's colour rising, 'there can be no want of Giants and Dragons while Oppression and Misery abound in the world.'

'To be sure,' said Euphranor; 'these old Romances are Symbols of the Truth: nay, the Truth itself, inasmuch as they record the Warfare which all Heroic men must wage for ever with Evil, under whatsoever shape it may appear.'

'Does not Carlyle somewhere tell us,' said I, 'that Chivalry must now seek and find its mission in the campaigns, not of War, but of Peace; which need no less Energy, Endurance, and Self-devotion? He talks of a "Chivalry of Labour," I think; the proper conquests for modern Heroes to be those of the Loom and the Steam engine; and that henceforward not "*Arms* and the Man," but "*Tools* and the Man," must be the Epic of the world.'

'O well,' said Lycion, 'if your Arthurs and Lancelots are to turn into peaceable Spinners, Stokers, and Tailors, I shall never quarrel with them. Let them go on conquering and to conquer; in the latter vocation especially; and more especially if, like true Knights, they charge nothing for their services.'

'Yes, my dear fellow,' said I laughing, 'but then you must not sit idle, smoking your cigar, in the midst of it; but, as your Ancestors led on mailed troops at Agincourt, so must you put yourself at the head of these Tailors, and become what Carlyle calls "a Captain of Industry," a Master-tailor, leading on a host of Journeymen to fresh fields and conquests new.'

'Besides,' said Euphranor, who did not relish this sudden descent of his hobby, 'surely Chivalry will ever find endless, if bloodless, engagement in the Laws, Education, and other such Advancement of a People; or, if you like it, of the World at large. As Tennyson so nobly says, King Arthur, who was carried away wounded to the island valley of Avilion, to be nursed by Queens, will, and does, return to us in the shape of a modern Gentleman 'of stateliest port.' And whatever Carlyle or any one else may say, War is not yet out of the world: there are still those ready to strike in a bad cause, and it would be hard if there were none to resist in a good.'

'Well,' said Lycion, who, often seeming inattentive to what was making against him, quickly caught at any turn in his favour—'we have a paid Army to do all that for us.'

'A paid Army!' repeated Euphranor with great indignation. 'And do you pretend to say, Lycion, that you, for one, would sit there smoking your eternal cigar, if England herself were to be invaded, for instance?'

Lycion, however, only turned that eternal cigar in his mouth, and glanced rather superciliously at his antagonist. And I, who had been all this while reading Godefridus at the page Euphranor had left open, said, 'Here we are, as usual, disputing without being as yet agreed upon the meaning of the terms we are using. Here, Euphranor, suppose you read us this passage, which defines what Digby himself understands by the word *Chivalry*, and then we shall see the way clearer perhaps.'

I gave him the book, and he read:

'Chivalry is only a name for that general Spirit or state of mind, which disposes men to Generous and Heroic actions; and keeps them conversant with all that is Beautiful and Sublime in the Intellectual and Moral world. It will be found that, in the absence of conservative principles, this Spirit more generally prevails in Youth than in the later periods of men's life: and, as the Heroic is always the earliest age in the history of nations, so Youth, the first period of life, may be considered as the Heroic or Chivalrous age of each separate Man; and there are few so unhappy as to have grown up without having experienced its influence, and having derived the advantage of being able to enrich their imagination, and to soothe their hours of sorrow, with its romantic recollections. The Anglo-Saxons distinguished the period between Childhood and Manhood by the term 'Cnithade,' Knighthood: a term which still continued to indicate the connexion between Youth and Chivalry, when Knights were styled 'Children,' as in the historic song beginning

Childe Rowlande to the dark tower came,—

an excellent expression, no doubt;—for every Boy and Youth is, in his mind and sentiment, a Knight, and essentially a Son of Chivalry. Nature is fine in him. Nothing but the circumstances of a singular and most degrading system of Education can ever totally destroy the action of this general law. Therefore, so long as there has been, or shall be, a succession of sweet Springs in Man's Intellectual World; as long as there have been, or shall be, Young men to grow up to maturity; and until all Youthful life shall be dead, and its source withered up for ever; so long must there have been, and must there continue to be, the spirit of noble Chivalry. To understand therefore this first and, as it were, natural Chivalry, we have only to observe the features of the Youthful age, of which examples surround us. For, as Demopho says of young men;

> *Ecce autem similia omnia: omnes congruunt:*
> *Unum cognoris, omnes noris.*[1] *

Mark the courage of him who is green and fresh in the Old world. Amyntas beheld and dreaded the insolence of the Persians; but not so Alexander, the son of Amyntas, *ἅτε νέος τε ἐὼν καὶ κακῶν ἀπαθὴς* (says Herodotus) *οὐδαμῶς ἔτι κατέχειν οἷος τεῆν.*[2] When Jason had related to his companions the conditions imposed by the King, the first impression was that of horror and despondency; till Peleus rose up boldly, and said,

> *Ὥρη μητιάασθαι ὅ κ' ἕρξομεν· οὐ μὲν ἔολπα*
> *Βουλῆς εἶναι ὄνειαρ, ὅσον τ' ἐπὶ κάρτεϊ χειρῶν.*[3]

* Translations of the excepts in Greek and Latin will be found on p. 259.

"If Jason be unwilling to attempt it, I and the rest will undertake the enterprise; for what more can we suffer than death?" And then instantly rose up Telamon and Idas, and the sons of Tyndarus, and Œnides, although

——*ὀυδε περ ὅσσον ἐπανθιόωντας ἰούλους*
'Αντέλλων.[1]

But Argus, the Nestor of the party, restrained their impetuous valour.'

'Scarce the Down upon their lips you see,' (said I), 'Freshmen;—so that you, Euphranor, who are now Bachelor of Arts, and whose upper lip at least begins to show the stubble of repeated harvests, are, alas, fast declining from that golden prime of Knighthood, while Lycion here, whose shavings might almost be counted—'

'Pshaw,' interrupted Lycion, 'I have no ambition to be one of his Heroes.'

'But you can't help it, it appears,' said I, 'and must not, like a bad bird, foul your own nest. And see here again,' I continued, having taken the book from Euphranor's hands—'after telling us that Chivalry is only Youth, he goes on to define what Youth is.'

"It is a remark of Lord Bacon, that 'for the Moral part, Youth will have the pre-eminence, as Age hath for the Politic;' and this has always been the opinion which is allied to that other belief, that the Heroic (the Homeric age) was the most Virtuous age of Greece. When Demosthenes was desirous of expressing any great and generous sentiment, he uses the term *νεανικὸν φρόνημα*"[2]—'and by the way,' added I looking up parenthetically from the Book, 'the Persians, I am told, employ the same word for Youth and Courage'—"and it is the saying of Plautus when surprise is evinced at the Benevolence of an old man, "Benignitas hujus ut

Adolescentuli est." There is no difference, says the Philosopher, between Youthful Age and Youthful Character: and what this is cannot be better evinced than in the very words of Aristotle. "The Young are ardent in Desire, and what they do is from Affection; they are tractable and delicate; they earnestly desire and are easily appeased; their wishes are intense, without comprehending much, as the thirst and hunger of the weary; they are passionate and hasty, and liable to be surprised by anger; for, being ambitious of Honour, they cannot endure to be despised, but are indignant when they suffer injustice: they love Honour, but still more Victory; for Youth desires superiority, and victory is superiority, and both of these they love more than Riches; for as to these, of all things, they care for them the least. They are not of corrupt manners, but are Innocent, from not having beheld much wickedness; and they are credulous, from having been seldom deceived; and Sanguine in hope, for, like persons who are drunk with wine, they are inflamed by nature, and from their having had but little experience of Fortune. And they live by Hope, for Hope is of the future, but Memory is of the past, and to Youth the Future is everything, the Past but little; they hope all things, and remember nothing: and it is easy to deceive them, for the reasons which have been given; for they are willing to hope, and are full of Courage, being passionate and hasty, of which tempers it is the nature of one not to fear, and of the other to inspire confidence; and thus are easily put to Shame, for they have no resources to set aside the precepts which they have learned: and they have lofty souls, for they have never been disgraced or brought low; and they are unacquainted with Necessity; they prefer Honour to Advantage, Virtue to Expediency; for they live by Affection rather than by Reason, and Reason is concerned with Expediency, but Affection with Honour: and they are warm friends and hearty companions, more than other men, because they delight in Fellowship, and judge of nothing by Utility, and therefore not their friends; and they chiefly err in doing all things over much, for they keep no medium. They love much, and they dislike much, and so in everything, and this arises from their idea that they know everything. And their faults consist more in Insolence than in actual wrong; and they are full of Mercy, because they regard all men as good, and more virtuous than they are; for they measure others by their own Innocence; so that they suppose every man suffers wrongfully." 'So that Lycion, you see,' said I, looking up from the book, 'is, in virtue of his eighteen Summers only, a Knight of Nature's own dubbing—yes, and here we have a list of the very qualities which constitute him one of the Order. And all the time he is pretending to be careless, indolent, and worldly, he is really bursting with suppressed Energy, Generosity, and Devotion.'

'If one can't help it then,' said Lycion rather sulkily, 'what is the use of writing books about it?'

'O yes, my dear fellow,' said I, 'it is like giving you an Inventory of your goods, which else you lose, or even cast away, in your march to Manhood—which you are so eager to reach. Only to repent when got there; for I see Digby goes on—"What is termed *Entering the World*"—which Manhood of course must do—"assuming its Principles and Maxims"—which usually follows—"is nothing else but departing into those regions to which the souls of the Homeric Heroes went sorrowing—

ὃν πότμον γοόωσα, λιποῦσ' ἁδροτῆτα καὶ ἥβην."'[1]

'Ah, you remember,' said Euphranor, 'how Lamb's friend,

looking upon the Eton Boys in their Cricket-field, sighed "to think those fine Lads should so soon turn into frivolous Members of Parliament!"'

'Why *frivolous?*' said Lycion.

'Ay, why *frivolous?*' repeated I.

But Euphranor went laughing on, 'Well, never mind, they needn't unless they like for some twenty years to come. Pythagoras, you know, Doctor, gives up the first forty years of his Man's allotted Eighty to Childhood and Youth; a dispensation which you and I at least shall not quarrel with.'

'No, nor any one else, I should suppose,' said I. 'Think, my dear Lycion, what a privilege for you to have yet more than twenty good years' expatiation in the Elysian Cricket-field of Youth before pent up in that Close Borough of your Father's! And Euphranor, who we thought fast slipping out of his Prime as his Youth attained a Beard, is in fact only just entering upon it. And, most wonderful of all, I, who not only have myself entered the World, but made my bread by bringing others into it these Fifteen years, am myself only just ceast to be a Boy!'

Lycion now called up to his friends in the Billiard room, one of whom appeared at the window, cue in hand, and shook his head, saying however, in a confidential way, that 'All would be right in a few minutes;' and so retired. On which Lycion had nothing for it but to light another cigar, and lying down on his back with his hat over his eyes, compose himself to Inattention.

Euphranor, who had been musing during this little episode, now said,

'You, however, Doctor, who have passed the Rubicon, will hardly confess the tract you have left behind you better than that you are entering upon?'

'Of course not,' I answered.

'And yet,' said he, 'in the passage you have read, you see he compares the Youth of Man to the Heroic age of a Nation.'

'Which, however, may not be its *Best* age,' answered I. 'Lycion and I may not agree that Argonautic expeditions, Trojan or Holy wars, mark the best epochs of a People, whatever you Heroic gentlemen think.'

'Well, but if what Digby says be true, that 't is this Spirit keeps Men and Nations most conversant with what is Beautiful and Sublime in the Moral and Intellectual world —And here is Bacon declaring that Youth excels in THE MORAL, and Age in the poor *Politic* only'—

'*Old* Age, he might mean,' I suggested smiling—'or such a Politic of Moral as Jeremy Bentham's.'

Euphranor however repudiated all such base Moral as this, and would have nothing whatever to do with Jeremy Bentham. 'And what mighty Virtues Aristotle attributes to Youth!' said he.

'And mighty Faults too, for that matter,' I returned. 'Does he not call it rash, ambitions, overbearing,—insolent even?—faults that we who have entered the World have learned to amend?'

'Well then,' said Euphranor, 'the sooner these Eton boys get there the better, after all.'

'But then, on the other hand,' said I, 'how much they owe to being *out* of it; for you see Aristotle says they are Innocent from not having beheld much Wickedness, Hopeful from not having been disappointed, Trustful from not having been deceived, Lofty of soul and despising Riches from never having been brought low; and so forth. Your friend Plato, if I remember, will not allow even those who are destined to be Judges in his Republic to make acquaintance with Crime till near Middle life, for fear they should harden into a distrust of human nature, and dry up those Generous Affections and Hopeful Energies of which Aristotle's Catalogue is almost made up.'

'Ah!' said Euphranor, 'and Bacon somewhere else observes, I think, that "Youth doth profit in the Affections, and Age in the Reason."'

'Age then has the best of it, according to Bacon, in the Reason as well as the Politic, whatever they may be; and Youth in the Affections and the Moral, whatever *they*.'

'No very high qualities, I doubt,' said he, smiling, 'if unconnected—I don't care for your Politic—but, with Reason,—The Moral of Dogs and Horses, Plato would call them.'

'Let me see,' said I, taking up the book again, and running my eye over the passage—'yes,—"*Ardent of desire*,"—"*Tractable*,"—some of them at least—"*Without comprehending much*"—"*Ambitious*"—"*Despisers of Riches*"—except the famous Dog and Shadow,—but that is a Fable—"*Warm friends and hearty Companions*"—really very characteristic of the better breed of Dogs and Horses. And why not? The Horse, you know, has given his very name to Chivalry, because of his association in the Heroic Enterprises of Men, —"*The most Hidalgo Brute of all*," Calderon calls him. And as for Dogs—Lord Byron says he never had but one Friend—"and—"'

'There *he lies!*' cried Euphranor, snorting. 'Lord Byron! —But there are other Affections—'

'Wife and children?' said I, as he paused. 'Birds, you know, have both; and your Knights are supposed as yet to know nothing of either.'

'I hope you like it, Euphranor,' said Lycion from under his hat.

'Pshaw! Doctor,' Euphranor called out rather impatiently

—'Religious Affections, for instance, which all Children feel, and Dogs and Horses never.'

'My dear Euphranor,' said I, more seriously, 'is not *all* Affection, *quoad* Affection, unreasonable? If you speak of the *Object* of Affection, that is another thing. Men only (as we suppose) comprehend the Idea of God;—And, by the way, does not Bacon say that Man looks up to God, as a Dog to his Master?'

'But meaning that Man looks up with a Reasonable Affection, as Dog to Man with *un*reasonable.'

'Well,' said I, 'when turn'd of Forty perhaps'—(humph!)-

'No, no,' urged Euphranor. 'To be able to look up to a God at all, *is* Reason; and so of Truth, and Justice, and other abstract Ideas, which are Intuitive in Children; remembered, Plato says, from some previous existence, and included by Bacon, I have no doubt, in what he calls the *Moral* of Youth.'

'And Wordsworth too,' added I, 'does not he affirm this Intuition is the more active the Younger we are, as being nearer to God, who is our home?'

Euphranor assented, and I said, 'But, Euphranor, if this Intuition be *Reason*, we overrule Bacon and Aristotle, and decide that not *Age* excels in it, but Childhood.'

'Unless,' said he, 'considering the *Intuitive* to be drawn out by the *Dialectic*, as music from an instrument, into the full harmony of *complete*, *REASON*, as we see done in Plato's Dialogues with the Young.'

'Hear these Metaphysicians, Lycion!' said I, '*Reason* drawn out by Reason into REASON!'

Lycion only answered with one long-drawn sigh of smoke, that went the way of most Metaphysics.

'Or,' said Euphranor, laughing, 'suppose I change the Terms, and put all into some—Coleridgean formula, such as—"*The Intuition + the Understanding = the whole Reason.*"'

We both laughed at this grand Proposition, which Euphranor gave out in a mock-heroic way. And then I said, 'This poor *Reason* has run the gauntlet of definition harder than any word in the language, I believe. Some make it an Instinct; some a process of that Instinct, confounding Reas*on* with Reason*ing*, perhaps. Milton says it is nothing but *Choice*. And, by the way, (what has escaped us before, Euphranor), Aristotle, or his Translator, seems to identify it with Bacon's *Politic*.—'Concerned with *Expediency*," he defines it. Jeremy Bentham, after all!'

'Aristotle had rather a leaning that way,' Euphranor said —'so unlike his glorious Master.'

'Well,' I said, 'I, for one, do not pretend to decide among such great authorities, all calling names. I stick to the common phraseology of the country, and when I want to name the Supreme faculty of human Judgment, whensoever and howsoever begun and completed, give the Idol its old name REASON, and so leave it. As for that Intuitive Moral-material which you say is innate with us, I should think your friend Plato would agree it should have full room to develope in; that the Instrument, as you call it, should be well seasoned and strung before played on by that same sceptical agent you told us of, the dialectic Understanding.'

'Only to be touched by so delicate a finger as his own Socrates,' answered Euphranor, smiling.

'And even he was accused of doing it unskilfully, was he not? of turning the harmonious Instincts of Youth into discord, and making Sophists of the Etonians of Athens?'

'A great calumny,' Euphranor declared.

'Well, at any rate he would not let this precious Intuition be tampered, or tamper, with the Finger of Worldly or Parliamentary Policy; though, by the bye, I doubt he was accused of some corruption of that kind also.'

'Aristophanes and Anytus were both of a piece,' persisted Euphranor.

'And as to those blinder Affections of Aristotle's Youth, Plato may say what he likes, but he would have been especially sorry could his Horses, Dogs, Servants, or Sons, have been argued out of them, even by his own Dialogues.'

'And why?'

'Because he probably wanted them to follow and *do* what he thought good for them, whether they understood it dialectically or not, as you will agree with me we want our Dogs and Children to do, and as those Children of old, your Knights, did.'

'And which they would not the less do for Understanding, surely.'

'*Perhaps* not, if with a very great Cerebellum at the back of all that Forehead; else you know my old "Native hue of Resolution," &c.,' said I, smiling. 'And by some of the more irreverent writers on Humanity, Reason itself is said to be the weakest governing part about us—a sign-post, somebody says, which points the way, but by no means urges us along it. But if it be not even Reason, but only such a Will o' the Wisp as most Men, and more Boys, mistake for her, pointing several, and wrong, ways? Whereas, once shown the Right road, these Blind Affections actually push on along it, being nearest allied in Growth and Energy to our *Animal* Affections, which are said to be the strongest governing part about us.'

'To which, however, you are not going to reduce Chivalry, I hope,' said Euphranor.

'Well,' said I, 'You and Plato must consider together, whether great part of the Dog's, Horse's, and Knight's *a*dialectic affections we spoke of does not indeed result from good *Bodily* condition in Dogs, Horses, and Knights.'

He looked incredulous.

'As, for instance, what we are always talking of as *Animal Spirits, Animal Courage, Sanguine Temper*, and so forth—all which, by the way, Aristotle says inflame Youth not at all like Reasonable people, but "*like persons drunk with wine*" —a kind of *moral* in which Youth proverbially surpasses Age, partly in virtue of its better Animal condition.'

He looked reproachfully.

'Why, you know,' said I, laughing, 'your starved Horse won't run, and your starved Soldier—*will*.'

'Chivalry an essence of Beef-steaks!' ejaculated he.

'I hope you like it,' said Lycion, from under his hat.

But I went on laughing—'No, no, not beef-steaks only, else your Alderman would be a Bayard—He must be well exercised as well as fed; at Cricket with those Eton lads, or Boating with you, in order to convert the Beef-steak and Turtle into pure Blood, Muscle, Sinew—and *Pluck*.'

Brute strength, however, Euphranor would have it, (on Plato's authority again, I believe, for Plato was his Oracle), brutalized the Soul. He must admit, however, that Telamon, and Idas, and Œnides, and those other youthful Knights we had read of, wanted a good stock of it to work that very heavy Craft, the Argo; as did also King Arthur's Knights in grappling with Giants and Dragons; and even those of our own time, 'the Modern Gentlemen,' if they were to lead to Conquest any more forcible Host than a Tailor's. And I asked him whether, apart from any influence such Exercises, or the Animal condition they helped to bring about, might have upon the Soul, Digby did not consider Bodily Strength *per se*, and the Riding, Swimming, Rowing, and so forth, which advanced it, and from whose equal Development of the Body a Gentleman might be known, as very necessary Accomplishments of his English Knighthood?

'No doubt,' Euphranor said; and then, recurring to what I had before hinted at, remembered some observation of Sir Walter Scott, (another Hero of his), that Strong men are usually good-humoured, Scott himself, as Euphranor remarked, being so good an instance. There was also Bacon's testimony as to Fretfulness being chiefly observable in Weakness, Old age, Childhood, and Sickness, and several other Authorities quoted in the same direction. 'So that, on the whole,' said I, tapping on the top of Lycion's hat, 'what with the keeping out of Knavery till one knows how to join in it properly; and a voiding Badair in more senses than one; and cultivating Good Affections, and Good Health, and perhaps (Euphranor says) Good Humour, and perhaps also some other Good things we cannot now think of—Lamb's friend might have been right after all in lamenting the departure of the Eton lads from the Fields of their Youth for a premature Manhood in St. Stephen's.

'Especially,' said Euphranor, 'as I assure you, whatever Aristophanes or Anytus may say, Plato will not have a man meddle with the Laws till he is past Thirty.'

'Well,' said Lycion, 'let your Ancients—or Moderns—say as they like, the law of England settles it otherwise.'

'You mean,' said I, 'in fixing on Twenty-one as the age of—Discretion?'

He nodded; and I said—'Discretion enough to pocket Rents, marry, make your Will, and so on.'

'Yes, and sit in Parliament,' said he.

I was obliged to admit this—'There is no denying it—only perhaps not to advise, but courageously to second, and carry out into vote, what some Nestor Russell or Ulysses Peel proposes—as the Knights of Greece and England obeyed the highest wisdom of Law or Church in their days.'

'Nay, nay,' interposed Euphranor, 'and to advise too, in

order that the Generous counsel, the *νεανικὸν φρόνημα*, of Youth, may vivify and ennoble the cold Politic of Age. As in the passage we read from Digby, Amyntas, the Man of Policy, was wrong, and his son Alexander right.'

But oddly enough, as I remember'd the story in Herodotus, by a device which smack'd more of Policy than Generosity. 'But in the other case, Argus, I suppose, was not so wrong in restraining the impetuosity of his Youthful Crew, who,—is it not credibly thought?—would have fail'd, but for Medea's unexpected Magical assistance?'

Euphranor was not clear about this.

'He was—Argus I mean—"the Nestor of the Party," says Digby. Brave old Nestor, who though more than two Generations old, Agamemnon, I think, declares that Troy walls would soon be down had he Ten such Generals! So Good-humoured and Conciliatory too, with a cheerful Garrulity about the gallant exploits of his Youth—a really fine Old Gentleman, whom one would I think have hailed as "Old Cock!" meeting him in the Grecian lines!—Ah, Euphranor! If, by so full an Apprenticeship of Youth, one could like him be so thoroughly seasoned with its Spirit, that all the Reason of Manhood, and Politic of Age, and Experience of the World, should serve not to freeze, but to direct, the Genial Current of the Soul,—Youth itself, a Perennial Spirit, independent of Time, so that

> *Ev'n while the vital Heat retreats below,*
> *Ev'n while the hoary head is lost in Snow,*
> *The* Life *is in the leaf, and still between*
> *The fits of falling Snow appears the streaky Green—*

that Boy's Heart within the Man's never ceasing to throb and tremble, even to remotest Age; nay, at the last breath of this Life giving it Elasticity to bound into another;—

Then indeed your Senate would need no other Youth than its Elders to vivify their Counsels, or could admit the Young without danger of corrupting them by ignoble Policy.'

Whether Lycion would have deigned any Comment, I know not; for just now his friend looked out again from the Billiard-room window, and called out to him, 'the Coast was clear.' On which Lycion getting up, and muttering something about its being a pity we did not go back to School for Trap-ball, and I retorting we could carry it forward into Life with us, he carelessly nodded to us both, and with and '*Au Revoir*' went with his Cigar into the House.

During this, Euphranor and I both applied to our Glasses; and, after a little pause, he began to rally me upon my ignominious subjection of the Soul to the Carcass—a Theory, he said, I was far too often harping upon. I laughed and said, we Doctors were of old infamous for such doctrine—we spoke up for our Craft, not choosing Plato and the Soul-doctors to carry off all the fees; we only wanting to divide the spoil, however, just as Nature was supposed to have divided it, and quite as ready to grant that Soul acted on Carcass as Carcass on Soul. He remember'd Sterne's Jerkin and Jerkin's lining?

'O base metaphor!' cried Euphranor, 'just like Sterne, whom I wonder you don't hate as I do,—Soul and Body all of one texture!'

'No, no,' said I, laughing; 'Jerkin, you know, may be lined with other and finer material than himself.'

'With coarser too,' replied Euphranor, 'as I believe Sterne's own Jerkin was, for his Body was a very delicate one, and his Soul one of the grossest the World has been contaminated with.'

I then asked him what he had to say to the old favourite

of the Body being a House, and the Soul its Tenant—"the Body's Guest"—Would that do for him?

'Well—' he nodded: and I said, that if inclined to argue, one might say the Tenant, whether Prince or Peasant, must be affected according as his Lodging is wholesome or not; thrive in it if compact, roomy, and sweet; but catch all kind of Fever, and Ague, if close, foul, and dilapidated. More especially, if he were not only a Tenant, but a Prisoner, as was the Soul in this Body; unless indeed, as some thought, she got abroad through the key-hole at night, when it was fast locked in sleep; making rather an odd use of her liberty in Dreams.—

But here Euphranor called out again that the Lodger I spoke of, whether Peasant or Prince, *was*, in some sort, of the very same matter composed as his lodging; —a Clay-built Body in a Clay-built shed,—as bad a Metaphor, after all, as Jerkin and lining. 'Besides,' he went on eagerly, 'is it not well known that persons at the last extremity of Illness, of Old age,—on the very verge of Death,—shine out brighter than ever in Piety, Wisdom, and Love.' And he went on to repeat those old lines;

The Soul's dark Cottage, batter'd and decay'd
Lets in new Light through chinks that Time has made;
Stronger by Weakness wiser men become,
As they draw near to their Eternal home.

'Halloo!' I called out, 'got back to the Clay Cottage again!'

'Only to escape from it, or prove,' said he, 'how its Inmate thrives upon its very Ruin and decay. What instances we have of the greatest Minds dwelling in the craziest and puniest Bodies! Look at Pascal now'—

'Well?'

'Whose Intellect—and Piety—'

'—Made him, I have read, dismiss his Family from his death Bed, lest their Love should divert his own from God. A strange twist of the Lining, surely, whether from within or without. But the profoundest Problems, wittiest Epigrams, or most Pious Sermons, are no further samples of THE MAN—Locke's "Whole, Sound, Roundabout MAN"—Heart as well as Head—Affections, Energies, Courage, Will, and Temper—than that famous Brick was of the whole House.'

'Oh, to be sure,' said Euphranor laughing, 'I forgot,—one must, according to you, be Half Horse to be Whole Man.' And, after a little silence on both sides, I smiling in my turn, said;

'Like some objects that will force themselves on one's eyes in a landscape for ever so long, this Confounded Clay Cottage will not be got out of sight. The Poets are fond of it. It now occurs to me in that inverse relation with its Lodger, as might have been Pascal's case, for what I know. You remember that restless Soul,

> *That o'er-informed its tenement of clay,*
> *Fretting the puny Body to decay?*

'Well,' said Euphranor, 'and so flies back to her proper home.'

'A great escape, doubtless,' I said. 'But if it has pleased God to lease her this same Clay Cottage for some Threescore Years (which she may well spare from Eternity) to work out her own and other's probation? Else she could doubtless break a window, and so fly out any day—with the chance of faring worse, however.'

'Well, perhaps,' said he.

'And then if your crazy Cottage won't fall of itself to

pieces at once, but, after the manner of creaking Gates and Cottages, go creaking on, calling on the Tenant too (which is doubly hard) for all Repairs; and this when he wants to be about other more important Business? To think how much time a Divine Soul has to waste over some little bit of Cheese, perhaps, that, owing to Bad Drainage, will stick in the Stomach of the most Universal Philanthrophist!'

Euphranor laughed. 'What could be done for her?' And I answered, 'Perhaps nothing better than, according to that old Prescription, the Physician's Curse, that "Prevention is better than Cure," build up for her, from the very Ground, a spacious, airy, and wholesome Tenement, (becoming so Divine a Tenant), of so strong foundation and masonry as to resist the wear and Tear of Elements without, and herself within. 'Yes; and a *handsome* house withal—unless indeed you think the handsome Soul will fashion that about herself from within—like a shell.'

'Ah,' said Euphranor, 'the most beautiful of all human Souls, as I think, could scarce accomplish that.'

'Socrates?' said I. 'No; but did not he profess that his Soul was naturally an ugly Soul to begin with? So, by the time he had beautified her within, it was too late to re-front her Outside, which had case-hardened, I suppose. Or perhaps he was not Dandy enough to care about the outward cut of his Jerkin, so long as the Stuff was good within. Well; *he* proved what his Soul was made of, not only by his Talk in the City, but his Deeds in the Field; by his Death as well as by his Life. But, to be sure, a Man comes down at once victoriously upon us, and without Deed or Dialectic, finds a royal road to all hearts—(except, as was said, of the Blind) —cloth'd with the beauty of the Divine Image in which Man was originally made.'

'Aye,' said Euphranor, 'but where refer to the Original for that?'

'Why, where, but in the Greek Statues, of *their* Gods, if you please, but made in the Image of Men furthest removed from the Beast, and instinctively accepted by all Nations similarly organised as the Type in which the Deity reflected himself. And Montaigne, who is *my* Plato you know, partly because he tells me nearly all I now read of *your's*—he somewhere quotes Aristotle saying, that we all of us owe a sort of *Worship* to the Beautiful, as to the Gods themselves, whose Images they resemble. And did not your Socrates thus worship Alcibiades, as well for his outward as for his inward Divinity? Who, by the way, might almost have set for the Original from which Aristotle drew this Portrait of Youth that we have been discussing, with all its splendid Virtues and Defects.'

'Ah,' said Euphranor, 'you should have heard what Skythrops said on that score in my Rooms, accidentally opening the Book on the very passage we have been reading.'

'Well, what did he say?'

'Oh, you can fancy—that Youth, so far from "drawing clouds of Glory from God who is its Home," draws clouds of Sulphur from—*his* home. He ran over Aristotle's Inventory as you call it; the old talk, he said, of Honour, Glory, and so on—Pagan virtues—very well for a Pagan to record and a Papist to quote; but he wondered I could keep such a book in my rooms. And he specially commented on the *ὕβρις*,[1] which as you observed, waits on the very Virtues Aristotle admires.'

'Well,' said I, 'dead wood doubtless makes best posts, and that is what Skythrops wants. *He*, you see, would nip the Flower of Youth as if it were Flower of Brimstone: then Lycion would stifle it in St. Stephen's; and how many now-a-days ruin by forcing it to blow before its time! Really, the Youth which Lycion says we all inherit, and *you* say has only to be sublimed by Cricket into a Chivalry which no Class of Men can afford to do without, seems to me in a bad way just now.'

'Our friend Charles Lamb says the Children of the Poor never can be Young,' said Euphranor.

'What,' said I, 'the Poor of the Plough, Yorkshire, or other? Whose Service, Sir Edward Coke says, is aptly placed against Knight's Service, "for that the Ploughman maketh the best Soldier?"'

'Aristotle's *βέλτιστος δῆμος*[1] too,' added Euphranor.

> *Sola relinquentes Pueris hæredia Rastros,*
> *Jugera pauca, Domum luteam, cultumque Supremi*
> *Numinis, et sanctos mores, studiumque Laboris.*[2]

'A Clay Cottage for the Clay Cottage of the Soul to dwell, and, it appears, *best* dwell, in,' said I, laughing. 'But Lamb was judging of the only Poor he saw—in London and great Cities—where, by the way, they now found Schools and Universities for the Rich.'

'No reflection on my own old Westminster, I hope,' said Euphranor, 'nor I think against our other great old schools.'

'Which yet,' I said, 'were accused of somewhat sacrificing the Living Man to the Dead languages, and of somewhat negligent Moral Discipline. However, the Rich are, we know, at least as hard to be saved as the Poor. Look at Lads lolling all day in Easy Chairs, stewing at Operas and in Feather-beds at Night, consuming and consumed by those Eternal Cigars which help to paralyze you all before Fifty! So as I never can get a case of strenuous old Gout now to deal with, for which I really have a Talent. Why, is not washy Claret almost superseding this Good Stuff,' tapping my Glass, 'which, with good old Port, used to be the Liquor of *my* College Days?'

'Not with me and mine, I assure you,' said Euphranor laughing, 'though perhaps not so much from Love of Heroism as want of Pence. Well, "*Medio tutissimus.*"[1] What if we Middle Classes have the best start after all?'

'*You!*' cried I, '*We!* Why, think how Jack and Tom are crammed, from their very Cradles, to work themselves into some Silk Gown or other, and become fine Gentlemen Themselves, and support innumerable poor Relations! A stout old Lady of the Old School, whose Grandson was put into my hands having lost his Senses in gaining a Medal, told me the other day, "She thought, Doctor, the World grew Wiser and Weaker every day." No; I think the Ploughboy has the best of it in these days after all—*Oh Fortunati Nimium!*[2]—His Knightly Childhood produced into extreme Old Age by Ignorance—of the World at least, into which he is never called to enter at all; still less into Parliament; learning Patience at Crowkeeping—Strength at the Plough—Temperance of Necessity—Hardihood by constant communion with rough Mother Nature, on whose Bosom he is almost cradled, and, from his very Birth, rolls, and roars, and grows as strong and happy, and, I think, as good—'

As hearing Skythrops tell of his predestined Depravity in a stived-up room,' guessed Euphranor.

'Skythrops is not aware,' rejoined I, 'that it is such unfettered Animal Activity most completely lays the very Devil of Mischief he then complains of—as a few years afterward of a Worse.'

'Ah, I remember,' said Euphranor, 'how you used to rouse us children to Rebellion when a Maiden Aunt ran out to warn us in, or reduce us to order.

'Or for fear your dresses should be dirtied; for we of your middle Class must always look *Respectable* you know. Then Noise and Shouting, without which Children can't play or work their Lungs, if out-doors, is *Vulgar*, and, in-doors, disturbs the serious and nervous Elders within. Then what shrieking from the window if a little Dew lay on the Grass, or Summer Cloud overcame the Sky, to prevent you enjoying what Richter calls the most wholesome and luxurious of all Baths—a Thunder-shower.'

'I suppose you would have a Child's Shoes made with holes in them on purpose to let in water, as Locke recommends,' said Euphranor, laughing.

'I wouldn't keep him within for having no whole Shoes, or whole Clothes—or *any*—only the Police would interfere.'

'But the Child catches cold.'

'Put him to bed and dose him.'

'But he dies.'

'Then, as a sensible woman said, "is provided for." Your own Plato, I think, says it is best the delicate should die at once; and the Spartans killed them.'

'Come, come, Doctor,' said Euphranor. 'However, we will suppose he survives,—what else?'

'My Plough-boy? Oh yes—where did I leave him? In the Mud—or, as Poets might say, on Nature's fragrant Bosom, shaded by her Leafy Tresses, under her Heaven-blue Eyes; learning at least *her* Grammar in many Modes and Tenses—in free Communion with Flowers, Woods, Streams, and Stars—with whom, by the by, beginning Acquaintance in Love, he has sometimes out-stript the Book-Student in Learning.'

'Pray don't forget Dog and Hog,' said Euphranor, 'whose Heroic virtues we are all to share you know. And, above all, Boxer, the Cart-horse.

'Who—if well fed—sometimes reveals a very inconvenient innate Chivalry,' said I, 'when he would carry *his* Argo after the Hounds, when they and their Music break through the sere November Covert.'

'And it is wonderful,' Euphranor observed, 'what forbearance the nobler animals show with Children; how great Dogs suffer themselves to be pulled about by them; and how Horses will carry Boys with a kind of proud docility, who would kick and plunge under a grown-up Rider. Perhaps they like Children's soft voices and light weights; for which very reason, I have heard, they are more manageable by Women than by Men.'

'Yes,' said I, 'beside a sense of Humour, perhaps, at being bestrid by Urchins; ay, and real Generosity too, that will not take advantage of weakness.'

'But come, Doctor,' said Euphranor, 'your Plough-boy even must not be for ever in the Mud—nor his Affections go wholly to the Dogs.'

'Well, he has a mother like the rest of us,' said I, 'from whose Bosom—*un*like many of us—he draws the Milk of Life and Love; whose very Eyes, it was well said, beam the Idea of the Unseen Parent, if that be what you are driving at, into his Soul—better again than Mr., Mrs., or Miss Cornelia Skythrops.'

'Or any shrill Teacher from one of their Model Schools,' said Euphranor.

'Then,' said I, 'think what an Element of Religion the Clown has in his Ghosts, Witches, Hobgoblins, Jack-o'-lanterns—'

'Doctor! Doctor!'

'And Fairies! who still drop testers in the shoes of the diligent. It has never been merry in England, says some old Writer, since They left dancing on the Green-sward.'

'Well, better perhaps a Child believe, than be able to disprove, them.'

'Oh! I'd make a Ghost of him who tried! Set himself up above Doctor Johnson indeed!—Sweep a Child's Mind clear of all this, and see if its dry Places don't get occupied with Devils seven times more tiresome at least. The Lord deliver me from a Child who can explain the Theory of the Pump! Why, does not punning Plato call WONDER, THAUMAS, the Father of PHILOSOPHY herself, in the person of IRIS, Ambassador from the Gods to Men? So *we* quote about the Beginning of Wisdom—'

'Come, Doctor, "*Fear*"—of something very different from Ghost and Goblin.'

'Well, well,' said I, laughing, 'but at any rate you must allow your Children *their* Fairies, Giants, Giant-killers, and Dragons, if not their Ghosts, if you expect Lycion to allow *you* King Arthur with *his;* Symbols, you say, of the Truth. if not the Truth itself; and sung even to my Plough-baby from old Border Ballad and Chap-book.'

'Part of what Plato may call the *Music of Education*, I suppose,' said Euphranor smiling.

'All, too, (here *We* have perhaps the advantage over my poor Clown), illustrated with Pictures, (which are indeed part of the Music), as also of the Good Horse, and the Great Dog—(*'Quorum Exempla nisi moveant, nihil unquam movebit!'*[1]) to be followed in due course by the Lion-hearted Heroes of what we call History: your Richards, Harrys, Elizabeths. Marlboroughs. Nelsons,—nay, your very Cæsars, Alexanders—nay, even your Homeric Heroes, who have found their way into the legendary Broad-sheet along with Jack and his Bean-stalk.'

'All of whom we shall one day read, as well as hear, of,' said Euphranor laughing; 'for even your Plough-boy wouldn't care to be left behind his friend the Learned Pig at the Country Show in the knowledge of his Letters.'

'Well, I don't know what to say to that. Does not your Plato somewhere declare against any but Oral Instruction? I think he does. And if frightened at MS., what would he say to PRINT? However, if *your* Boy must learn his Alphabet, he may do so in the most Musical manner of all. Don't you know?'

> *To Master John, the Chamber-maid*
> *A Horn-book gives of Ginger-bread;*
> *And, that the Child may learn the better,*
> *As he can name he eats the Letter.*

I only wish my poor Clown had such facilities—for anything but Learning. However, take you care to give *your* Boy very little of his Alphabet daily, Gingerbread or other; and that again not in Skythrops' stived-up room, which will go far to turn the stomach. It seems a Truism till you come to apply it—Never tax a Child's—stomach—beyond its strength. As in *our* way of life (not in the Cottage, where the Child finds his own Legs) Mother and Nurse are as apt to make their Child walk before he can stand, as Skythrops to forbid the free play of his limbs when he should be doing little else than use them.'

'Ah,' said Euphranor, 'and beside being put to learn what one could not understand, how often wrongly taxed with Obstinacy for blundering what one was thought to have understood an hour or two before!'

'Perhaps a Fall in the Barometer being to blame,' said I. 'Yes, so we misinterpret the far finer Barometer of the Child's mind, whose variations might yet be read by the wiser Eye in the Child's face. If good with Men, how much better with Children, Rich or Poor, to lean to Indulgence rather than Severity. And still truer with regard to Morals than Intellect. You at least get at *Truth*, if ugly Truth, by letting a child display his character without fear; and evil humours that determine outwardly, are far more likely to disperse than when repressed to rankle within. And, any how, the ugliest Truth is better than the handsomest Falsehood.'

'But if,' said Euphranor, 'our Hero really, and with *malice prepense* rebel against such harmonious Music as we have provided for him?'

'"*The Birch Tree still grows in the depth of thy valleys,*"' said I, 'and doubtless followed Orpheus with the rest. Then there is the Cane—an Exotic Luxury. My Ploughman's Fist and home-bred Oak-stick supply all the Medicine needed for *his* Ginger-bread.'

'Somewhat too much for the Disease, I doubt,' said Euphranor, 'judging from what I have seen of their Discipline. Come, Doctor, Rod and Stick are almost gone out of date.'

'Going,' said I; 'and, as of so many other branches of Education, the less of them the better. I may not go the whole old-fashioned length of *Spare the Rod, Spoil the Child*, but I must say I am for an occasional dose; rare and rememberable; a last resort of *just* Authority over Child, as over Dog and Horse, like whom he is not to reason, but to obey, when Obedience is manifestly in his power.'

'My Mother,' said Euphranor musing, 'who I suppose never struck one of us in her life, though we were no better than the rest—I remember her observing to a neighbour one day, that so far as she saw, Children generally grew up with just contrary likings and ways of thinking from their Parents.'

'Yes,' said I; 'you know how one Generation is known

to swerve away to the opposite extreme from its Predecessor, —Pious to Infidel—Poetical to Practical, and so on.—And our Children are our next Generation, Your Great Men, I believe, generally leave no Posterity at all, or turn out something quite other than themselves; which touches at some other law of Nature. As for us common folks, we generally bring the reaction on ourselves, by dragging, or over-coaxing, the Horse to the water we ourselves like to drink of. Your mother, I dare say—as good and wise a Woman as ever I knew—knew better than this; she might insist, for instance, on your attending Family Prayer—a short one—twice a day, and Sunday Church once a week, but not tease your Conscience as to whether you really felt yourself a miserable sinner, loved the Missions—though by your High-Church—'

'Not she! oh, never, never!' cried Euphranor, 'and we now catch ourselves constantly saying how right she was in the few things we ever thought her mistaken about. God bless her!'

He took a long pull at his glass, and was silent some little while—she had died a few years ago.—And then he said—'Well, come Doctor, How far have we brought your Hero? Out of the Women's Apartments where the old Persian would have him kept for the first Seven years of Life? and where he was, one might hope, pretty safe from the Stick?'

'Yes, *that*,' I said, 'might advantageously be carried over to the account of the next Seven years. But, in the meanwhile, what had become of Lexilogus?

'Ah, what indeed?' But Euphranor thought nothing was to be done but wait quietly for him, at least till our Tipple was out. And as I had insensibly carried Sir Lancelot through his First Septenniad, I should e'en carry him on through his Second. Which, I answered, was not my Business at all in any Walk of Life; that, as Plough-boy, he never had any need of me, almost from his very Birth; and that even in the *Higher Circles* I had only to consult with Mother and Nurse for those first Seven Years when, as you tell us—from Xenophon, I believe—he was in the Women's Apartments; and then only about his Jerkin,—nothing to do with its Lining then or after.'

'Then,' replied Euphranor laughing, 'I must give him up to Skythrops, who is now coming up the Garden.'

'In a white neck-cloth, and with a face of determined Reprobation! Yes, he has often condoled with me heretofore on the poor Child's backwardness and depravity: and now his hour is come.'

'Well, and you give him up?'

'Not I, but rather in the doorway fast oppose to him my portly personage—thin as he is he slips no further in—he cannot melt me with his Vinegar, direct the Torrent on me as he may.'

'Come, come,' said Euphranor laughing at my modern prose, 'you shall let him pass, and hear what he has got to say for himself.'

'Very well,' said I, 'into the parlour with him then, where the luncheon is happily spread, from which Skythrops very largely partakes, proposing, between full mouthfuls and glaring spectacles, the scheme he has already tried on several Victims;—some Twelve hours' a-day Indoor instruction, Greek, Latin, Mathematics, Modern Languages, Geography, and general Christianity, to perhaps Two hours' Recreation, —videlicet, an improving Walk with Skythrops himself and his decaying pupils. To all which I listen deferentially as you advise, not fretting the current with a single Objection; on the contrary, mixing it with a third glass of Sherry, which he duly imbiles with a protest against Wine being his habit; and then, proposing to show him a late improvement in the place, I fairly escort him *down* the Garden again, and so out of the Premises.'

'Hilloa, Doctor,' cried Euphranor, 'here we have got your Plough-boy out of his Mud into a House with Sherry and *Premises!*'

'The more the Pity,' said I. ''Twas you did it. However, there having got him, there keep him, if you please, so long as you keep Skythrops out.'

'He and his Scheme do not suit you?'

'No,' said I. 'There is Magnetism in these things. Boys cannot learn of one who has nothing of the Boy in him. As for his scheme it only wanted reversing;' and I told him of a Table I had lately seen made by a German Physiologist, who, proposing to begin serious application at Seven years old (and not a whit earlier) with but *One* hour's in-door study, keeps adding on an Hour every Year, so as, by Fourteen years old, the Boy studies Eight hours of the Twenty-four.

'Distinctions,' Euphranor remarked, 'which, ever so good, could never be made in Schools.'

'That *were* made, however, in one School,' I replied, 'and that a German. Not only the hours of Exertion, whether bodily or mental, proportioned to the ages of the pupils, but even the hours of Sleep—no Lesson lasting longer than an Hour—and wholesome changes of Subject, Master, and School-rooms, to refresh the Boy's mind. Only to glance at Nature's own out-o'-door Academy, where, at any rate, so much of herself is to be learned.'

'Ah,' said Euphranor, 'I remember envying those who had time and money to follow Sedgwick in his Geological Hunt—across country—mounted on Hacks and Screws of all sorts and sizes.'

'Why, even your Greeks,' I said, 'taught abstract Philosophy in the Porch, and walking abroad; though, to be sure, in a better climate than our's; and, as you say, how much better the Philosophy of Nature, which, since Bacon's time, has continued to grow and bear fruit, while Metaphysic and Moral remain pretty much where they were 2000 years ago. Come! what say you now to Sir Lancelot beginning a Course of Anatomy with me?'—

'My dear Doctor!—At Eight!'

'Oh, out of doors, of course—say, in the straw-yard—on a Dead Horse to begin with. As to witnessing any Pig in the Parish killed and cut up, of course all Boys with a Spark of healthy Destructiveness in them will flock to that of Themselves.'

'One need not wonder,' said he, 'at the Brutes so many of them grow into.'

'You mean,' said I, 'the many Men of Feeling who turn away from the sight of Blood just when wanted to stop it?'

'Come, come, Doctor, I would rather have him into the School-room at once—and now we have made a Parlour-boarder and got him well into English, he shall learn that very Greek and Latin, which, say what you will, I know you venerate in your heart.'

'Yes,' said I, 'for the grand Languages themselves, and for some dozen Master-works untranslatable into any other. Otherwise I am tempted to agree with the Boy in one of Crabbe's Stories—I forget which—

Heav'ns! if a language once be fairly dead,
Let it be buried, not preserv'd and read.
If any good these crabbèd books contain,
Translate them well, and let them so remain;
To one huge vault convey the useless store,
Then lose the key, and never find it more.

'Well,' said Euphranor laughing, 'But to get the Boy into Latin and Greek, or into any other Language but his own, he must learn Grammar;—itself about as hard an Abstraction as may be. I am sure I now wonder at the jargon I had to learn and repeat when I was a Boy, and only now in happy hour light upon the *Reason* of the rules I then mechanically repeated.'

'True,' said I, 'but you were then only expected, I hope, mechanically to *use* them; by some formal terminations in *ùs, a, um, do, das, dat,* and such like, learning to distinguish the different parts of Speech, and by other empirical Rules their connexion, or Syntax; till able to put the scattered words together, and so ford through a Sentence. And the Repetition by heart of those rules fixed them in your mind, and was a fair exercise of Memory and Attention. I hate your modern Philosophical Grammars, which deaden the Boy's faculties to the *how*, while hammering at the *why*. "*Floreat Etona!*"[1] with her old Lily, and *Propria quæ maribus.*[2] Why, you might as well keep a Boy starving till he had learned the Theory of Digestion.'

'Which you were for teaching him however, with your dead Horse,' said Euphranor laughing. 'Well, come, however he may fare with the dead Horse, I suppose he is coming on all this while with the Living.'

'No doubt,' said I, 'the Horse he was taken to look at, feed, and be held on, he now bestrides alone—a Pony at any rate—trots, gallops, gets a peep at the Hounds throwing off; in due time a Run with them—fleshes his maiden courage at a Leap—'

'Ah,' said Euphranor, 'we poorer fellows, as I said, are cut out of this.'

'Well, there are the Ditches and Rivers for you to fall into, and be drowned in, whether Leaping, Skating, Swimming, or Boating; nay, in this dear Old England of ours, the Sea herself ready to embrace and strangle the whole Youth of Britain in her arms.'

'Ah, there again,' said Euphranor—'if Mamma was frightened at her boy dabbling in the Dew, what will she say now he is brought home half drowned, or his Arm broken by a fall from his Pony?'

'I must console her as before,' said I—

If he fall in, Good night!
Send Danger from the East unto the West,
So Honour cross it from the North to South.

'"Better a Broken arm than the Fear of one,' says Richter; Better die well ever so Young, than grow up a Valetudinary and Poltroon. One can only grow Strong in Body and Soul by such exercises as carry Danger along with them; and Strong in Body and Soul our Knight must be, must he not?'

'Nay, but,' said Euphranor, '*I* have not yet agreed that the Soul's strength depends on the Body's; nor Mamma perhaps that the Body can only be made strong by dangerous Exercises.'

'Well—by Strong Exercises, however.'

'Perhaps.'

'And is not all Strong Exercise more or less Dangerous? In Digging, Rolling, or even Running over, Mamma's Garden, we may sprain, strain, and rupture, if we do not break, limbs. There is no end to finding dangers if you look for them. Men have died of grapestones sticking in the throat—are we never to eat unpicked grapes again? And as for strength of Soul—Courage, for instance,—that includes so much beside—How is this, if not born in the Man, to be attained, and if innate, how *main*tained, but in the Demand for it; so repeated upon the yet plastic Mind of

Youth as, if not an Instinct, to become a *Habit* of the Soul, and act with the Force and promptitude of Instinct?'

'Mamma may say, in good Example, great Object, Religious Principle, and so on,' said Euphranor.

'And there may be found the long-concocted Determination, that, after all the struggles of natural Fear, may nerve a man to be a Cranmer at last. But while it succeeds in one, it fails in a thousand. For here, as with WILL and DECISION also, comes the ancient difference between *Resolving* and *Doing;* which latter is what we want. Nay, you know, the habit of Resolving without Acting (as we necessarily do in Books and in the Closet) is worse for us than never resolving at all, inasmuch as it gradually snaps the natural connexion between Thought and Deed, and the Man's last state is worse than his first.'

'Ah,' said Euphranor, 'you stole that from the Newman I lent you, Doctor; how true and good it is!'

'Very true and very good,' answered I, 'and I dare say stolen from him; though I had long before been familiar with a Proverb, as old as the Fathers for anything I know, as to the result of Thought's lying a-bed.'

Euphranor laughed, and said my old 'Native Hue of Resolution' was a cleanlier Comparison.

'And then,' said I, 'if this Closet-Courage could certainly brace us up for any long foreseen Emergency, would it help us at the sudden pinches of Accident for which our Knight must assuredly be prepared;—I mean, when there is no time to *make up our Minds.* But the Mind must act at once, ready made.'

'What is called *Presence of mind,*' said Euphranor.

'A very wonderful thing,' said I; 'as, for instance, such a sudden Resolution as the mind is put upon, whereby, should his Horse chance to fall and roll over, Full Cry, the Rider as instantly between Saddle and ground, braces himself up to pitch, not a flaccid heap of Flesh only fit to squash, but Nerve-compact, and out of his horse's reach—a Presence of Mind which Fielding tells us that brave old Parson Adams had, when even most Absent-minded—'

'I have often thought,' said Euphranor, 'what a wonderful act of the Soul it is in Cricket, where the Batter has to make up his mind whether to hit, tip, or block, all in the twinkling of an eye, between the Ball's being delivered from the Bowler's hand, and its arrival at his own Wicket. How much to be "Willed, Done, and Performed," in that moment of time!'

'Yes,' said I, 'and the Boxer, whose mind is to decide, and his fists to follow his mind so instantly, as to put in a blow at the very moment of guarding one off.'

'*Gladiatorem in Arena capere Consilium*,'[1] said Euphranor. 'But granting your Heroic Games *do* provoke those Powers of the Soul—by the bye, why wouldn't Battledore and Shuttlecock do, for DECISION at least?'

'Not where Danger is concerned, however,' said I.

'Well, even the Gladiator's Arena skill will hardly help on horseback; and would any, or all, of these noble Arts avail us in the Emergencies of actual modern Life when the Gladiator may be looked on as gone, the Boxer going, and even the Fox almost stole away for ever?'

'So far help,' said I, 'that the Soul having learned to abide unshaken in one (especially if a Greater) Trial will be better able so to face another, and at least bring to bear all the resources she has. Like Logic and Mathematics, you know, whose particular Problems do not specially resolve any other, but dispose us to a solution of all—especially all minor Dilemmas—though perhaps not so convincingly as the Fist. And what is any modern Life you like, but all a Battle against the Blows and Buffets of Fortune, whose lightest Taps will count as Blows if we be not armed against her hardest, and which if Man, unprovided with Woman's natural passive Submission, did not *actively* Resist, he was sure to make himself and all about him wretched. Or, if you like that better, what but a Chase after something more fugitive, and when found, no sweeter than a Fox? where the Heart, if not the Neck, was in danger of Breaking? Why, DECISION was necessary in taking a Lodging as a Leap, and, if tampered with, more difficult and distressing: *In*decision of all kinds being, as Bacon says, really a Decision, of such a kind as, after all distractions, generally ends in deciding on a course which unites the Inconveniences of all Alternatives. So the weak WILL spills itself in contradictory Wishes;—all these irritating the Owners with Themselves and all around them. Depend upon it,' said I, 'your Carpet-Knight will have his Battles *on* the Carpet—with Wife, Children, Friends, and Servants, Destiny, and Himself. Besides,' I went on laughing, 'the Noble Arts you laugh at are not so obsolete in even the pipingest days of Peace. Accidents will still happen in the best-regulated families. The House will take fire, the Coach will break down, the Boat will upset;—is there no gentleman who can swim, to save himself and others; no one do more to save the Maid snoring in the garret, than merely repeating, "How *very* awful!" Some one is taken ill at midnight; John is drunk in bed; Is there no Gentleman can saddle Dobbin—much less get a Collar over his Head, or the Crupper over his tail, without such awkwardness as brings on his Abdomen the kick he fears, and spoils him for the journey?'

Euphranor laughed, and I went on, '"I tell you, my Lord Fool, out of this Nettle *Danger*, we pluck this Flower *Safety*." Why, the most timid Valetudinary is ordered a gentle Ride; the quietest Cob is bought; but only he trots safely who has galloped hard: no one so sure to come down in the road as your heavy Sack of a Sitter, with no seat in his saddle, nor hand on his bridle; and no one so sure to break his nose when down he does come. Besides,' I continued, 'what after all is the amount of danger in all the Hunting, Wrestling, Boating, &c., that Boys go through? Half a dozen are drowned, half a dozen shot for rabbits by their friends, half a dozen get broken arms or collarbones in the course of the year; and for this little toll paid to Death and disaster, how large a proportion of the Gentry of this Country are brought up manfully fitted for War; —such "Manly Sports being," Fuller says, "the Grammar of Military Performance—" and *I* say for Peace also. If I have to do with Sir Lancelot, he shall take his chance, to grow up a MAN fit to live, or honourably to die in striving toward it. And so I leave him at the end of his Second Septenniad.'

'Close upon the age of those young Argonauts,' said Euphranor, 'upon whose lips the Down as yet was not.'

'Yes,' said I; 'push him on three or four years, and you may dub him Knight according to ancient usage, I believe.'

'Fitted in Body and Mind to his Calling?'

'Well, Euphranor, I cannot tell: my mind misgives me when about to send my Pupil into the Lists, whether Nature originally endowed him well enough, and whether I have helped to make the best of Nature's bounty. My Idea of Knighthood may fall very far short of yours and Digby's.

'Well, what sort of a fellow do you turn out, at any rate?'

'At Sixteen or Seventeen, say? Why, Euphranor, with how much of his first Septenniad about him! And why not? Being yet, according to your computation, a Child for some twenty years to come!—his Locks as thick, if not so long—Locks never to fall, but some Fifty years hence to begin May-whitening over a Green old Age; his Eye as full, clear, and direct, but settling toward a more constant Object; his Nose at least with something of a turn to Romanism; still, of course, not a furrow on face or brow, over which the blood mantles as before, only higher and deeper at the mention of what is Noble or Shameful—Ah, Euphranor, would he but bring me back this face of his Second Septenniad at the expiration of his Third!—His Body striking out into manly proportion not yet filled up, —Flesh giving way to Fibre and Muscle,—his Voice changed from Childish Treble to the Ringdove Register of Youth, 'sweet and tuneable," as were those of the Family of Margaret Newcastle; she does not mean, she says, (nor do I), *Singing* Voices; but "no husking or wharling in the Throat" —that is her word;—ringing out upon occasion clear and cheery as Chanticleer, and telling always of a roomy Chest, and in some measure, I think, of a candid Soul. However that may be,' continued I, seeing Euphranor shake his head at me with a smile—'Candid of Soul I trust he is; for I have ever sought his Confidence and never used it against himself; never arraigned him for the honest out-break of Youthful Spirit; nor exacted Sympathy when it was out of the nature of Youth to Sympathize. Inflamed to the full with Aristotle's Wine of Life, he is eager as before—after the Fox perhaps instead of the Hoop; Fearless, Generous, Giving and Forgiving,—if still passionate, yet less easily moved, and by deeper causes; if as stubborn against Force, yet helpless against Helplessness and an appeal to those Affections and Remembrances now lodged in a longer Past, and that deeper Heart whose shadowiest recesses also the Mystery of Woman is beginning to haunt. Ambitious perhaps, but of Honour in Action rather than Talk, in Riding than in

Reading; yet perhaps thinking more of what he reads than he cares to tell—somewhat awkwardly disposed perhaps to Dancing and other Drawing-room Accomplishments, which even now he shirks to go Earth-stopping with Tom and Jack who used to set him upon Topsail's back in days gone by. Apt, I am afraid, to yawn under Lulham's discourse; yet not ceasing to repeat Morning and Evening the short Prayer he learned at his Mother's knee—"Make me a good Boy!" and still less to go to Rest without her Blessing. In short, I should be content to find him with the Faults as well as with the Virtues of a vigorous Constitution of Mind and Body, which Time and good Object may direct into a Channel that will find room and outlet for all.'

'Rather a Tom Jones tendency, I doubt,' observed Euphranor, as I ceased speaking.

'Better than a Blifil, any how,' retorted I. '"The dry Rogue who sets up for Judgment being incorrigible," says virtuous Berkeley, whereas "the Errors of the lively Rake, lying in his Passions, may be cured." But I will not admit even Fielding's—and still less my—Tom to be a Rake; though I admit I must have him launch into Life with a Vigour that might run into an Extreme of Evil as well as Good. Only VIGOUR he must have, as the one needful thing: subject like all best things to worst Corruptions; vigour of Body and Soul, whether implicate or individual; Strength itself, even of Evil, being a kind of Virtue, which Time, if not good Counsel, is sure to moderate; whereas Weakness is the one radical and Incurable Evil, increasing with Every Year of Life.—Which fine sentence, or to that effect, you will find somewhere in the Newman you lent me, and whose Authority I know you cannot doubt.'

'And all this without regard to a Lad's Profession or natural Genius?'

I asked him 'if it would not do very well at least for the Profession of Shooting Partridges or Hunting the Fox; nay, even serving as High Sheriff?'

'He could not deny that,' laughing.

'Or if obliged, poor fellow,—a Younger son perhaps,—to *do* something to earn him Bread—or Claret—for his Old Age, whether not fairly qualified to be knocked on the Head as Soldier or Sailor?'

'Nor that.'

'As for the Church, (which is your other Gentlemanly Profession), you know your Bishop can consecrate Tom or Blifil equally by that Imposition—'

'Doctor, Doctor,' broke in Euphranor, 'you have been talking very well, don't spoil it by one of your Grimaces.'

'Well, well,' said I,—'Oh, but there is still THE LAW.'

'For which I am sure he needs all the Chivalry you can ingraft upon him,' said Euphranor.

'And in which I would rather trust myself with Tom than Blifil,' added I, 'Lawyer as the latter is in grain. Well, what else? Surgery? But that is an Ungentlemanly Profession, into which you would not let me initiate him; though it is said to need "the Lion's Heart" as much as another.'

'But also the Lady's Hand,' replied he, smiling.

'Not in drawing one of the Molares, I assure you. However, thus far I do not seem to have indisposed him for the Professions his Rank usually opens to him; perhaps even, if he have what you call a Genius that way, not to some of those *Ologies* we thought he might pick up a liking for in the Mud, and even light upon some discovery which the more systematic Explorer missed; as Pan a-hunting found out Ceres, whom the more seriously-searching Gods could not.'

'Perhaps.'

'Or even a turn for searching into Digby and Plato for qualities he already unconsciously possesses.'

Euphranor, on whose earnest face no Sign of Self-consciousness appeared, sat meditating a-while by himself as I drew the last draught from my Tumbler: and then observed that, if my Notions were right, the Body needed to be made as much a matter of Discipline as the Brain, whether at Home or Abroad; a matter which the Great Schools at least (which Arnold thought the only good ones) ignored, taking for granted Boys would only give up too much time that way without any Encouragement. A mistake, I thought, in these days, when, beside School-work, there were so many sedentary Muses soliciting the Hours allotted to Active Recreation. A Mistake also, looking to Holiday Activity as a due Compensation for School Study; Mind and Body needing ever to be kept in proportionate Action—certainly not to Mind's over-exertion, who had so many years of Growth before her, unless, by premature Energy, she shook the Foundations of that House of hers, then so rapidly completing for better or worse. The Greeks we knew made Gymnastic a part of their Discipline; so do the modern Germans; so, I thought, might and should our Schools; the larger the better, as affording all the more efficient means not only for Individual but Collective Gymnastic,—Military Drills, Exercises, Watches, expressly enjoined by Milton, I remembered, beside the Good they did the Body, and as Preparation for possible War, carrying a Sense of Order, Duty, Submission, mutual Dependence, and wholesome Companionship into the Soul. Even as to rarer Appliances, which we think the Rich only can have or want, and those mainly *at Home:* Fellenberg had them in his so much poorer Establishments than our Harrows and

Etons. Not only the Swimming-Bath, which he found one best remedy for Indolence or Inertness of Mind as well as Body—(our Seas and Rivers supply us with that of the best Water)—but also his Riding-School for Poor as well as Rich; beside Gardens and Ploughing-fields for Rich as well as Poor,—'Where, as I was saying before,' said Euphranor, 'our young Tailor might have a turn at the Bat, and our young Lord at the Plough, now and then.'

'And all the better, if the young Lord were put to earn his Bread there for a week or so every now and then,' said I, 'affording him light as to the condition of the Poor, "unquenchable by logic and statistics," Carlyle says, "when he comes, as Duke of Logwood, to legislate in Parliament."'

'To hear you talk, Doctor, one might suppose you would send your son to Germany for his Schooling; but I know your inveterate prejudice for an Englishman being brought up in England, imbibing English air and English associations into his very nature from the very first.'

'Yes,' said I, 'I am for growing up by the Thames under Windsor Castle, not by the Rhine under Heidelberg.'

'Not forgetting glorious Westminster Abbey!' cried he with exultation.

'No,' said I, 'we will not transplant our Youth to Fellenberg, but have a slip of him over here if needful. For even that I suggest with hesitation, and under Awe of the Old Genius of those Nobler Schools of ours, which, in blunder and out of blunder, perhaps from having better Stuff to work upon, had somehow managed to send abroad a better article of Manhood than Germany, who indeed somewhat overlaid the Free Spirit of her Youth by Discipline of many kinds. But for our little Schools—(I don't speak of such hideous Spectres as *Dotheboys*, now laid, I trust, for ever, by a more potent Wand than mine),—you scarcely know, my dear Euphranor, what sordid, pusillanimous, Soul-and-Body-stunting things the most of these are, which, if English Good Sense should not explode just before it is too late, (as English Good Sense has somehow a knack of doing), would almost extirpate half the Middle (and that how large a Class!) of English Chivalry. Nor are the poor Masters only to blame. The Fathers who send are quite as base and ignorant as the Masters who receive, as anxious to get their full pennyworth as the others to give it. On your Suburban Minerva Academies, and Classical and Commercial Seminaries, where young Gentlemen are boarded, taught, and indeed Done for, for some twenty or thirty Pounds a year: their "Moral and Intellectual Culture carefully attended to;" the "strictest Attention" paid to what is called "their Health" —some Mrs. Apollo perhaps superintending the Pupils' Stomachs as her Husband their Souls. Some Ten hours a day of Indoor Desk-work, of a kind too most indigestible by the Young; the little Play-time cut up into intercalary shreds, precluding any Generous invigorating Game, even if the few square yards of heartless gravel and the strict Edict against whatever ever so remotely threatens the Boy's limbs or the Master's windows, should permit; perhaps, a so-called Gymnastic Gallows in the centre, up which you see creatures with the Bodies of Babies and the faces of Old Men climbing and turning over with a feeble squeak of Emulation. No Rowing, no Sailing, no Sliding even, no stolen Ride on Horse, Donkey, or Coach-Box, no wild Chase over the Meadows, Hedge, and Ditch, animated by the pursuit of some infuriate and over-blown Gamekeeper; but a walk, Two and Two, along the road, dogged by the sallow, spectacled, and still-reading Usher. Sunday, that comes a day of Rest to all beside, revisiting these poor things only with a worse increase of hypocritical restriction of the Spirits and unnatural tension of the Mind; having to endure, and afterwards record, two long Sermons—perhaps to indite a short one—'

'Of course no Fighting,' said Euphranor, 'and, I suppose, no Flogging neither.'

'And yet,' said I, 'the clenched Fist so soon resolved into the Open hand, when once the question of Might and Right was settled—how much better than the perpetual canker of a grudge never suffered to explode!—and Flogging had its humour too—soon passed away, shame and smart, from fore and aft—how much better than the Heart-pining, Body-contracting Confinements and Repetitions which double the already overloaded task-work, and revenge a temporary fault with lasting injury.'

'You get excited about it, Doctor,' said Euphranor as I paused almost for Breath.

'Oh, it succeeds, it succeeds,' I went on. 'The little Fellow who came with but little Colour in his Cheek and troublesome Activity in his Blood, soon loses what he had; contracts instead of expanding,—dwindles instead of Growing, —and becomes a Credit to the School, and a blessing to his parents. Only one of Nature's "best earthly mould," with the spirit of her Chivalry strong in his blood, it is who kicks over the traces, throws the whole "very eligible Establishment" into disorder, and finally rouses the dastard Skythrops into a meagre attitude of Expulsion, however unwilling to part with any Victim who pays. But "Go he must—nothing can be done with him—" He goes: is sent to Sea—rolls and tosses over the World—returns a good-humoured, active, lively, sun-burnt fellow, with tobacco and cheroots for his old Dad; silks for Mother and Sisters; a parrot for old aunt Deborah; a bamboo which he says he would give old Skythrops but for fear of his licking the boys with it. So he travels, and returns, and travels again; has at last scraped a little money together; marries a good-humoured girl who has even less world's wealth than himself; nay, I believe had married her long before he was half as rich as he is—; has a large family of children healthy as himself—the more the merrier, he says; and so whistles through and over the ups and down of life; his healthy, courageous Good-humour, and Activity of soul, radiating a more happy Atmosphere throughout a little circle, and through that, imperceptibly, to the whole World, than shop-loads of Poems, Sermons, and Essays, by dyspeptic Divines, sickly Poets, and universal Philanthropists, whose fine feelings and bad stomachs generally make them Tyrants in their own families, and whose Books go to draw others into a like unhappy condition with themselves.'

'And the *Good* boy,' said Euphranor,—'what becomes of him?'

'I have no heart to follow him,' said I. 'Poor fellow! the last I heard of him was, that after a most unimpeachable progress through School and College, he was either dying at some German Bath covered with Blotches and Boils; or, still worse, surviving—a highly Respectable, and indeed Religious, Attorney in large practice.'

'Do you remember,' said Euphranor, 'that fine passage in the Clouds—little as I love Aristophanes, by the bye—between the *Δίκαιος* and *Ἄδικος Λόγος*?'[1]

I had forgotten, I said, my little Latin and less Greek: and he declared I must however read this Scene over again with him. 'It is, you see, Old Athens pleading against Young; whom after denouncing, for relinquishing the hardy Discipline and simple severe exercises that reared the *Μαραθωνομάχους Ἄνδρας*,[2] for the Warm Bath, the intricate, lascivious Dance, and the Law Court; he suddenly turns to the Young Man who stands hesitating between them, and in those Verses, musical as the whisper of the Trees they tell of—

'Ἀλλ' οὖν λιπάρος γε καὶ εὐανθὴς—'[1]

'Come, my good fellow,' said I, 'you must interpret.' And Euphranor, with a little sly smile, and looking down, recited—

O listen to me, and so shall you be stout-hearted and fresh as
a Daisy:
Not ready to chatter on every matter, nor bent over Books till
you're hazy:
No Splitter of straws, no dab at the Laws, making Black seem
White so cunning;
But wandering down out o' the town, and over the green
Meadow running.
Ride, wrestle, and play with your fellows so gay, all so many
Birds of a feather,
All breathing of Youth, Good-humour, and Truth, in the time
of the jolly Spring weather,
In the jolly Spring time, when the Poplar and Lime dishevel
their tresses together.

'Well, but go on,' said I, when he stopped, 'I am sure there is something more of it, now you recall the passage to me—about broad Shoulders and little—'

'But this was all he had cared to remember,' he said.

I then asked him who was the Translator; to which he replied, it was more a Paraphrase than a Translation, and I might criticise as I liked. To which I had not much to object, I said—perhaps the Trees 'disheveling their tresses' was a little Cockney, which he agreed it was, beside missing that very Whisper, which in Sound and Sense is most delightful of all, and might so easily have been retained. And he then observed how the degradation Aristophanes satirized in the Athenian youth went on and on, so that, when Rome came to help Greece against Philip of Macedon, the Athenians, Livy says, could contribute little to the common cause but Declamation and Despatches—"quibus solum valent," he says.'

'Ay,' said I, 'and to think that when Livy was so writing of Athens, his own Rome was just beginning to go downhill in the same way and for the same causes:

> *Nescit equo rudis*
> *Hærere ingenuus puer,*
> *Venarique timet, ludere doctior*
> *Græco seu jubeas trocho,*
> *Seu malis vetita legibus alea:* [1]

how unlike those early times, when Heroic Father begot and bred Heroic Son; Generation following Generation through ages of national glory, crowned with Laurel and with Oak; under a system of Education, the same Livy says, handed down, as it were an Art, from the very foundation of Rome, and filling her Senate with Generals, each equal, he declares, to Alexander.—But come, my dear fellow,' said I, jumping up, 'here have I been discoursing away like a little Socrates, while the day is passing over our heads. We have forgotten poor Lexilogus, who (I should not wonder) may have stolen away to Cambridge.'

Euphranor, who yet seemed to linger with the subject, nevertheless rose up. On looking at my watch I saw we could not take anything like the Walk we had proposed and be at home by their College dinner; so as it was I who had wasted the day, I would stand the expense, I said, of Chops and Ale at the Inn: after which we could all return at our ease to Cambridge in the Evening. As we were leaving the Bowling-green, I called up to Lycion, who thereupon appeared at the Billiard-room window with his coat off, revealing a rather gorgeous waistcoat, and asked him if he had nearly finished his Game? In reply, he asked us if we had finished our Ogres and Giants? Whom, on the contrary, I said, we were now running away from that we might live to fight another day—would he come with us into the Fields for a walk? or, if he meant to go on playing Billiards, would he dine with us on our return? 'He could not walk with us, certainly,' he said; and when I spoke of dinner again, seemed rather to hesitate; but at last said, 'Very well;' and, nodding to us, retired with his cue and waistcoat back into the room.

Then Euphranor and I, leaving the necessary orders within, sallied out towards the Church, observing, as we went along, how much pains Lycion took to spoil the good that nature had given him. For, at Harrow, he was (as Euphranor understood) a good-humoured, lively, and rather gallant boy. But dining with Ambassadors, and the Clubs, and Almack's was spoiling him. And Euphranor spoke of the levity and indifference, now so fashionable,—so unnatural to Youth,—especially ungraceful, he thought, (and so did I), in Women. And he observed, I remember, that even if there were no other ill effects of London dissipation on them, yet the simply being present in so many Crowds was a sort of prostitution, especially of the Eye; and noticed the hackneyed look which even young and delicate Women soon acquired. In all of which we judged, both of us, rather from what we heard, and read, and saw of fine people in their carriages, than from any personal knowledge; for neither of us were much in Great company. We were talking thus, when, on coming close to Chesterton Church, we saw

Lexilogus passing through a turnstile on his way towards us. In half a minute we had met; and he explained to us why he was so late: delayed by one of Aunt Martha's fits of Asthma; and he did not like to leave the house till it was over. She had now fallen into a quiet Sleep.

After shortly expressing our sympathy, we again turned back with him; and I told him how, after all, Euphranor and I had played no Billiards, but had been arguing all the time about Digby and his Books.

Lexilogus smiled, but made no remark, being naturally slow of Speech, and perhaps of Thought also. But the day was delightful, and we walked briskly along the road, conversing on many topics, till a little further on we got into the Fields. These were now in their Prime, (and that of the Year, Crabbe used to say, fell with the Mowing), crop-thick of Grass full charged with Daisy, Clover, and Buttercup; and, as we went along, Euphranor quoted,

Embroidered was he as it were a Mede,
All full of fresh Flowris, both white and rede,

and instantly added, 'What a lovely picture was that, by the way, of a young Knight!'

I agreed, and asked Lexilogus did he not think so too? but he had never read Chaucer: so I begged Euphranor to repeat it to us; which he did, with an occasional pause in his Memory, and jog from mine.

With him there was his Sonn, a yongé Squire,
A Lover, and a lusty Bachelire,
With Lockis curle, as they were leid in press;
Of Twenty yere of age he was, I ghesse;
Of his Stature he was of evin length,
Wonderly deliver, and of grete Strength;

And he had ben somtime in Chevauchie
In Flandris, in Artois, and Picardie,
And born him wel, as of so litil space,
In hope to standin in his Lady's grace.
Embroidered was he as it were a Mede,
All full of fresh Flowris, both white and rede;
Singing he was or floyting all the day;
He was as fresh as is the month of May:
Short was his Goun with slevis long and wide,
Well couth he set an Hors, and fair yride;
And Songis he couth make, and well endyte,
Just, and eke daunce, and well portraye and write.
So hote he lovid that by nighter tale
He slept no more than doth the Nightingale.
Curteys he was, lowly, and servisable,
And karft before his Fadir at the table.

'Chaucer, however,' said Euphranor when he had finished the passage, 'allows his young Squire more Accomplishments than you would trust him with, Doctor. See, he dances, draws, and even writes songs—quite a *Petit-maître*.'

'But also,' I added, 'is of "grete Strength," "fair y-rides," having already "born him well in Chevauchie." Besides,' continued I, (who had not yet subsided, I suppose, from the long roll of my former Sententiousness), 'in those days, you know, there was scarce any Reading, which usurps so much of Knighthood now. Men left that to Clerk and Schoolman; contented, as we before agreed, to follow their bidding to Pilgrimage and Holy war. Some gentler Accomplishments were then needed to soften manners, just as rougher ones now to fortify ours.'

'As we may see among ourselves,' said Euphranor. 'Music, *you* will say, only helps to *mollyfy* the rich,—pardon the vile pun,—but the Education people agree it is of excellent use among the Poor.'

'And who was it,' said I, 'that, when some one grumbled at a Barrel-organ in the street, said prettily, one should tolerate, and even respect, the instrument that carried Orpheus down into dark alleys and cellars. It has struck me strangely to hear in one of our Yorkshire Sears all of a sudden some delicate Air of Modern Art breathing into the old Hills and almost as primitive Inhabitants.'

Euphranor then observed, that in the days of Elizabeth and the Stuarts the Lute and Viol were common Accomplishments of young Gentlemen: so, to be sure, were all Martial exercises.

'And more than Exercises,' added I; 'young fellows going to serve as Soldiers abroad as part of their Education, if there were no Wars in hand at home. Sir Philip Sidney might well be permitted a little Sonneteering; and one would not quarrel with a Midshipman practising his Flute in the Cockpit now.'

'Even Pepys, Tailor as he was,' Euphranor said, 'takes Horse and rides to Huntingdon from London and back without comment.'

'And without a sore bottom, I dare say,' rejoined I. 'People could only so travel in those days; and could hardly help being hardily brought up in all respects. There is a delightful little Horseback tour in Derbyshire, made and recorded by a Son of Sir Thomas Browne—Edward, and one friend,—I think; with all their wet jackets, stumbles, benightings, and weariness, so well compensated by the welcome Inn with its jovial Host at last. Travelling has lost its proper relish for the Young now,—there is no Fun, no Adventure, no Endurance. And look at old Chaucer himself,' said I, 'how the fresh air of the Kent hills, over which he rode Four hundred years ago, breathes in his Verses still. They have a perfume like fine old hay, that will not lose its sweetness, having been cut and carried so fresh.

'Lydgate too, I remember,' said Euphranor, 'tells lovingly of Chaucer's Good-humour and Generosity—I cannot now recollect the lines,' he added, after pausing a little. *

'A famous Man of Business too,' said I, 'employed by Princes at home and abroad. And ready to fight as to write; having, he says, when some City people had accused him of Untruth, "prepared his body for Mars his doing, if any contraried his Saws."'

'A Poet after your own heart, Doctor, sound in Wind and Limb. In general, however, they are said to be a sickly, irritable, inactive, and solitary tribe.'

'The Great ones?' I asked, 'who, I think, are the only ones worth naming—Homer, Æschylus, Shakspeare, for instance?'

'We don't know much of them—of the two first, at any rate,' said he.

I asked if Homer did not go about Camp and Court singing his verses? To which Euphranor answered, the stories of his Beggarhood were quite exploded by those omniscient critics the Germans, whom he knew how much I reverenced; and I said, 'About as much a Beggar, I suppose, as his own divine Demodocus at Alcinous' palace, or as the Bards at a Celtic Banquet. Then as to Æschylus, pray is his presence at Salamis only a *Myth*, as you call it?'

* The verses Euphranor could not remember are these:

For Chaucer that my Master was and knew
What did belong to writing Verse and Prose
Ne'er stumbled at small faults, nor yet did view
With scornful eyes the works and books of those
That in his time did write, nor yet would taunt
At any man, to fear him or to daunt.

Euphranor laughed, and believed we must admit this to be authentic, so clearly as the Trumpet that woke the Greeks to Battle on that morning still rung in his Verse. I then asked laughingly about Shakspeare's Poaching, which Euphranor said of course I should vindicate, however discredited by German and English critics too.

'Well,' said I, 'whether Shakspeare were a Poacher or not, (and I firmly believe he *was*, in the days of his Knighthood), he, at least, was no dyspeptic Solitary, but, like Chaucer, a good Man of Business, managing a Theatre so unlike modern Managers, who are not great Poets, that he made a sufficient fortune; which when he got, desiring no more, he retired from London and all his Glory, to dear old Stratford, the town of his Birth—the fields of his Knighthood—and Poaching—and there spent the rest of his life, an active Burgess of the town, esteemed by all the neighbouring Gentry, Aubrey tells us, for his pleasant Conversation.'

Shakspeare did not however, Euphranor thought, quite bear out my old Theory: his very sound Mind appearing to have dwelt in a rather heavy Body, to judge by the figure on his Tomb. And he died young.

Which Monument, a very clumsy one, however, only indicates that he grew plump at last, I said. But the only probable Pictures of him exhibit great Beauty of Face, and every appearance of its growing on a well-proportioned and well-developed Body.

'Ward's Journal,' said Euphranor, 'says he died of a kind of Fever, I think, resulting from a Carousal with Ben Jonson, who came to visit him from London.'

'Not unlikely,' said I; 'he would, no doubt, pledge Ben handsomely, having no notion his own Life was at all necessary to the World. And, after all, Fifty-two (the age he died at) was not so Young in those days, when people drank Sack and Ale for breakfast, and were much less careful of their Health.'

'Without such good Doctors as now we have,' added Euphranor, slily. 'Well, who does not wish *his* clay cottage had been built so strong, or patched so well, as to have stood out the Dictation of many more Imperial Manifestos to Posterity! However, Doctor, if you save your Theory one way with him, (I am not quite sure you have, though), what will you say to Dante—and, if you will allow him of the front rank, Milton—both Morose, Solitary kind of fellows, I doubt.'

I replied, that supposing this were so, both lived in Times to try the temper of the Strongest and Best—Civil War—Neighbour opposed to Neighbour—Friend to Friend—even Kinsman to Kinsman—and, even after Might had carried the quarrel, Victor and Vanquisht having to settle down cheek by jowl again. Dante was forced by Banishment into Solitude, or to that worst pang, he says, of climbing another's stair for Eleemosynary Bread—no wonder he put—into a Poetic Hell at least—those who had so reduced him. As to Milton, when he had worn out his eyes "in Liberty's Defence," and when the Restoration made that Defence Treason, he was obliged to live in Seclusion, besides being compelled by Poverty. Certainly, if his own word were to be believed, he never bated a jot of Heart or Hope to the last: and, in my turn, I asked Euphranor from what *myths* he drew his conclusion about the Temper of these Two Men?

Euphranor did not like the bitterness of Milton's Prose tracts, and fancied he was an awkward Husband. Something in his Portraits too—

'Ah, Lexilogus,' said I, 'Euphranor cannot forgive the

Republicans, and their treatment of his Martyrs, Charles and Laud. Were, however, Shakspeare ever so fat, and Milton and Dante ever so surly, I should not give in. For who doubt sthat men, however nobly constituted, may ruin all by misuse; as Burns by Intemperance of all kinds, and Walter Scott by the forced redemption of his own and his friend's credit? The Poetic spirit in itself is a fiery one, most apt to fret its Body to decay, made up of some dangerous elements, which, as you say, and as Wordsworth has hinted, may lead to Melancholy and Madness, unless aired by perpetual contact with Reality, Action, and wholesome Communion with men.'

'I suppose,' said Euphranor, 'you would knock about a young Apollo like the rest of us coarser Vessels.'

'To be sure I would.'

'And so break half the Tribe in Moulding.'

'And live the better with the other half,' I replied.

'Yes, decidedly, I would pass them all through such a Fire as only the true Poetic Metal should abide, and that come forth all the purer and stronger. A great gain both ways; and it has been said to be the mark of Genius that it never can be crushed; only *Talent*, which in Poetry assuredly we do not want to survive. I would forthwith set young Edwin on a rough Colt, and pit a Cockney and a Laker at a Wrestling match, and see if some external Bruises would not draw off that inner Sensibility which is the main stock of many-so-called Poets.'

'And not of the True also?' said Euphranor. 'It has also been said the Poet has more of the Woman than Man in him.'

'Which were it true,' answered I, 'what a final argument for smothering the whole Tribe as early as possible, Great and Small, if they are not only to be Women themselves, but affeminate us also with their Incantations! But, mark you, I don't believe a word of this; I believe the true Poetic Sensibility to be wholly different from the Feminine; no Tenderness of Nerves, but Susceptibility of Imagination, or some essential difference which I, who am neither Poet nor Metaphysician, may not comprehend.'

'Yet that Vision of Marcellus that moved Octavia to tears; and patient Grizel; and Juliet; and Cordelia; and the Baby Star in Andromache's Bosom, frighted at the Helmet of the Father he is so soon to lose—'

'Yes,' said I as he paused, 'not to be found in any Laura Matilda, Male or Female.'

'But where the Woman must have been very strong'—

'But not strong*est;* not running away in Elegiac Tears, but moulded into Form by yet stronger Imagination and Understanding. They who tell of Andromache and Cordelia told of Achilles and Lady Macbeth; and left it for *us* to weep, while they conjured up those Forms of common Passion which only they ennobled in reflecting back on us.'

And Euphranor recalled to me that passage in the Last Years of Scott's Life where the Strong Man, broken not by Time but Over-work, could no longer repeat his so oft-repeated Chevy Chase without Tears, which even the Sighing of the Summer-wind, he says, would bring into his Eyes 'not unpleasantly,' as he Drove—no longer *Rode*—among his Woods by Tweedside: Bodily weakness, Lockhart finely says, having laid bare the delicacy of Organization whose finer Vibrations,—'*Nerves* you may call them, Doctor,'—once kept under by a Strong WILL, now 'trembled to the Surface.'

'No longer able to Create a Jeanie Deans,' said I, 'but only *feel* for her like the rest of us—The Man of Genius degraded to the Man of Taste!—Let us contemplate that no longer.

And *his* Jerkin too one of those which Sterne goes on to say, (only you would not let him), seemed Stout enough to resist any Rumple from within.'

'Oh that Jerkin,' said Euphranor laughing, 'returning on us as obstinately as ever my Clay Cottage did. and, I declare, far less ornamentally.'

'Why think, my dear Fellow,' I went on laughing, 'how, wrapt up in one of the stoutest, your Poet is enabled, like my Ploughman, to face, conquer, and consort with Nature in all her humours, Storm as well as Calm, and penetrate into all her Mysteries, Sea and Land, Mountain and Valley, Day and Night: and bring them back—in its Pockets—for us. Really the only Great Poet I had seen was of great Mould and Muscle; having used as a Boy, I was told, to be out upon the Hills Night after Night with Shepherd and Sheep, whose individual Faces and Voices he not only grew to distinguish, but, both in Heaven above and Earth beneath, many of those uncertain phenomena of Night—the sound of falling Weirs and creeping Brooks, and Copses muttering to themselves afar off, perhaps the yet more impossible Sea—all inaudible to the Ear of Day; and not only the "Consistory of the Nightly Stars,' and their gradual Dispersion by the Dawn, but also certain unsurmised Apparitions of the Northern Aurora, by some shy Glimpses of which silverying some low-lying Horizon Cloud in their customary quarter of the Heavens, scarce any Winter—no, nor even Summer—Night, he said, was utterly unvisited. Then there is Wordsworth, whom *You* at least think a great Poet, and the Idleness of whose Youth, we read, was lamentably—promising—He, I am told. is still to be seen, at near Eighty, moving with the Shadow of the Cloud up Helvellyn. Whereas your young Cockney can only strain laboriously up Hampstead Hill, with an Umbrella, Cork soles, and a cold Muffin in his pocket, having promised Miss Briggs by the sacred Moon to be at home in Bidborough Street before the dews fall. And even if the Daisies and Buttercups there were at this time of day sufficient Object for the Muses, yet cannot he make even *his* best of them: for has he not gone out *prepared* to be Poetical? Whereas Poetry is said to be an Instinct—an Inspiration—a Madness, (the Platonic Ion argues), that will not come at call like a Laureate's Odes, but leap out of its own accord from unpremeditated Contact with Nature, (of, the recollection of such at least), which alone dashes Reality into his words. Just as those Physical Emergencies we were talking of called out the Moral Instinct of Decision and Courage. In such a way one fancies Language itself began; so Adam named all Things as each presented itself before him, appealing to the divine organ of Speech within. Let any of your *Esemplastic* Scholars sit down in his Study and try to invent *Words* now; whereas one *does* see something of the faculty among the more Illiterate,—Sportsmen for instance, and the Brethren of the Ring,—where some new sudden Occasion somehow calls out a suitable Word from the unconscious Poet of the Field—the very name "Slang," we give to all such Vocabulary, being itself perhaps an instance of such felicitous Invention, and spontaneously sprung from some such Occasion.'

Euphranor then read to us as we walked a delightful passage from his Godefridus, to this effect, that, if the Poet could not invent, neither could his Reader understand him, when he told of Ulysses and Diomed listening to the Crane clanging in the Marsh by night, without having *experienced* something of the kind. And so we went on, partly in Jest, partly in Earnest, drawing Philosophers of all kinds into the same net in which we had entangled the Poet and his Critic

—How the Moralist who worked alone and dyspeptic in his closet was most apt to mismeasure Humanity, and be very angry when his System would not fit—how the best Histories were written by those who had been themselves Actors in them—Gibbon, one of the next best, recording how the Discipline of the Hampshire Militia he served as Captain in—how odd he must have looked in the uniform! —cleared up his ideas as to the evolutions of a Roman Legion—and so on a great deal more, till I, suddenly observing how the Sun had declined from his Meridian, looked at my watch, and asked my companions did not they begin to feel Hungry, as I did? They agreed with me; and we turned homeward: and as Lexilogus had hitherto borne so little part in the Conversation, I began to question him about Herodotus and Strabo, (whose books I had seen lying open upon his table), and drew from him some information about the courses of the Nile and the Danube, and the Geography of the Old World: till, all of a sudden, our conversation stepped from Hymettus to the Hills of Yorkshire—our own old Hills—and the old Friends and Neighbours who dwelt among them. And as we were talking of old Places, and old People, and old Times, we suddenly heard the galloping of Horses behind us, (for we were now again in the main road), and, looking back as they were just coming up, I recognised Phidippus for one of the riders, with two others whom I did not know. I held up my hand, and called out to him as he was passing; and Phidippus, drawing up his Horse all snorting and agitated with her arrested course, wheeled back to us and held out his hand.

I asked him what he was about, galloping along the road; I thought Scientific men were more tender of their Horses' legs and feet. But the roads, he said, were quite soft with late rains; and they were only trying each other's speed for a mile.

By this time his two Companions had pulled up some way forward, and were calling to him to come on; but he said, laughing, 'they had quite enough of it,' and addressed himself with many a 'Steady!' and 'So! So!' to pacify Miss Middleton, as he called her, who still curvetted about, and pulled at her Bridle; his friends shouting louder and louder —'Why the Devil he didn't come on?'

He waved his hand, and shouted to them in return not to wait for him; and with a 'Confound' and 'Deuce take the Fellow,' they set off away toward the town. On which Miss Middleton began to caper afresh, plunging, and blowing out a Peony nostril after her flying fellows, until, what with their dwindling in distance, and some expostulation addressed to her by her Master as to a fractious Child, she seemed to make up her mind to the Indignity, and composed herself to go pretty quietly beside us.

I then asked him did he not remember Lexilogus,—(Euphranor he had already recognised),—and Phidippus who really had not hitherto seen who it was, (Lexilogus looking down all the while), called out heartily to him, and, wheeling his Mare suddenly behind us, took hold of his hand, and began to inquire about his family in Yorkshire.

'One would suppose,' said I, 'you two fellows had not met for years.'

'It was true,' Phidippus said, 'they did not meet so often as he really wished; but Lexilogus would not come to his rooms, and he did not like to disturb Lexilogus at his Books.'

I then inquired about his own Reading, which, though not large, was not neglected, it seemed; and he said he had meant to ask one of us to beat something into his stupid head this summer in Yorkshire.

Lexilogus, I knew, meant to stop at Cambridge all the long Vacation: but Euphranor said he should be at Home, for anything he then knew; and they could talk the matter over when the time came. We then again fell to talking of our County: and among other things I asked Phidippus if his Horse were Yorkshire,—of old famous for its Breed, as well as of Riders,—and how long he had her, and so on.

Yorkshire she was, a present from his Mother, 'and a great Pet,' he said, bending down his head, which Miss Middleton answered by a dip of hers, shaking the Bit in her teeth, and breaking into a little Canter, which however was easily suppressed.

'Miss Middleton?' said I—'what, by Bay Middleton out of Coquette, by Tomboy out of High-Life Below-Stairs, right up to Mahomet and his Mares?

'Right,' he answered laughing, 'as far as Bay Middleton is concerned.'

'But, Phidippus,' said I, 'she's as Black as a coal!'

'And so was her Dam, a Yorkshire Mare,' he answered; which, I said, saved the credit of all parties. Might she perhaps be descended from our famous 'Yorkshire Jenny,' renowned in Newmarket Verse? But Phidippus had never heard of 'Yorkshire Jenny' in Ballad or Calendar. And then I began to ask him some questions as to his mode of Making up his mind in some of those Equestrian emergencies Euphranor and I had talked of: all which Phidippus thought was only my usual Banter,—'he was no judge,—I must ask older hands,—he never made up his mind at all,'— and so on; till suddenly he declared he must be off directly to get marked in Hall. But I told him we were all going to dine at Chesterton, now close at hand; he must come too: all Yorkshiremen, except Lycion, whom he knew a little of. There was to be a Boat race, however, in the evening, which

Phidippus said he must leave us to attend, if dine with us he did; for though not one of the Crew on this occasion, (not being one of the best), he must yet see his boat (the Trinity) keep the head of the River. As to that, I said, we were all bound the same way, which indeed Euphranor had proposed before; and so the whole affair was settled.

On reaching the Inn, I begged Euphranor to order Dinner directly, while I and Lexilogus accompanied Phidippus to the Stable. There, after giving his Mare in charge to the hostler with due directions as to her toilet and table, he took off her Saddle and Bridle himself, and adjusted the head-stall. Then, followed out of the Stable by her flaming Eye and pointed Ears, he too pausing a moment on the Threshold to ask me, 'was she not a Beauty?' (for he persisted in the delusion of my knowing more of Horses than I chose to confess), we left the Stable and went into the House.

There, having first washed hands and faces, we went up into the Billiard-room, where we found Euphranor and Lycion playing,—Lycion very lazily, like a man who had already too much of it, but yet nothing better to do. After a short while, the Girl came to tell us Dinner was ready: and, after that slight hesitation as to Precedence which Englishmen rarely forego on the least ceremonious occasions, —Lexilogus, in particular, pausing timidly at the door, and Phidippus pushing him gently and kindly before him,—we got down to the little Parlour, very airy and pleasant, with its window opening on the Bowling-green, the table laid with a clean white cloth, and upon that a good dish of smoking Beef-steaks, at which I, as master of the Feast, sat down to officiate. For some time the clatter of Knife and Fork, and the pouring of Ale, went on, mixed with some conversation among the young men about College matters:

till Lycion began to tell us of a gay Ball he had lately been at, and of the Families there; among whom he mentioned three young Ladies from a neighbouring County, by far the handsomest Women present, he said.

'And very accomplished too, I am told,' said Euphranor.

'O, as for that,' replied Lycion, 'they *Valse* very well, which is enough for me,'—he hated 'your accomplished women.'

'Well, there,' said Euphranor, 'I suppose the Doctor will agree with you.'

I said, certainly *Valsing* would be no great use to me personally—unless, as some Lady of equal size and greater Rank had said, I could meet with a concave Partner.

'One knows so exactly,' said Lycion, 'what Accomplishments the Doctor would choose,—a Woman

Well versed in the Arts
Of Pies, Puddings, and Tarts,
And the lucrative skill of the Oven,

as one used to read somewhere, I remember.'

'Not forgetting,' said I, 'the being able to help in compounding a Pill or a Plaister; which I dare say your Great-grandmother knew something about, Lycion, for in those days, you know, Great ladies studied Simples. Well, so I am fitted,—as Lycion is to be with one who can *Valse* through life with him.'

And follow so the ever-rolling Year
With profitable labour to their graves,

added Euphranor laughing.

'I don't want to marry her,' said Lycion testily.

'Then Euphranor,' said I, 'advertises for a "Strong-minded" Female, able to read Plato's Republic with him, and Wordsworth, and Digby, and become a Mother of Heroes. As to Phidippus, there is no doubt—Diana Vernon—

But Phidippus disclaimed any sympathy with Sporting ladies.

'Well, come,' said I, passing round a bottle of Sherry I had just called for, 'every man to his Taste, only all of you taking care to secure the Accomplishments of Health and Good-humour.'

'Ah! there it is, out at last!' cried Euphranor, clapping his hands; 'I knew the Doctor would choose as Frederic did for his Grenadiers.'

'Well,' said I, 'you wouldn't breed from an ill-made, ill-conditioned Mare, would you, Phidippus?'

He smiled, and asked me if I remembered Miss Prince, a Governess his Mother had for his Sisters, and who really worked them so hard he was obliged to appeal in their behalf.

I did not remember Miss Prince; but I asked what effect his Appeal had on his Mother.

'O, I was a School-boy then,—she patted my head, and said Miss Prince knew best; she had perfect confidence in her. And then, you know, if one of them did not get on with her Music, there was no use suggesting she had perhaps no Talent, and had better not learn at all; the Master only concluded she must practise double at it.'

'Yes, that is the way,' I answered. 'Well?'

Well, after a time, his Mother herself, he said, took notice the girls began to look pale and dispirited. 'Why, I assure you, Doctor, Miss Prince would scarce let them run alone, even in Play-hours, but followed them about with a Book, so that if they plucked a Daisy, they told me, out came a little Wordsworth from her reticule, for a Poem about it. Not a moment, she said, to be left unimproved.'

'Better that Wordsworth had been tied about her neck, and she cast—Well,' I went on, seeing Euphranor look grave, 'I presume Miss Prince was not fitted for a Dam of Heroes, or Hunters.'

Poor thing, Phidippus said, she was an excellent woman—he used to be vexed with himself for getting out of patience with her. She worked hard for her Bread, and Duty, as she thought.

'And besides, your remonstrances came to nothing, said I.

'I don't know,' answered he, laughing; 'Though I was accused of making them romp, which I assure you I never meant, they used to tell me I had more power with her than any one else, even my Mother. I don't know how that was.'

Poor Governesses! so much to be pitied, and reverenced, as Phidippus said, only not to be Governed by! Early divorced from their own Home and its Affections, and crammed themselves in order to cram others, they are most ignorant of the Nature of the very Childhood they are to rule. I was almost going to be Didactic about it all, but thinking I had preached quite enough for that day, I only filled up my Glass, passed the Bottle round, told them to drink Miss Prince's health, and then, unless they would have more Wine, we might have a Game of Bowls, which Euphranor would tell us was the noble custom of our Forefathers after dinner.

'Not however till we have the Doctor's famous Ballad about Miss Middleton's possible Great-Great-Grandmother,' cried Euphranor, 'by way of Pindaric close to this Heroic Entertainment—sung from the Chair, who probably composed it—'

'—As little as could sing it,' I assured him.

'Oh, I remember, it was the Jockey who rode her!'

'Perhaps only his Helper,' answered I; 'such bad Grammar,

and Rhyme, and altogether want of what your man—how do you call him—G. O. E. T. H. E.?—"*Gewty*," will that do? —calls, I believe, *Art*.'

'—Who however said that, if not the simplest People, it was only those who could reduce their minds to the simplest Impressions who could indite a Ballad at all: the reason it becomes ever less possible as Thought complicates. Beside,' added he smiling, 'as we have agreed those best can Paint who Feel the most, Pindar's Jockey and Homer's Ajax, against Pindar and Homer, any day.'

'Fair presumption, however,' said I, 'why my poor Lad should at least sing of his Mare better than Shenstone of Strephon and Delia.'

'Who might yet be more at home with the China Shepherds on his Mantel-piece than more modern Gentlemen with Cocles in the River, or Regulus in the Tub,' said Euphranor slily. 'But come, Song, Song, from the Chair!' he broke out, tapping his Glass on the Table and appealing to Phidippus, who, looking with a smile to me, gently echoed with his.

So with a prelusive 'Well then,' I began—

I'll sing you a Song, and a merry, merry Song—

'—By the way, Phidippus, what an odd notion of merriment is a Jockey's, if this Song be a sample. I think I have observed they have grave, taciturn faces, especially when old, which they soon get to look. Is this from much Wasting, to carry little Flesh, and large—Responsibility?'

'Doctor, Doctor, leave your—faces, and begin!' interrupted Euphranor. 'I must call the Chair to Order'—

Thus admonished, with very slight interpolations, (which may be jumped by the Æsthetic), I repeated the poor Ballad which, dropt I know not how into my Childish ear, had, as so often happens, managed to crevice itself in some chink of a seemingly uncongenial Memory, and wave its almost worthless Verse over much that was—Obstetric—there—

I

I'll sing you a Song, and a merry, merry Song,
Concerning our Yorkshire Jen;
Who never yet ran with Horse or Mare,
That ever she cared for a pin.

II

When first she came to Newmarket town,
The Sportsmen all view'd her around;
All the Cry was, 'Alas, poor Wench,
Thou never can run this Ground!

III

When they came to the Starting Post,
The Mare look'd very smart;
And let them all say what they will,
She never lost her Start—

—which I don't quite understand, by the way: do you, Lycion?'—No answer.

IV

When they got to the Two-mile Post,
Poor Jenny was cast behind:
She was cast behind, she was cast behind,
All for to take her Wind—

V

When they got to the Three-mile Post,
The Mare look'd very pale—

(Phidippus!'—His knee moved under the table—)

SHE LAID DOWN HER EARS ON HER BONNY NECK
  AND BY THEM ALL DID SHE SAIL!

VI *(Accelerando)*

Come follow me, come follow me,
  All you who run so neat;
And ere that you catch me again
  I'll make you well to Sweat.

VII *(Grandioso)*

When she got to the Winning Post,
  The People all gave a Shout:
And Jenny click'd up her Lily-white foot,
  And jump'd like any Buck.

VIII

The Jockey said to her, 'This Race you have run,
  This Race for me you have got;
You could Gallop it all over again,
  When the rest could hardly Trot!'

'They were Four-mile Heats in those days, you see, would pose your Modern Middletons, though Miss Jenny, laying back her Ears—away from catching the Wind, some think—and otherwise Homerically "*pale*," with the distended Vein and starting Sinew of that Three-mile Crisis, nevertheless on coming Triumphantly in, clicked up that Lily-white foot of hers, (of which *one*, I have heard say, is as good a Sign, as all four White are a bad), and could, as the Jockey thought, have gallop'd it all over again. Can't you see him, Phidippus, for once forgetful of his professional Stoicism, (but I don't think Jockeys were quite so Politic then), bending forward to pat the bonny Neck that measured the Victory, as he rides her slowly back to the—*Weighing-house*, is it? followed by the Scarlet-coated Horsemen and shouting People of those Days?—all silent and pass'd away for ever now, unless from the Memory of one pursy Doctor, who, were she but alive, would hardly know Jenny's Head from her Tail!'

Conticuere omnes.[1]

'And now *will* you have any more Wine?' said I, holding up the reverst Decanter.

Phidippus, hastily finishing his glass, jumped up; and the others following him with more or less alacrity, we all sallied forth on the Bowling-green. As soon as there, Lycion of course pulled out his 'Eternal Cigars' (which he had eyed, I observed, with really good-humoured Resignation during the Ballad) and offered them all round, telling Phidippus he could recommend them as some of Pontet's best; but Phidippus did not Smoke, he said; which, together with his declining to bet on the Boat race, caused Lycion, I thought, to look on him with some indulgence.

And now Jack was rolled upon the Green; and I bowled after him first, pretty well; then Euphranor, still better; then Lycion, with great Indifference, and indifferent Success; then Phidippus, who about rivalled me; and last of all, Lexilogus, whom Phidippus had been instructing in the mystery of the Bias with little side-rolls along the turf, and who, he said, only wanted a little practice to play as well as the best of us.

Meanwhile, the Shadows lengthened along the Grass, and, after several bouts of Play, Phidippus said he must be off to see his friends start. We should soon follow, I said; and Euphranor asked him to his rooms after the race. But Phidippus was engaged to sup with his Crew.

'Where you will be drunk,' said I.

'No—there,' said he, 'you are quite mistaken, Doctor.'

'Well, well,' I said, 'away, then, to your Race, and your Supper.'

'"*Μετα σωφρονος ἡλικιωτου*,"'[1] added Euphranor, smiling.

'"*Μετα*" "with," or "after,"' said Phidippus, putting on his gloves.

'Well, go on, Sir,' said I,—' "*Σωφρονος*?" '

'A temperate—something or other—'

'"'*Ηλικιωτου*?"'

'—Supper?'—he hesitated, smiling—'After a temperate supper?"'

'Go down, Sir; go down this instant!' I roared out to him as he ran from the Bowling-green. And in a few minutes we heard his Horse's feet shuffling over the threshold of the Stable, and directly afterwards breaking into a retreating canter outside the gate.

Shortly after this, the rest of us agreed it was time to be gone. We walked along the Fields by the Church, (purposely to ask about the sick Lady by the way), crossed the Ferry, and mingled with the Crowd upon the opposite Shore. Townsmen and Gownsmen, with the tassell'd Fellow-commoner sprinkled here and there—Reading men and Sporting men—Fellows, and even Masters of Colleges, not indifferent to the prowess of their respective Crews—all these, conversing on all sorts of topics, from the Slang in Bell's Life to the last new German Revelation, and moving in everchanging groups down the Shore of the River, at whose farthest visible bend was a little knot of Ladies gathered up on a green Knoll faced and illuminated by the beams of the setting Sun. Beyond which point was at length heard some indistinct shouting, which gradually increased, until 'They are off—they are coming,' suspended other

Conversation among ourselves: and suddenly the head of the first Boat turned the corner; and then another close upon it; and then a third; the Crews pulling with all their Might compacted in perfect Rhythm; and the Crowd upon the shore turning round to follow along with them, waving hats and caps, and Cheering, 'Bravo, St. John's,' 'Go it, Trinity,'—the high Crest and blowing Forelock of Phidippus's Mare, and he himself shouting Encouragement to his Crew, conspicuous over all—until, the Boats reaching us, we also were caught up in the returning tide of Spectators, and hurried back toward the Goal; where we arrived just in time to see the Ensign of Trinity lowered from its pride of place, and the Eagle of St. John's soaring there instead. Then, waiting a little while to hear how the Winner had won, and the Loser lost, and watching Phidippus engaged in eager conversation with his defeated brethren. I took Euphranor and Lexilogus one under each arm, (Lycion having got into better company elsewhere), and walked home with them across the Meadow leading to the Town, whither the dusky troops of Gownsmen with all their confused Voices were evaporating, while Twilight gradually gathered over all, and the Nightingale began to be heard among the flowering Chestnuts of Jesus.

APPENDIX

FROM ECKERMANN'S CONVERSATIONS WITH GOETHE

[I am indebted to John Oxenford, Esq., and Messrs. Smith and Elder, his Publishers, for permission to quote from his Translation the following Passages, not to be found in the earlier German Edition.]

'THERE is something more or less wrong among us old Europeans; our relations are far too Artificial and Complicated; our Nutriment and Mode of life are without their proper Nature, and our Social Intercourse is without proper Love and Goodwill. Every one is Polished and Courteous; but no one has the Courage to be Hearty and True, so that an Honest man, with Natural views and feelings, stands in a very bad position. Often one cannot help wishing that one had been born upon one of the South Sea Islands, a so-called Savage, so as to have thoroughly enjoyed Human existence in all its purity, without any adulteration.

'If in a depressed mood one reflects deeply upon the wretchedness of our Age, it often occurs to one that the world is gradually approaching the Last day. And the Evil accumulates from Generation to Generation! For it is not enough that we have to suffer for the sins of our Fathers; but we hand down to Posterity these inherited vices increased by our own.'

'Similar thoughts often occur to me,' answered I, 'but if, at such a time, I see a Regiment of German Dragoons ride by me, and observe the Beauty and Power of these Young People, I again derive some consolation, and say to myself, that the Durability of Mankind is after all not in such a desperate plight.'

'Our Country people,' returned Goethe, 'have certainly kept up their Strength, and will I hope long be able not only to furnish us with good Horsemen, but also to secure us from total Decay and Destruction. The Rural population may be regarded as a Magazine, from which the Forces of Declining Mankind are always recruited and refreshed. But just go into our great Towns, and you will feel quite differently.' *

'The Scotch Highlanders under the Duke of Wellington,' rejoined Goethe, 'were doubtless Heroes of another description.'

'I saw them in Brussels a Year before the Battle of Waterloo,' returned I. 'They were, indeed, fine Men; all strong, fresh, and active, as if just from the Hand of their Maker. They all carried their heads so Freely and Gallantly, and stepped so lightly along with their strong Bare legs, that it seemed as if there were no Original Sin, and no Ancestral Failing, as far as they were concerned.' †

* While Christopher North understood the Breed of Cocknies to be on the Increase, 'the Females marriageable long before, and prolific long after, the Season usually allowed to our Species—the period of Gestation shorter too, varying from Four to Five Months;' Sir A. Carlisle declares his Conviction that 'the Destroying influence of Large Cities and Manufactories more than counterbalances the alleged Increase of British Population, while they give rise to a Degenerate, Enfeebled, and Demoralized Race. 'I believe,' he says, 'that no Persons, Town-bred in both the Male and Female lines, ever extend their Children to the Fourth Generation.'

† See a fine passage in Haydon's Life, where he describes seeing, among the half Savage Allies in Paris, the English Officer's 'Boy's Face and Broad Shoulders,' which latter, with those of his Men, occupied, as is well known, a larger ground in the Reviews there than any equal Number of any other Country's Shoulders.

'There is something peculiar in this,' said Goethe. 'Whether it lies in the Race, in the Soil, in the Free Political Constitution, or in the healthy tone of Education,—certainly the English in general appear to have certain Advantages over many others. Here in Weimar we see only a few of them, and, probably, by no means the best; but what Fine, Handsome people they are! And however Young they come here, they feel themselves by no means strange or embarrassed in this Foreign Atmosphere; on the contrary, their Deportment in Society is as full of Confidence, and as easy, as if they were Lords everywhere, and the whole World belonged to them. This it is which pleases our Women, and by which they make such havoc in the hearts of our Young Ladies. As a German Father of a Family, who is concerned for the tranquillity of his Household; I often feel a slight shudder, when my Daughter-in-law announces to me the expected arrival of some fresh young Islander. I already see in my Mind's eye the Tears which will one day flow when he takes his Departure. They are dangerous young people; but this very quality of being Dangerous is their Virtue.'

'Still I would not assert,' answered I, 'that the Young Englishmen in Weimar are more Clever, more Intelligent, better informed, or more excellent at Heart than other people.'

'The secret does not lie in these things, my good friend,' returned Goethe. 'Neither does it lie in Birth or Riches; it lies in the Courage which they have to be that for which Nature has made them. There is nothing vitiated or spoilt about them; there is nothing half way or crooked; but such as they are, they are thoroughly Complete Men. That they are also sometimes complete Fools, I allow with all my heart; but that is still something, and has still always some weight in the scale of Nature.'

'You know that scarcely a day passes in which I am not visited by some travelling Foreigner. But if I were to say that I took great pleasure in the Personal Appearance especially of young learned Germans from a certain North-eastern quarter, I should tell a falsehood.

'Short-sighted, Pale, Narrow-chested, Young without Youth; that is a picture of most of them as they appear to me. And if I enter into a conversation with any of them, I immediately observe that the things in which one of us takes Pleasure seem to them Vain and Trivial, that they are entirely absorbed in THE IDEA, and that only the highest Problems of Speculation are fitted to interest them. Of sound Senses or Delight in the Sensual there is no trace; all Youthful feeling and all Youthful pleasure are driven out of them, and that irrecoverably; for if a man is not Young in his Twentieth year, how can he be so in his Fortieth?'—Goethe sighed and was silent.

'In our own dear Weimar I need only look out at the window to discover how matters stand with us. Lately, when the Snow was lying upon the ground, and my Neighbour's Children were trying their little Sledges in the Street, the Police was immediately at hand, and I saw the poor little things fly as quickly as they could. Now, when the Spring Sun tempts them from the houses, and they would like to play with their Companions before the door, I see them always constrained, as if they were not safe, and feared the approach of some Despot of the Police. Not a Boy may crack a whip, or sing, or shout; the Police is immediately at hand to forbid it. This has the effect with us all of taming Youth prematurely, and of driving out all Originality and Wildness, so that in the end nothing remains but the Philistine.'

'If we could only alter the Germans after the model of the English, if we could only have less Philosophy and more Power of Action, less Theory and more Practice, we might obtain a good share of Redemption.

'Thus, for instance, I cannot approve the requisition, in the studies of future Statesmen, of so much Theoretically-learned Knowledge, by which Young people are ruined before their time, both in Mind and Body. When they enter into Practical service, they possess, indeed, an immense stock of Philosophical and Learned matters; but in the narrow circle of their calling this cannot be Practically applied, and must therefore be forgotten as Useless. On the other hand, what they most needed they have lost; they are deficient in the necessary Mental and Bodily Energy which is quite indispensable, when one would enter properly into Practical life. And then, are not Love and Benevolence also needed in the life of a Statesman, in the management of Men? And how can any one feel and exercise Benevolence towards another, when he is ill at ease with himself?

'But all these people are in a dreadful bad case. The Third part of the Learned men and Statesmen, shackled to the Desk, are ruined in Body, and consigned to the Demon of Hypochondria.

'In the mean time,' continued Goethe, smiling, 'let us remain in a state of hopeful Expectation as to the condition of us Germans a Century hence, and whether we shall then have advanced so far as to be no longer *Savants* and *Philosophers*, but MEN.'

'Does this Productiveness of Genius,' said I, 'lie merely in the Mind of an important Man, or does it also lie in the Body?'

'The Body has, at least,' said Goethe, 'the greatest Influence upon it. There was indeed a time when in Germany a Genius was always thought of as Short, Weak, or Hunchbacked; but commend me to a Genius who has a well-proportioned Body.'

'When it was said of Napoleon that he was a Man of Granite, this applied particularly to his Body.'

'Whilst we read Shakspeare we receive the impression of a man thoroughly Strong and Healthy, both in Mind and Body.'

*

What should be expected of German Youth, when Richter himself, from whose Levana many Wise things shall be quoted, tells us of an Anthology he made of his Pupils' 'Bon Mots,' to encourage them in the Practice of Wit—with such samples as follow?

A Boy of Twelve, oldest and Cleverest of all, said, 'Man is mimicked by Four things—An Echo, a Shadow, an Ape, and a Looking-Glass.' 'Windpipes, Spaniards, and Ants, expel all that is alien to them.' 'The Greeks in the Trojan Horse were a Living Transfiguration of Souls,' &c.

The Younger Brother, Ten-and-a-Half-Old, said, 'God is the only *Perpetuum mobile*.' His Sister, of Seven, 'Every Night we are seized with Apoplexy, but in the Morning are well again.' 'The Spartans wore Red in Battle to prevent Blood—as some Italians Black to prevent Fleas—being seen,' &c.

A Five-year-old Boy says to his Four-year-old Sister, 'God has made all Things; so if one offers him Anything, he has made it.' Whereupon the Four-year-old, 'He makes Nothing.' To which the Sage of Five, 'He makes Nothing because he *has* made it.'

When Richter was writing his Book, Four-year-old had

grown to Five, and to this increase of Philosophy; 'Number has a One and Begins: what Begins must End,' and showing a Stick asks, 'Whether that did not end on all Sides?' An Argument that might have been handled much to that Child's Edification.

Seven-year-old maintained that 'If the Soul in the Brain had, with another set of Legs, Arms, &c., another Head, that Head must have another Soul; which Soul again another Head,' &c.

The little Fleas, you 'll hardly guess,
Have little Fleas that bite 'em;
Those little Fleas have others less.
And so ad Infinitum!

Sometimes, says Richter, there were several Fathers and Mothers to the same Thought: all jumping at once: and then all 'justly claimed' the Parentage in the Anthology.

Niebuhr tells us his Boy Marcus already contemplated a New Tense to the Verb! Lucky for his Schoolfellows—and, reckoning on their righteous Vengeance, for Himself—that he did not Accomplish it.

FROM RICHTER'S LEVANA

SAVAGES, Hunters, Soldiers—all such develope their Powers to the Full in the Fresh Air. All who have lived to a Century and Half were Beggars; indeed should one only wish for old Age, and Health all the while, no better Exercise than Begging. Nevertheless a Mother believes that her Child set at an Open Window half an hour a Day will inhale from the Town (itself only a larger Room filled with Street instead of House Breath) as much pure Air as will ventilate Three and Twenty Hours and a half of Foul! Will no one remind her of the Three wretched Autumn days she travelled with that same Child in an open Carriage with no further Injury than—coming hither! Will no Chemist, by *showing* her the Bad Airs that *can* be seen, teach her the Value of the only Element that can*not?*

A Grown-up Man pursued all Day by some moveable Pulpit and Confessional would lose all Moral Freedom and Activity. How much more a Child entangled every Step with 'Stop!' 'Go on!'—his whole Day crammed too with Lesson upon Lesson,—Seed upon Seed, of which no Living Harvest comes! The Watch stops while you wind it; and to be for ever winding up your Child!—

The Jesuit Laws limit Study to Two Hours. And We force Children to Attend so long as their Elders can Teach!

Attention is surely not what Bonnet calls her, the Mother of Genius, but her Daughter—whence born but of the Wedlock made in Heaven between the Object and the Desire for it? Imagine Swift at a Musical—Mozart at a Philosophical—Lecture; Raffaelle at a Political Club—Frederic the Great at a 'Cour d'Amour!'—each a grown Man—of Genius too in his own way, and not ignorant of others. And you expect Children in Years and Understanding to Attend on Subjects as foreign perhaps to their Genius! their Senses more open to every External Influence,—the Hum of the Market without, the Bough waving over the School-room window, the very Stripe of Sunshine on the Floor—still more to the delicious consciousness of some coming Holiday!—For, attach Reward and Punishment to the Exercise of a Child's Attention, do you not at once direct it to *another* Object?

Repetition, one Main Spring of Attention, is also its Clog. Give a Child the same Writing-Copy through a whole Page, each Line will be worse written than the preceding. Change the Copy—even then the First Line will be the Best.

To write up the Ten Commandments on the Wall is precisely the best way to prevent their being seen.

Body is the Anchor-ground of Courage, the Mail-Armour of the Soul; therefore to be hardened into Steel by Heat and Cold. Not for Long life's sake, (Invalids, Nuns, and Court Ladies reach that), but as a Strong-hold of Cheerfulness, Activity, and Courage.

The Weak must Lie: hate the Net of Sin as they may, a Frown drives them in.

Always let Singleness of Purpose rule a Boy. He wanted to Do, or Have, such a thing; *make* him Take or Do it. And never Command *Twice*.

Children's Gravity is rarely as Innocent as their Fun.

Boys close upon Manhood often appear most Heartless, Mischievous, and Destructive; just as Night is coldest close to Dawn. But the Sun rises and warms the World; Vigour dawns into Love; the Teasing Lad into an Affectionate Young Man.

If even Travelled *Men* return with full Heads and Empty Hearts, having gone through the World as in a Country Dance, presenting the Hand indifferently to all—how much more, and more unnaturally, the Travelled Child! whose Affections are only cherished by long and close living with the same People in the same Places, Houses, and Playgrounds; nay, with the same Furniture about them.

There is one Remark very general and very pitiable in the History of the Learned—that so many Admirable Men have so many Years determined to get up earlier of a Morning without much Result—unless it be visible at the Last Day.

῎Οιμοι φιλοσοφεῖς—τοὺς δε φιλοσόφους ἀεί
'Εν τοῖς λόγοις φρονοῦντας εὑρισκω μόνον
'Εν τοὶσι δ' ἔργοις ὄντας ἀνοήτους ὁρῶ.[1]

*

An Emigrant Gentleman visiting England for a while was Wonder-struck at the Indolence of the Middle Classes, especially at such places as Sidmouth; People lounging about throwing Stones into the Sea, and carrying about Three Volumes of Novels from the Circulating Library. 'It seemed to me as if they were all Mad. In Canada every one is seen at work—hacking away at something or other, awkwardly perhaps, but still at Work.' Then the fretful movements of the Children in an opposite house Genteelly confined to a Nursery that reflected all their imprisoned Energies back on Themselves, and looking to him like 'caged Birds beating their Breasts against the Wires!' Whereas he had just left in Canada his own little Boy of Three Years old feeding the Poultry out of doors, and even then able to distinguish one kind of Grain from another in the Field; his little Sister with her little Batch of Bread ready for the Oven, when Baking was going forward—'Both of them insensibly acquiring the most indispensable of the Arts of Life'—while Richeter's Children of the same Age were cultivating Wit for the Anthology!

Instructions how to throw Boys' Minds into a Fever, that shall work itself off in Bodily Sweat—quoted in the Athenæum (864), from the Seventh Annual Report of our Massachusetts Board of Education by Horace Mann, Esq., Boston, 1844.

A Scotch School (*Proximus ardet*[1])

'I entirely despair of exciting in any other person, by a description, the vivid impressions of Mental activity or celerity which the daily operations of these Schools produced on my mind—actual Observation can alone give anything approaching to the true idea. I do not exaggerate when I say, that the most active and lively Schools I have ever seen in the United States must be regarded almost as Dormitories, if compared with the fervid life of the Scotch Schools: and, by the side of theirs, our Pupils would seem to be Hybernating Animals, just emerging from their Torpid state, and as yet but half-conscious of the possession of Life and Faculties. It is certainly within bounds to say, that there were Five times as many Questions put, and Answers given, in the same space of time, as I ever heard put or given in any School in our own country. But a few preliminary observations are necessary to make any description of a Scotch School intelligible. In the numerous Scotch Schools which I saw, the custom of Place-taking prevailed not merely in Spelling, but in Geography, Arithmetic, Reading, Defining, &c. Nor did this consist solely in the passing up of the one giving a Right answer above the one giving a Wrong; but, if a Scholar made a very Bright answer, he was promoted at once to the Top of the Class—if he made a very Stupid one, he was sentenced no less summarily to the Bottom. Periodically Prizes are given, and the fact of having been "Dux" (that is, at the Head of the Class) the greatest number of times, is the principal ground on which the Prizes are awarded. In some Schools, an auxiliary stimulus is applied. The fact of having passed up so many places (say ten or twelve) entitles the pupil to a Ticket; and a given number of these tickets is equivalent to being "Dux" once. When this sharper goad to Emulation is to be applied, the spectator will see the Teacher fill his hand with small bits of pasteboard, and, as the Recitation goes on, and Competition grows keen, and places are rapidly lost and won, the Teacher is seen occasionally to give one of these Tickets to a Pupil as a counter, or token, that he has passed up above so many of his fellows; that is, he may have passed up above four at one time, six at another, two at another—and if Twelve is the number which entitles to a Ticket, One will be given without any stopping or speaking—for the Teacher and Pupil appear to have kept a Silent reckoning, and when the latter extends his Hand, the former gives a Ticket without any suspension of the lesson. This gives the greatest intensity to Competition, and at such times the Children have a look of almost Maniacal eagerness and anxiety.'

'A Boy errs, giving, perhaps, a wrong Gender, or saying that the word is derived from a Greek Verb, when, in fact, it is derived from a Greek Noun of the same family. Twenty Boys leap forward into the area—as though the house were on Fire, or a Mine or Ambush had been sprung upon them—and shout out the True answer, in a voice that could be heard forty rods. And so the Recitation proceeds for an hour. To an unaccustomed spectator, on entering one of these rooms, all seems Uproar, Turbulence, and the Contention of angry voices; the Teacher traversing the space before his Class in a state of high Excitement, the Pupils springing from their seats, darting to the Middle of the floor, and sometimes, with extended arms, forming a Circle around him, two, three, or four deep—every Finger quivering from the intensity of their Emotions, until some more sagacious Mind, outstripping its rivals, solves the difficulty—when all are in their seats again, as though by magic, and ready for another Encounter of wits. I have seen a School kept for two hours in succession in this state of intense Mental activity, with nothing more than an alteration of subjects during the time, or, perhaps, the relaxation of Singing. At the end of the Recitation, both Teacher and Pupils would glow with heat, and be covered with perspiration, as though they had been contending in the Race or the Ring. It would be utterly impossible for the Children to bear such fiery excitement if the Physical exercise were not as violent as the Mental is intense.'

Here is 'an exact account of a *Religious* lesson which I saw and heard:'—

'*Teacher.*—What sort of Death was denounced against our first Parents for Disobedience?

'*First Pupil.*—Temporal Death!

'*T.* No—(and pointing instantaneously to the Second)—

'*Second* P. To Die!

'The Teacher points to the Third, crying, "Come away!" and then to the Fourth. A dozen Pupils leap on the floor, a dozen hands are held out, all quivering with eagerness.

'*Fourth P.* Spiritual Death!

'*T.* Go up, Dux—(that is, to the Head of the Class).'

And so of the following, from the Westminster Catechism, which, with all the proofs, is committed to Memory.

'*Teacher.* What is the Misery of that Estate whereinto Man fell?

'*Pupil.* All Mankind by their Fall lost Communion with God, &c.

'*T.* What sort of a place is Hell?

'*P.* A place of Devils.

'*T.* How does the Bible describe it?

'*First P.* (Hesitates.)

'*T.* Next?—Next?—

'*Fifth P.* A lake of Fire and Brimstone.

'*T.* Take 'em down Four!

'And thus on these awful themes, a Belief and Contemplation of which should turn the eyes into a fountain of Tears, and make the heart intermit its beatings, there is the same Ambition for Intellectual superiority as on a question in the Multiplication table. There is no more apparent Solemnity in the one case than the other.'

Were one to preach a Sermon on Health, as really were worth doing, WALTER SCOTT ought to be the Text. Theories are demonstrably True in the way of Logic; and then in the way of Practice they prove True, or Not true. But here is the Grand Experiment—Do they turn out well? What boots it that a Man's Creed is the Wisest, that his System of Principles is the superfinest, if when set to work the Life of him does nothing but jar, and fret itself into Holes: They are Untrue in that, were it in nothing else, these Principles of his; openly convicted of Untruth—fit only, shall we say, to be rejected as Counterfeits and flung to the Dogs? We say not that: but we do say that Ill-health of Body or Mind is Defeat—is Battle in a Good or Bad Cause with Bad success: that Health alone is Victory. Let all men if they can contrive it manage to be Healthy.—*Carlyle.*

And *how* Healthy—in Body at least?

Porro ne in Corpore quidem Valetudinem Medici probant quæ nimia Anxietate continget; parum est Ægrum non esse; FORTEM ET LŒTUM ET ALACREM VOLO. Prope abest ab Infirmitate in quo sola Sanitas laudatur.—*Tacitus, Dial.* c. 23.[1]

THE END

In the [illegible]

[illegible]

1. Overbearing pride.

[illegible]

TRANSLATIONS AND SOURCES OF QUOTATIONS IN GREEK AND LATIN

P. 175

1. Look—it's all of a piece; every one agrees; know one and you know all. — TERENCE, *Phormio* 264–5.

2. (Who), since he was young and inexperienced in the evil ways of the world, could control himself no longer. — HERODOTUS, V, 19.

3. It is indeed time to deliberate about what we are going to do: but I think that taking counsel will profit us less than the might of our hands. — APOLLONIUS RHODIUS, *Argonautica*, III, 506–7.

P. 176

1. Though he had not yet grown so much as the soft down on his cheeks. — APOLLONIUS RHODIUS, *Argonautica* III, 519–20.

2. A gallant (lit. youthful) resolution. — [e.g.] DEMOSTHENES, 37, 10.

P. 178

1. Bewailing their fate, and the loss of vigour and youth. — HOMER, *Iliad* XVI, 857.

P. 192

1. Overbearing, pride.

P. 193

1. Excellent communers.

2. To their sons as their only inheritance they leave their mattocks, a few acres of land and a mud hut: also the worship of the Supreme Divinity, the habits of right living, and the will to work.

P. 194

1. Safest in the middle. — OVID, *Metamorphoses*, ii, 137.

2. Oh extraordinarily happy men! — cf. VERGIL, *Georgics*, II, 458.

P. 197

1. If the pictures of these animals have no influence, nothing ever will.

P. 204

1. May Eton flourish!
2. The terminations proper to masculine nouns.

P. 207

1. A gladiator does not make plans until he is in the arena. — *Proverb quoted in* SENECA, *Ep.* 22, 1.

P. 217

1. Just *and* Unjust Reason.
2. The heroes of Marathon. — ARISTOPHANES, *Clouds*, 986.

P. 218

1. (This is the first half-line of the passage Euphranor recites).

P. 219

1. The callow delicate lad is unable to sit a horse, and fears to hunt: he would show more proficiency if you told him to play with his Greek hoop or with dice, which are forbidden by law. — HORACE, *Odes* III, 24, 54–8.

P. 241

1. Everyone fell silent. — VERGIL, *Aeneid* II, 1.

P. 242

1. With a temperate companion. — ARISTOPHANES, *Clouds* 1006.

P. 252

1. I am sorry that you are a philosopher—for I find philosophers consistently rational only in theory, while I see that they are fools in practice.

P. 253

1. Your neighbour is aflame (*originally said of a burning house*). — HORACE, *Epistles* I, xviii, 84.

P. 257

1. Indeed doctors do not approve of the sort of bodily well-being which is maintained only by excessive worry. Freedom from illness is not enough: I would have men strong and exuberantly vigorous, for if a man's only boast is mere Health, he is not far from Decrepitude.

SALÁMÁN AND ABSÁL

An Allegory

TRANSLATED FROM THE PERSIAN OF JÁMI

SALÁMÁN AND ABSÁL

An Allegory

I

PROLOGUE

Oh Thou whose memory quickens lovers' souls,
Whose Fount of Joy renews the Lover's Tongue.
Thy Shadow falls across the World, and they
Bow down to it; and of the Rich in Beauty
Thou art the Riches that make Lovers mad.
Not till thy Secret Beauty through the Cheek
Of Laila smite does she inflame Majnún, *
And not until Thou have sugar'd Shírín's Lip
The Hearts of those Two Lovers fill with Blood, †
For Lov'd and Lover are not but by Thee,
Nor Beauty;—Mortal Beauty but the Veil
Thy Heavenly hides behind, and from itself
Feeds, and our Hearts yearn after, as a Bride
That glances past us Veil'd—but ever so
As none the Beauty from the Veil may know.
How long wilt thou continue thus the World
To cozen with the Fantom of a Veil.
From which Thou only peepest?—Time it is
To unfold thy perfect Beauty. I would be
Thy Lover, and Thine only—I, Mine Eyes

* All well-known Types of Eastern Lovers. Shírín and her Suitors figure in Section xx.

† The Persian Mystics also represent the Deity Diceing with Human Destiny behind the Curtain.

Seal'd in the Light of thee to all but Thee:
Yea, in the Revelation of Thyself
Self—Lost, and Conscience—quit of Good and Evil.
Thou movest under all the Forms of Truth,
Under the Forms of all Created Things;
Look whence I will, still nothing I discern
But Thee in all the Universe, in which
Thyself Thou dost invest, and through the Eyes
Of Man, the subtle Censor * Scrutinise.
No Entrance finds—no Word of THIS and THAT;
Do Thou my separate and Derivéd Self
Make One with thy Essential! Leave me room,
On that Diván which leaves no Room for Two; †
Lest, like the Simple Kurd of whom they tell,
I grow perplext, O God, 'twixt 'I' and 'Thou;'
If *I*—this Dignity and Wisdom whence?
If *Thou*—then what this abject Impotence?

A Kurd perplext by Fortune's Frolics
Left his Desert for the City.
Sees a City full of Noise and
Clamour, agitated People,
Hither, Thither, Back and Forward
Running, some intent on Travel,

* 'The Appollonius of Keats's *Lamnia.*'

† This Súfi Identification with Deity (further illustrated in the Story of Section xix.) is shadowed in a Parable of Jeladdin, of which here is an outline. 'One knocked at the Belovéd's Door; and a Voice asked from within, "Who is there?" and he answered, "It is I." Then the Voice said, "This house will not hold Me and Thee." And the Door was not opened. Then went the Lover into the Desert, and fasted and prayed in Solitude. And after a Year he returned and knocked again at the Door. And again the Voice asked, "Who is there?" and he said, "It is Thyself!"—and the Door was opened to him.'

Others home again returning,
Right to Left, and Left to Right,
Life-disquiet everywhere!
Kurd, when he beholds the Turmoil,
Creeps aside, and Travel-weary,
Fain would go to sleep; 'But,' saith he,
'How shall I in all this Hubbub
Know myself again on waking?'
So by way of Recognition
Ties a Pumpkin round his Foot,
And turns to sleep. A Knave that neard him
Crept behind, and slily watching
Slips the Pumpkin off Sleeper's
Ancle, ties it round his own
And so down to sleep beside him.
By and by the Kurd awaking
Looks directly for his Signal—
Sees it on another's Ancle—
Cries aloud, 'Oh, Good-for-nothing
Rascal to perplex me so!
That by you I am bewilder'd,
If I—the Pumpkin why on You?
If You—then Where am I, and Who?'

Oh God! this poor bewilder'd Kurd am I,
Than any Kurd more helpless!—Oh, do thou
Strike down a Ray of Light into my Darkness!
Turn by thy Grace, these Dregs into pure Wine,
To recreate the Spirits of the Good!
Or if not that, yet, as the little Cup
Whose Name I go by, * not unworthy found

* The Poet's name, '*Jámí*,' also signifying '*A Cup*.' The Poet's 'Yúsuf and Zulaikha,' opens also with this Divine Wine, the favourite

I listen in the Tavern of Sweet Songs,
And catch no Echo of their Harmony:
The Guests have drunk the Wine and are departed,
Leaving their empty Bowls behind—not one
To carry on the Revel Cup in hand!
Up Jámí then! and whether Lees or Wine
To offer—boldly offer it in Thine!

2

And yet how long, Jámí, in this Old House
Stringing thy Pearls upon a Harp of Song?
Year after Year striking up some new Song,
The Breath of some Old Story? * Life is gone,
And yet the song is not the Last: my Soul
Is spent—and still a Story to be told!
And I, whose Back is crooked as the Harp
I still keep tuning through the Night till Day!
That Harp untun'd by Time—the Harper's hand
Shaking with age—how shall the Harper's hand
Repair its cunning, and the sweet old Harp
Be modulated as of old? Methinks
'Tis time to break and cast it in the Fire;
Yea, sweet the Harp that can be sweet no more,
To cast it in the Fire—the vain old Harp
That can no more sound Sweetness to the Ear,
And burn'd may breathe sweet Attár to the Soul,
And comfort so the Faith and Intellect,
Now that the Body looks to Dissolution.
My Teeth fall out—my two Eyes see no more

symbol of Háfiz and other Persian Mystics. *The Tavern* spoken of is The World.

* 'Yúsuf and Zulaikha,' 'Laila and Majnún,' etc.

Till by Feringhi Glasses * turn'd to Four;
Pain sits with me sitting behind my knees,
From which I hardly rise unhelpt of hand;
I bow down to my Root, and like a Child
Yearn, as is likely, to my Mother Earth,
With whom I soon shall cease to moan and weep,
And on my Mother's Bosom fall asleep.

The House in Ruin, and its Music heard
No more within, nor at the Door of Speech,
Better in Silence and Oblivion
To fold me Head and Foot, remembering
What that BELOVED to the Master whisper'd:—
'No longer think of Rhyme, but Think of ME!'—
Of WHOM?—Of HIM whose Palace THE SOUL is,
And Treasure House—who notices and knows
Its Income and Out-going, and *then* comes
To fill it when the Stranger is departed.
Whose Shadow being Kings—whose Attributes
The Type of Theirs—their Wrath and Favour His—
Lo! in the Celebration of His Glory
The King Himself comes on me unaware,
And suddenly arrests me for his own.
Wherefore once more I take—best quitted else—
The Field of Verse to Chaunt that double Praise,
And in that Memory refresh my Soul
Until I grasp the Skirt of Living Presence.

One who travel'd in the Desert
Saw Majnún where he was sitting
All alone like a Magician
Tracing Letters in the Sand.

* First notice of Spectacles in Oriental Poetry, perhaps.

'Oh distracted Lover! writing
What the Sword-wind of the Desert
Undecyphers soon as written.
So that none who travels after
Shall be able to interpret!' —
Majnún answered, 'I am writing
"LAILI" were it only "LAILI,"
Yet a Book of Love and Passion;
And, with but her Name to dote on,
Amorously I caress it
As it were Herself and sip
Her Presence till I drink her Lip.'

3

When Night had thus far brought me with my Book
In middle Thought Sleep robb'd me of myself;
And in a Dream Myself I seem'd to see,
Walking along a straight and even Road,
And clean as is the Soul of the Súfí;
A Road whose spotless Surface neither Breeze
Lifted in Dust, nor mix'd the Rain to Mire.
There I, methought, was pacing tranquilly,
When, on a sudden, the tumultuous Shout
Of Soldiers behind broke on mine Ear
And took away my Wit and Strength for Fear.
I look'd about for Refuge, and Behold!
A palace was before me; whither running
For Refuge from the coming Soldiery,
Suddenly from the Troop a Sháhzemán, *

* 'Lord of the World, SOVEREIGN; HASAN, BEAUTIFUL, GOOD.' HASAN BEG of Western Persia, famous for his Beauty, had helped Jámí with Escort in a dangerous Pilgrimage. He died (as History and

By name and Nature HASAN—on the Horse
Of Honour mounted—robed in Royal Robes,
And wearing a White Turban on his Head,
Turn'd his Rein tow'rd me, and with smiling Lips
Open'd before my Eyes the Door of Peace.
Then, riding up to me, dismounted; kiss'd
My Hand, and did me Courtesy; and I,
How glad of his Protection, and the Grace
He gave it with!—Who then of gracious Speech
Many a Jewel utter'd; but of these
Not one that in my Ear till Morning hung.
When, waking on my Bed, my waking Wit
I question'd what the Vision meant, it answered;
'This Courtesy and Favour of the Shah
Foreshows the fair Acceptance of thy Verse,
Which lose no moment pushing to Conclusion.'
This hearing, I address'd me like a Pen
To steady Writing; for perchance, I thought,
From the same Fountain whence the Vision grew
The Interpretation also may come True.

Breathless ran a simple Rustic
To a Cunning Man of Dreams;
'Lo, this Morning I was dreaming—
And, methought, in yon deserted
Village wander'd—all about me
Shatter'd Houses—and Behold!
Into one, methought, I went—and
Search'd—and found a Hoard of Gold!'
Quoth the Prophet in Derision,
'Oh Thou Jewel of Creation,

a previous line in the Original tell) before *Salámán* was written, and was succeeded by his Son Yácúb.

Go and sole your Feet like Horse's,
And returning to your Village
Stamp and scratch with Hoof and Nail,
And give Earth so sound a Shaking,
She must hand you something up.'
Went at once the unsuspecting
Countryman; with hearty Purpose
Set to work as he was told;
And, the very first Encounter,
Struck upon his Hoard of Gold!

Until Thou hast thy Purpose by the Hilt,
Catch at it bodily—or Thou never wilt.

4

THE STORY

A SHAH there was who ruled the Realm of Yún,
And wore the Ring of Empire of Sikander;
And in his Reign A SAGE, who had the Tower
Of Wisdom of so strong Foundation built
That Wise Men from all Quarters of the World
To catch the Word of Wisdom from his Lip
Went in a Girdle round him.—Which THE SHAH
Observing, took him to his Secresy;
Stirr'd not a Step nor set Design afoot
Without that Sage's sanction; till, so counsel'd,
From Káf to Káf † reach'd his Dominion:

* Or 'YAVAN,' Son of Japhet, from whom the Country was called 'YÚNAN,'—IONIA, meant by the Persians to express Greece generally. Sikander is, of course, Alexander the Great, of whose Ethics Jámí wrote, as Nizami of his Deeds.

† The Fabulous Mountain supposed by Asiatics to surround the World, binding the Horizon on all sides.

No Nation of the World or Nation's Chief
Who wore the Ring but under span of his
Bow'd down the Neck; then rising up in Peace
Under his Justice grew, and knew no Wrong,
And in their Strength was his Dominion strong.
The SHAH that has not Wisdom in Himself,
Nor has a Wise Man for his Counsellor,
The wand of his Authority falls short,
And his Dominion crumbles at the Base.
For he, discerning not the Characters
Of Tyranny and Justice, confounds both,
Making the World a Desert, and the Fount
Of Justice a Serâb. * Well was it said,
'*Better just Káfir than Believing Tyrant.*'

God said to the Prophet David,—
'David, speak, and to the Challenge
Answer of the Faith within Thee.
Even Unbelieving Princess,
Ill-reported if Unworthy,
Yet, If They be Just and Righteous,
Were their Worship of THE FIRE—
Even These unto Themselves
Reap Glory and redress the World.'

* Miráge; but, of two Foreign Words, why not the more original Persian?—identical with the Hebrew Shâráb, as in Isaiah xv., 7, 'The *Shárâb* (or *Miráge*) shall become a Lake;' —rather, and better, than our Version, 'The parched Ground shall become a Pool.' *See* Gesenius.

5

One Night THE SHAH of Yúnan, as his wont,
Consider'd of his Power, and told his State,
How great it was, and how about him sat
The Robe of Honour of Prosperity;
Then found he nothing wanted to his Heart,
Unless a Son, who his Dominion
And Glory might inherit after him,
And then he turn'd him to THE SHAH, and said;
'Oh, Thou, whose Wisdom is the Rule of Kings—
(Glory to God Who gave it!)—answer me;
Is any Blessing better than a Son?
Man's prime Desire; by which his Name and He
Shall live beyond Himself; by whom his Eyes
Shine living, and his Dust with Roses blows;
A Foot for Thee to stand on, he shall be
A Hand to stop thy Falling; in his Youth
Thou shalt be Young, and in his Strength be Strong;
Sharp shall he be in Battle as a Sword,
A Cloud of Arrows on the Enemy's Head;
His Voice shall cheer his Friends to better Plight,
And turn the Foeman's Glory into Flight.'
Thus much of a Good Son, whose wholesome Growth
Approves the Root he grew from; but for one
Kneaded of Evil—Well, could one undo
His Generation, and as early pull
Him and his Vices from the String of Time.
Like Noah's, puff'd with Ignorance and Pride,
Who felt the Stab of 'HE IS NONE OF THINE!
And perish'd in the Deluge. * And because

* In the Kurán God engaged to save Noah and his Family—meaning all who believed in the Warning. One of Noah's Sons

All are not Good, be slow to pray for One,
Whom having you may have to pray to lose.

Crazy for the Curse of Children,
Ran before the Sheikh a Fellow,
Crying out, 'Oh hear and help me!
Pray to Allah from my Clay
To raise me up a fresh young Cypress,
Who my Childless Eyes may lighten
With the Beauty of his Presence.'
Said the Sheikh, 'Be wise, and leave it
Wholly in the Hand of Allah,
Who, whatever we are after,
Understands our Business best.'
But the Man persisted, saying,
'Sheikh, I languish in my Longing;
Help, and set my Prayer a-going!'
Then the Sheikh held up his Hand—
Pray'd—his Arrow flew to Heaven—

(Canaan or Yam, some think) would not believe. 'And the Ark swam with them between waves like Mountains, and Noah called up to his Son, who was separated from him, saying, "Embark with us, my Son, and stay not with the Unbelievers.' He answered, "I will get on a Mountain which will secure me from the Water." Noah replied, "There is no security this Day from the Decree of God, except for him on whom he shall have Mercy." And a Wave passed between them, and he became one of those who were drowned. And it was said, "Oh Earth, swallow up thy waters, and thou, oh Heaven, withhold thy Rain!" and immediately the Water abated and the Decree was fulfilled, and the Ark rested on the Mountain Al Judi, and it was said, "Away with the ungodly People!"—Noah called upon his Lord and said, "Oh Lord, verily my Son is of my Family, and thy Promise is True; for Thou art of those who exercise Judgment." God answered, "Oh Noah, verily he is not of thy Family; this intercession of thine for him is not a righteous work."' —*Sale's Kurán*, vol. ii, p. 21.

From the Hunting-ground of Darkness
Down a musky Fawn of China
Brought—a Boy—who, when the Tender
Shoot of Passion in him planted
Found sufficient Soil and Sap,
Took to Drinking with his Fellows;
From a Corner of the House-top
Ill affronts a Neighbour's Wife,
Draws his Dagger on the Husband,
Who complains before the Justice,
And the Father has to pay.
Day and Night the Youngster's Doings
Such—the Talk of all the City;
Nor Entreaty, Threat, or Counsel
Held him; till the Desperate Father
Once more to the Sheikh A-running,
Catches at his Garment, crying—
'Sheikh, my only Hope and Helper!
One more Prayer! that God who laid
Will take that trouble from my Head!'
But the Sheikh replied: 'Remember
How that very Day I warn'd you
Better not importune Allah;
Unto whom remains no other
Prayer, unless to pray for Pardon.
When from this World we are summon'd
On to bind the pack of Travel
Son or Daughter ill shall help us;
Slaves we are, and unencumber'd
Best may do the Master's mind:
And, whatever he may order,
Do it with a Will Resign'd.'

6

When the Sharp-witted SAGE
Had heard these Sayings of THE SHAH, he said,
'Oh SHAH, who would not be the Slave of Lust
Must still endure the Sorrow of no Son.
—Lust that makes blind Reason; Lust that makes
A Devil's self seem Angel to our Eyes;
A Cataract that, carrying havoc with it
Confounds the prosperous House; a Road of Mire
Where whoso falls he rises not again;
A Wine of which whoever tastes shall see
Redemption's face no more—one little Sip
Of that delicious and unlawful Drink
Making crave much, and hanging round the Palate
Till it become a Ring to lead thee by *
(Putting the rope in a Vain Woman's hand),
Till thou thyself go down the Way of Nothing.'

'For what is Woman? A Foolish, Faithless Thing—
To whom The Wise Self-subjected, himself
Deep sinks beneath the Folly he sets up.
A very Káfir in Rapacity;
Clothe her a hundred Years in Gold and Jewel,
Her Garment with Brocade of Susa braided,
Her very Night-gear wrought in Cloth of Gold,
Dangle her Ears with Ruby and with Pearl,
Her House with Golden Vessels all a-blaze,
Her Tables loaded with the Fruit of Kings,
Ispahan Apples, Pomegranates of Yazd;

* '*Mihar*'—a Piece of Wood put through a Camel's Nose to guide him by.

And, be she thirsty, from a Jewell'd Cup
Drinking the Water of the Well of Life—
One little twist of Temper—all you've done
Goes all for Nothing. "Torment of my Life!"
She cries, "what have you ever done for Me!—
Her Brow's White Tablet—Yes—'tis uninscrib'd
With any Letter of Fidelity;
Who ever read it there? Lo, in your Bosom
She lies for Years—you turn away a moment,
And she forgets you—worse, if as you turn
Her Eye should light on any Younger Lover.'

Once upon a Throne of Judgment,
Telling one another Secrets,
*Sat SULAYMAN and BALKIS;**
The Hearts of Both were turn'd to Truth,
Unsullied by Deception.
First the King of Faith SULAYMAN
Spoke—'Though mine the Ring of Empire,
Never any Day that passes
Darkens any one my Door-way
But into His Hand I look—
And He who comes not empty-handed
Grows to Honour in mine Eyes.'
After this BALKIS a Secret
From her hidden Bosom utter'd,
Saying—'Never Night or Morning
Comely Youth before me passes
Whom I look not longing after;
Saying to myself, "Oh, were he
Comforting of my Sick Soul!—"'

* Solomon and the Queen of Sheba.

'If this, as wise Ferdúsi says, the Curse
Of Better Women, what should be the Worse?'

7

THE SAGE his Satire ended; and THE SHAH
With Magic-mighty WISDOM his pure WILL
Leaguing, its Self-fulfilment wrought from Heaven.
And Lo! from Darkness came to Light A CHILD,
Of Carnal Composition Unattaint,—
A Rosebud blowing on the Royal Stem—
A Perfume from the Realm of Wisdom wafted;
The Crowning Jewel of the Crown; a Star
Under whose Augury triumph'd the Throne.
For whose Auspicious Name they clove the Words
'SALÁMÁT'—Incolumity from Evil—
And 'AUSEMÁN'—the Heav'n from which he came—
And hail'd him by the title of SALÁMÁN.
And whereas from no Mother Milk he drew,
They chose for him a Nurse—her name ABSÁL—
Her Years not Twenty—from the Silver Line
Dividing the Musk-Harvest of her Hair
Down to her Foot that trampled Crowns of Kings,
A Moon of Beauty Full; who thus elect
SALÁMÁN of Auspicious Augury
Should carry in the Garment of her Bounty,
Should feed Him with the Flowing of her Breast.
As soon as she had opened Eyes on him
She closed those Eyes to all the World beside.
And her Soul crazed, a-doting on her Jewel,—
Her Jewel in a Golden Cradle set;
Opening and Shutting which her Day's Delight,
To gaze upon his Heart-inflaming Cheek,—

Upon the Darling whom, could she, she would
Have cradled as the Baby of her Eye. *
In Rose and Musk she wash'd him—to his Lips
Press'd the pure Sugar from the Honeycomb;
And when, Day over, she withdrew her Milk,
She made, and having laid him in, his Bed,
Burn'd all Night like a Taper o'er his Head.

Then still as Morning came, and as he grew,
She dress'd him like a Little Idol up;
On with his Robe—with fresh Collyrium Dew
Touch'd his Narcissus Eyes—the Musky Locks
Divided from his Forehead—and embraced
With Gold and Ruby Girdle his fine Waist.—

So rear'd she him till full Fourteen his Years,
Fourteen-day full the Beauty of his Face,
That rode high in a Hundred Thousand Hearts;
Yea, when SALÁMÁN was but Half-lance high,
Lance-like he struck a wound in every One,
And burn'd and shook down Splendour like a Sun.

8

Soon as the Lord of Heav'n had sprung his Horse
Over the Horizon into the Blue Field,
SALÁMÁN rose drunk with the Wine of Sleep,
And set himself a-stirrup for the Field;
He and a Troop of Princes—Kings in Blood,
Kings too in the Kingdom-troubling Tribe of Beauty,
All Young in Years and Courage, † Bat in hand

* Literally *Mardumak*—the *Mannikin*, or *Pupil*, of the Eye, corresponding to the Image so frequently used by our old Poets.

† The same Persian Word serving for both.

Gallop'd a-field, toss'd down the Golden Ball
And chased, so many Crescent Moons a Full;
And, all alike Intent upon the Game,
SALÁMÁN still would carry from them all
The Prize, and shouting 'Hál!' drive Home the Ball.
This done, SALÁMÁN bent him as a Bow
To Shooting—from the Marksmen of the World
Call'd for an unstrung Bow—himself the Cord
Fitted unhelpt, † and nimbly with his hand
Twanging made cry, and drew it to his Ear:
Then, fixing a Three-feather'd Fowl, discharged
No point in Heaven's Azure but his Arrow
Hit; nay, but Heaven were made of Adamant,
Would overtake the Horizon as it roll'd;
And, whether aiming at the Fawn a-foot,
Or Bird on wing, his Arrow went away
Straight—like the Soul that cannot go astray.

When Night came, that releases Man from Toil,
He play'd the Chess of Social Intercourse;
Prepared his Banquet Hall like Paradise,
Summon'd his Houri-faced Musicians,
And when his Brain grew warm with Wine, the Veil

* The Game of Chúgán, for Centuries the Royal Game of Persia, and adopted (Ouseley thinks) under varying modifications of Name and Practice by other Nations, was played by Horsemen, who, suitably habited, and armed with semi-circular-headed Bats or Sticks so short the Player must stoop below the Saddle-bow to strike, Strove to drive a Ball through a Goal of upright Pillars. *See* Appendix.

† Bows being so gradually stiffened, to the Age and Strength of the Archer, as at last to need five Hundredweight of Pressure to bend, says an old Translation of Chardin, who describes all the Process up to bringing up the String to the Ear, '*as if to hang it there*' before Shooting. Then the First Trial was, who could shoot highest; then, the Mark, etc.

Flung off him of Reserve. Now Lip to Lip
Concerting with the Singer he would breathe
Like a Messias Life into the Dead;
Now made of the Melodious-moving Pipe
A Sugar-cane between his Lips that ran
Men's Ears with Sweetness: Taking up a Harp,
Between its dry String and his Finger fresh
Struck Fire, or lifting in his arms a Lute
As if a little Child for Chastisement,
Pinching its Ear such Cries of Sorrow wrung
As drew Blood to the Eyes of Older Men.
Now Sang He like the Nightingale alone,
Now set together Voice and Instrument;
And thus with his Associates Night he spent.

His Soul rejoiced in Knowledge of all kinds;
The fine Edge of his Wit would Split a Hair,
And in the Noose of Apprehension catch
A Meaning ere articulate in Word;
His Verse was like the PLEIADS; * his Discourse
The MOURNERS OF THE BIER; his Penmanship
(Tablet and running reed his Worshippers),
Fine on the Lip of Youth as the First Hair,
Drove PENMEN, as with LOVERS, to Despair.

His Bounty was as Ocean's—nay, the Sea's
Self but the Foam of his Munificence,
For it threw up the Shell, but he the Pearl;

* 'i.e., compactly strung, as opposed to Discursive Rhetoric, which is compared to the scattered Stars of THE BIER AND ITS MOURNERS or what we call THE GREAT BEAR. This contrast is otherwise prettily applied in the Anvari Soheili—' When one grows Poor, his Friends, heretofore compact as THE PLEIADS, disperse wide asunder as THE MOUPNERS.'

He was a Cloud that rain'd upon the World
Dirhems for Drops; the Banquet of whose Bounty
Left Hátim's * churlish in Comparison—

9

Suddenly that Sweet Minister of mine
Rebuked him angrily; 'What Folly, Jámí
Wearing that indefatigable Pen
In celebration of an Alien SHAH
Whose Throne, not grounded in the Eternal World,
YESTERDAY was, TO-DAY is not!' † I answer'd;
Oh Fount of Light!—under an Alien Name
I shadow One upon whose Head the Crown
Both Was and Is TO-DAY; to whose Firmán
The Seven Kingdoms of the World are subject,
And the Seas Seven but droppings of his Largess.
Good Luck to him who under other Name
Taught us to veil the Praises of a Power
To which the Initiate scarce find open Door.'

Sat a Lover solitary
Self-discoursing in a Corner,
Passionate and ever-changing
Invocation pouring out;
Sometimes Sun and Moon; and sometimes
Under Hyacinth half-hidden
Roses; or the lofty Cypress,
And the little Weed below.

* The Persian Type of Liberality, infinitely celebrated.

† The Hero of the Story being of YUNAN-IONIA, or GREECE generally (the Persian Geography not being very precise)—and so not of THE FAITH.

Nightingaling thus a Noodle
Heard him, and, completely puzzled,—
'What!' quoth he, 'and you, a Lover,
Raving not about your Mistress,
But about the Moon and Roses!'
Answer'd he; 'Oh thou that aimest
Wide of Love, and Lover's Language
Wholly misinterpreting;
Sun and Moon are but my Lady's
Self, as any Lover knows;
Hyacinth I said, and meant her
Hair—her Cheek was in the Rose—
And I myself the wretched Weed
That in her Cypress Shadow grows.'

10

Now was Salámán in his Prime of Growth,
His Cypress Stature risen to high Top,
And the new-blooming Garden of his Beauty
Began to bear; and Absál long'd to gather;
But the Fruit grew upon too high a Bough,
To which the Noose of her Desire was short.
She too rejoiced in Beauty of her own
No whit behind Salámán, whom she now
Began enticing with her Sorcery.
Now from her Hair would twine a musky Chain,
To bind his Heart—now twist it into Curls
Nestling innumerable Temptations;
Doubled the Darkness of her Eyes with Surma
To make him lose his way, and over them
Adorn'd the Bows * that were to shoot him then;

* With dark Indigo Paint, as the Archery Bow with a thin Papyrus-like Bark.

Now to the Rose-leaf of her Cheek would add
Fresh rose, and then a grain of Musk * lay there,
The Bird of the Belovéd Heart to snare.
Now with a Laugh would break the Ruby Seal
That lockt up Pearl; or busied in the Room
Would smite her Hand perhaps—on that pretence
To lift and show the Silver in her Sleeve;
Or hastily rising clash her Golden Anclets
To draw the Crowned Head under her Feet.
Thus by innumerable Bridal wiles
She went about soliciting his Eyes,
Which she would scarce let lose her for a Moment;
For well she knew that mainly by THE EYE
Love makes his Sign, and by no other Road
Enters and takes possession of the Heart.

Burning with Desire ZULAIKHA
Built a Chamber—Wall and Ceiling
Blank as an untarnisht Mirror,
Spotless as the Heart of YUSUF.
Then she made a cunning Painter
Multiply her Image round it;
Not an Inch of Wall but echoed
With the Reflex of her Beauty.
Then amid them all in all her
Glory sat she down, and sent for
YUSUF—she began a Tale
Of Love—and Lifted up her Veil.
From her Look he turn'd, but turning
Wheresoever, ever saw her
Looking, looking at him still.
Then Desire arose within him—

* A Patch, sc.—'*Noir comme le Musc.*' De Sacy.

He was almost yielding—almost
Laying Honey on her Lip—
When a Signal out of Darkness
Spoke to him—and he withdrew
His Hand, and dropt the Skirt of Fortune.

II

Thus day by day did ABSÁL tempt SALÁMÁN,
And by and bye her Wiles began to work.
Her eyes Narcissus stole his Sleep—their Lashes
Pierc'd to his Heart—out from her Locks a Snake
Bit him—and bitter, bitter on his Tongue
Became the Memory of her honey Lip.
He saw the Ringlet restless on her Cheek,

And he too quiver'd with Desire; his Tears
Burn'd Crimson from her Cheek, whose musky spot
Infected all his soul with Melancholy.
Love drew him from behind the Veil, where yet
Withheld him better Resolution—
'Oh, should the Food I long for, tasted, turn
Unwholesome, and if my Life to come
Should sicken from one momentary Sweet!'

On the Sea-shore sat a Raven,
Blind, and from the bitter Cistern
Forc'd his only Drink to draw.
Suddenly the Pelican
Flying over Fortune's Shadow
Cast upon his Head, * *and calling—*

* Alluding to the Phœnix, the Shadow of whose wings fore-told a Crown upon the Head it passed over.

'Come, poor Son of Salt, and taste of
Sweet, sweet Water from my Maw.'
Said the Raven, 'If I taste it
Once, the Salt I have to live on
May for ever turn to Loathing;
And I sit a Bird accurst
Upon the Shore to die of Thirst.'

12

Now when SALÁMÁN's heart turn'd to ABSÁL,
Her Star was happy in the Heavens—Old Love
Put forth afresh—Desire doubled his Bond:
And of the running Time she watch'd an Hour
To creep into the Mansion of her Moon
And satiate her soul upon his lips.
And the Hour came; she stole into his Chamber—
Ran up to him, Life's offer in her Hand—
And, falling like a Shadow at his Feet,
She laid her Face beneath. SALÁMÁN then
With all the Courtesies of Princely Grace
Put forth his Hand—he rais'd her in his Arms—
He held her trembling there—and from that Fount
Drew first Desire; then Deeper from her Lips,
That, yielding, mutually drew from his
A Wine that ever drawn from never fail'd—

So through the Day—so through another still—
The Day became a Seventh—the Seventh a Moon—
The Moon a Year—while they rejoiced together,
Thinking their Pleasure never was to end.
But ruling Heaven whisper'd from his Ambush,
'So in my License is it not set down.
Ah for the sweet Societies I make,

At Morning and before the Nightfall break;
Ah for the Bliss that with the Setting Sun
I mix, and, with his Rising, all is done!'

Into Baghdad came a hungry
Arab—after many days of waiting
In to the Khalífah's Supper
Push'd, and got before a Pasty
Luscious as the Lip of Beauty,
Or the Tongue of Eloquence.
Soon as seen, Indecent Hunger
Seizes up and swallows down;
Then his mouth undaunted wiping—
'Oh Khalífah, hear me Swear,
Not of any other Pasty
Than of Thine to sup or dine.'
The Khalífah laugh'd and answer'd;
'Fool! who thinkest to determine
What is in the Hands of Fate—
Take and thrust him from the Gate!'

13

While a Full Year was counted by the Moon,
Salámán and Absál rejoiced together,
And for so long he stood not in the face
Of SAGE or SHAH, and their bereavéd Hearts
Were torn in twain with the Desire of Him.
They question'd those about him, and from them
Heard something; then Himself in Presence summon'd,
And, subtly sifting on all sides, so plied
Interrogation till it hit the Mark,
And all the Truth was told. Then SAGE and SHAH
Struck out with Hand and Foot in his Redress.

And First with REASON, which is also Best;
REASON that rights the Retrograde—completes
The Imperfection—REASON that unties the Knot:
For REASON is the Fountain from of old
From which the prophets drew, and none beside.
Who boasts of other inspiration lies—
There are no other prophets than the Wise.

14

First spoke THE SHAH;—SALÁMÁN, oh My Soul,
Oh Taper of the Banquet of My House,
Light of the Eyes of my Prosperity,
And making bloom the Court of Hope with Rose;
Years Rose-bud-like my own Blood devoured
Till in my hand I carried thee, my Rose;
Oh do not tear my Garment from my Hand,
Nor wound thy Father with a Dagger Thorn.
Years for thy sake the Crown has worn my Brow,
And Years my foot been growing to the Throne
Only for Thee—Oh spurn them not with Thine;
Oh turn thy face from Dalliance unwise,
Lay not thy Heart's Hand on a Minion!
For what thy Proper Pastime? Is it not
To mount and manage RAKHSH * along the Field;
Not, with no stouter weapon than a Love-lock,
Idly reclining on a Silver Breast.
Go, fly thine Arrow at the Antelope
And Lion—let not me my Lion see
Slain by the Arrow eyes of Ghazal.
Go flash thy Steel among the Ranks of Men,

* 'LIGHTNING.' The name of RUSTUM's famous horse in the SHAH-NAMEH.

And smite the Warriors' Necks; not, flying them,
Lay down thine own beneath a Woman's Foot.
Leave off such doing in the Name of God
Nor bring thy Father weeping to the Ground.
Years have I held myself aloft, and all
For Thee—Oh Shame if thou prepare my Fall!'

When before Shirueh's Feet
*Drencht in Blood feel Kai Khusrau**
He declared this Parable—
'Wretch!—There was a Branch that, waxing
Wanton o'er the Root he drank from,
At a Draught the Living Water
Drain'd Wherewith Himself to crown;
Died the Root—and with it died
The Branch—and barren was brought down!'

15

SALÁMÁN heard—the Sea of his Soul was moved,
And bubbled up with Jewels, and he said;
'OH SHAH, I am the Slave of Thy Desire,
Dust of the Throne ascending Foot am I
Whatever thou desirest I would do,
But sicken of my own Incompetence;
Not in the Hand of my infirmer Will
To carry into Deed mine own Desire.
Time upon Time I torture mine own Soul,
Devising liberation from the Snare
I languish in. But when upon that Moon

* KHUSRAU PARVÍZ (Chosroe The Victorious), Son of Noshiravan The Great; slain, after Thirty Years of Prosperous Reign, by his Son Shirueh, who, according to some, was in Love with his Father's Mistress, Shírín. See further Section xxi., for one of the most dramatic Tragedies in Persian History.

I think, my Soul relapses—and when *look*—
I leave both Worlds behind to follow her!'

16

THE SHAH ceased Counsel and THE SAGE began.
'Oh Thou new Vintage of a Garden Old,
Last Blazon of the Pen of "LET THERE BE" *
Who read'st the SEVEN and FOUR; † interpretest
The Writing on the Leaves of Night and Day—
Archetype of the Assembly of the World,
Who hold'st the Key of Adam's Treasury—
(Know Thine own Dignity and Slight it not,
For Thou art greater yet than all I tell)—
The Mighty Hand that mix't thy Dust inscribed
The Character of Wisdom on thy Heart;
Oh Cleanse thy Bosom of the Material Form,
And turn the Mirror of thy Soul to Spirit,
Until it be with Spirit all possest,
Drowned in the Light of Intellectual Truth.
Oh veil thine Eyes from Mortal Paramour.
And follow not her Step!—For what is She?—
What is She but a Vice and a Reproach
Her very Garment-hem Pollution!
For such Pollution Madden not thine Eyes,
Waste not thy Body's Strength, nor taint thy Soul,
Nor set the Body and the Soul in Strife!
Supreme is thine Original Degree,
Thy Star upon the Top of Heaven; but Lust
Will fling it down even unto the Dust!'

* The Pen of 'KUN'—'Esto!' The Famous Passage of Creation stolen from Genesis by the Kurán.

† Planets?—adding Sun, Moon. and the Nodal Dragon's Head and Tail; according to the Sanskrit Astronomy adopted by Persia.

Quoth a Muezzin unto Crested
Chanticleer—'Oh Voice of Morning,
Not a Sage of all the Sages
Prophesies of Dawn, or startles
At the Wing of Time, like Thee
One so Wise methinks were fitter
Perching on the Beams of Heaven
Than with these poor Hens about him
Raking in a Heap of Dung.
'And,' replied the Cock, in Heaven
Once I was; but by my Evil
Lust am fallen down to raking
With my wretched Hens about me
On the Dunghill. Otherwise
I were even now in Eden
With the Bird of Paradise.'

17

When from THE SAGE these words SALÁMÁN heard,
The breath of Wisdom Round his Palate blew;
He said—'Oh Darling of the Soul of Plato,
To whom a hundred Aristotles bow;
Oh thou that an Eleventh to the Ten
Original INTELLIGENCES addest, *—
I lay my Face before thee in the Dust,
The humblest Scholar of Thy Court am I;
Whose every word I find a Well of Wisdom,
And hasten to imbibe it in my Soul.
But Clear unto the Clearest Eye it is,
That Choice is not within Oneself—To Do,
Not in the Will, but in The POWER, to Do.

* This passage finds its explanation in the last Section.

From which I originally am
How should I swerve? or how put forth a Sign
Beyond the Power that is by Nature Mine?'

18

Unto the Soul that is confused by Love
Comes Sorrow after Sorrow—most of all
To Love whose only Friendship is Reproof,
And overmuch of Counsel—whereby Love
Grows stubborn and increases the Disease.
Love unreproved is a delicious flood;
Reproved, is Feeding on one's own Heart's Blood.

SALÁMÁN heard; his Soul came to his Lips;
Reproaches struck not ABSÁL out of him
But drove Confusion in; bitter became
The Drinking of the sweet Draught of Delight,
And waned the Splendour of his Moon of Beauty.
His Breath was Indignation, and his Heart
Bled from the Arrow, and his Anguish grew
—How bear it?—Able to endure one Wound
From Wound on Wound no Remedy but Flight;
Day after Day, Design upon Design,
He turned the Matter over in his Heart,
And, after all, No Remedy but Flight.
Resolv'd on that, he victuall'd and equipp'd
A Camel, and one Night he led it forth,
And Mounted—he and ABSÁL at his side,
The fair SALÁMÁN and ABSÁL the Fair,
Together on one Camel side by side,
Twin Kernels in a single Almond packt.
And True Love murmurs not however small
His Chamber—nay, the straitest, best of all.

When the Moon of Canaan YUSUF
Darken'd in the Prison of Ægypt,
Night by Night ZULAIKHA went
To see Him—for her Heart was broken.
Then to her said One who never
Yet had tasted of Love's Garden:
'Leavest thou thy Palace-Chamber
For the Felon's narrow Cell?'
Answer'd She, 'Without my Lover,
Were my Chamber Heaven's Horizon,
It were closer than an Ant's eye;
And the Ant's Eye wider-were
Than Heaven, my Lover with me there!'

19

Six Days SALÁMÁN on the Camel rode,
And then Remembrance of forgone Reproach
Abode not by him; and upon the Seventh
He halted on the Sea-Shore, and beheld
An Ocean Boundless as the Heaven above,
That, reaching its Circumference from Kaf
To Kaf, down to the back of GAU and MAHI *
Descended, and its Stars were Creature's Eyes.
The Face of it was as it were a Range
Of Moving Mountains; or as endless Hosts
Of Camels trooping from all quarters up,
Furious, with the Foam upon their Lips.

* The Bull and Fish—the lowest substantial base of earth. 'He first made the mountains; then cleared the face of the Earth from Sea; then fixed it fast on Gau; Gau on Mahi; and Mahi on Air and Air on what? on NOTHING; Nothing upon Nothing, all is Nothing—Enough!' Attár; quoted in De Sacy's Pendnamah, xxxv.

In it innumerable glittering Fish
Like Jewels polish-sharp, to the sharp Eye
But for an Instant visible, glancing through
As Silver Scissors Slice a blue Brocade;
Though were the Dragon from its Hollow roused,
THE DRAGON of the Stars * would stare Aghast.
SALÁMÁN eyes the Sea, and cast about
To Cross it—and forthwith upon the Shore
Devised a Shallop like a crescent Moon,
Wherein the Sun and Moon in Happy Hour
Entered as into some Celestial Sign;
That, figured like a Bow, but Arrow-like
In Flight, was feathered with a little Sail,
And, pitcht upon the Water like a Duck,
So with her Bosom sped to her Desire.

When they had sailed their Vessel for a Moon
And marred their Beauty with the Wind o' the Sea,
Suddenly in mid-Sea revealed itself
An Isle, beyond Description beautiful;
An Isle that all was Garden; not a Bird
Of Note or Plume in all the world but there;
There as a Bridal Retinue arrayed
The Pheasant in his Crown, the Dove in her Collar;
And those who tuned their Bills among the Trees
That Arm in Arm from Fingers paralysed
With any Breath of Air Fruit moist and dry
Down scattered in Profusion to their Feet,

* The Sidereal Dragon, whose Head, according to the Pauranic (or Poetic) Astronomers of the East, devoured the Sun and Moon in Eclipse. 'But *we* know,' said Ramachandra to Sir W. Jones, 'that the supposed Head and Tail of the Dragon mean only the Nodes, or Points formed by Intersections of the Ecliptic and the Moon's Orbit.' Sir W. Jones's Works. vol. iv., p. 74.

Where Fountains of Sweet Water ran, and round
Sunshine and Shadow chequer-chased the Ground.
Here Iram Garden seemed in Secresy
Blowing the Rosebud of its Revelation;
Or Paradise, forgetful of the Day
Of Audit, lifted from her Face the Veil.
SALÁMÁN saw the Isle, and thought no more
Or Further—there with ABSÁL he sat down,
ABSÁL and He together side by side
Rejoicing like the Lily and the Rose,
Together like the Body and the Soul.
Under its Trees in one another's Arms
They slept—they drank its fountains hand in hand—
Sought Sugar with the Parrot—or in Sport
Paraded with the Peacock—raced the Partridge
Or fell a-talking with the Nightingale.
There was the Rose without the Thorn, and there
The Treasure and no Serpent to beware—
What sweeter than your Mistress at your side
In such a Solitude, and none to Chide!

Whisper'd one to WAMIK *—'*Oh Thou*
Victim of the Wound of AZRA,
What is it that like a Shadow
Movest thou about in Silence
Meditating Night and Day?'
WAMIK *answered, 'Even this—*
To fly with AZRA *to the Desert;*
There by so remote a Fountain
That which e'er way one travell'd
League on League, one yet should never,
Never meet the Face of Man—

* Another typical Lover of Azra, A Virgin.

There to pitch my Tent—for ever
There to gaze on my Belovéd:
Gaze, till Gazing out of Gazing
Grew to BEING *Her I gaze on,*
SHE *and I no more but in one*
Undivided Being blended.
All that is not ONE *must ever*
Suffer from the Wound of Absence;
And whoever in Love's City
Enters, finds but Room for ONE
And but in ONENESS Union.'

20

When by and bye THE SHAH was made aware
Of that Soul-wasting Absence of his Son,
He reach'd a cry to Heaven—his Eye-lashes
Wept Blood—Search everywhere he set a-foot
But none could tell the hidden Mystery.
Then bade he bring a Mirror that he had,
A Mirror like the Bosom of the Wise,
Reflecting all the World, * and lifting up
The Veil from All its Secrets, Good and Evil

* Mythically attributed to the East—and in some wild Western Avatar—to this Shah's Predecessor, Alexander the Great. Perhaps (V. Hammer thinks) the concave Mirror upon the Alexandrian Pharos, which by Night projected such a fiery Eye over the Deep as not only was fabled to exchange glances with that on the Rhodian Colossus, and in Oriental Imagination and Language to Penetrate 'THE WORLD,' but by Day to reflect it to him who looked therein with Eyes to see. The Cup of their own JAMSHID had, whether full or empty, the same Property. And that Silver Cup found in Benjamin's Sack—'Is not this it in which my Lord drinketh, and whereby indeed he *Divineth?*' Gen. xliv., 5. Our Reflecting Telescope is going some way to realise the Alexandrian Fable.

The Mirror bade he bring, and, in its Face
Looking, beheld the Face of his Desire.
He saw those Lovers in the Solitude,
Turn'd from the World, and all its Ways, and People,
And looking only in each other's Eyes,
And Never finding any Sorrow there.
THE SHAH Beheld them as they were, and Pity
Fell on his Eyes and he reproached them not;
And, gathering all their Life into his hand,
Not a Thread Lost, disposed in Order all.
Oh for the Noble Nature, and Clear Heart,
That, seeing Two who draw one Breath, together
Drinking the Cup of Happiness and Tears
Unshatter'd by the Stone of Separation
Is loath their sweet Communion to destroy,
Or cast a Tangle in the Skein of Joy.

The Arrows that Assail the Lords of SORROW
Come from the Hand of Retribution.
Do well, that in thy Turn Well may betide Thee;
And turn from Ill, that Ill may turn beside Thee.

> FIRHAD, *Moulder of the Mountain,*
> *Love-distracted look'd to* SHÍRÍN
> *And* SHÍRÍN, *the Sculptor's Passion*
> *Saw, and turned her Heart to Him.*
>
> *Then Fire of jealous Frenzy*
> *Caught and carried up the Harvest*
> *Of the might of* KAI KHUSRAU.
>
> *Plotting with that ancient Hag*
> *Of Fate, the Sculptor's Cup he poison'd*
> *And remain'd the Lord of Love.*

So—but Fate that Fate avenges
Arms SHIRUE *with the Dagger,*
And at once from SHÍRÍN *tore him,*
Hurl'd Him from the Throne of Glory *

21

But as the days went on, and stil THE SHAH
Beheld SALAMAN now sunk in ABSÁL,
And yet no Hand of better Effort lifted;
But still the Crown that should adorn his Head,
And still the Throne that waited for his Foot,
Trampled from Memory by a base Desire,
Of which the Soul was still Unsatisfied—
Then trom the Sorrow of THE SHAH fell Fire;
To Gracelessness ungracious he became,
And, quite to shatter his rebellious Lust
Upon SALÁMÁN all his WILL discharged, †
And lo! SALÁMÁN to his Mistress turn'd
But could not reach her—looked and looked again
And palpitated toward her—but in Vain!
Of Misery! What to the Bankrupt worse
Than Gold he cannot reach! To one athirst
Than Fountain to the Eye that Lip forbid!
Or than Heaven opened to the Eyes in Hell!-

* One Story is that Khusrau had promised if Firhád cut through a mountain, and brought a stream through, Shírín should be his. Firhád was on the point of achieving his Work when Khusrau sent an Old Woman (here, perhaps, purposely confounded with Fate) to tell him Shírin was dead: whereon Firhád threw himself headlong from the Rock. The Sculpture at Beysitún (or Besitún) where Rawlinson has deciphered Darius and Xerxes, was traditionally called Firhád's.

† He Mesmerises Him!—See also further on this Power of the Will in Sections xxiii. and xxvi.

Yet, when SALÁMÁN Anguish was extreme,
The Door of Mercy open'd in his Face;
He saw and knew his Father's Hand outstretch
To lift him from Perdition—timidly,
Timidly tow'rd his Father's Face his own
He lifted, Pardon-pleading, Crime-confest,
As the stray Bird one day will find her Nest.

A Disciple asked a Master,
'By what Token should a Father
Vouch for his reputed Son?'
Said the Master—'By the Stripling,
Howsoever Late or Early,
Like to the reputed Father
Growing—whether Wise or Foolish.'

'Lo the disregarded Darnel
With itself adorns the Wheat-field,
And for all the Early Season
Satisfies the Farmer's Eye;
But come once the Hour of Harvest,
And another Grain shall answer,
"Darnel and no Wheat, am I."'

22

When THE SHAH saw SALÁMÁN's face again,
And breath'd the Breath of Reconciliation,
He laid the hand of Love upon his Shoulder,
The Kiss of Welcome on his Cheek, and said,
'Oh Thou, who lost, Love's Banquet lost its Salt,
And Mankind's Eye its Pupil!—Thy Return
Is as another Sun to Heaven; a new
Rose blooming in the Garden of the Soul.

Arise, Oh Moon of Majesty unwaned!
The Court of the Horizon is thy Court,
Thy Kingdom is the Kingdom of the World!—
Lo! Throne and Crown await Thee—Throne and Crown
Without thy Impress but uncurrent Gold,
Not to be stamped by one not Worthy Them;
Behold! The Rebel's Face is at thy Door;
Let him not triumph—let the Wicked dread
The Throne under thy Feet, the Crown upon thy Head.
Oh Spurn them not behind Thee! Oh my Son,
Wipe Thou the Woman's Henna from thy Hand:
Withdraw Thee from the Minion who from Thee
Dominion draws; * the Time is come to choose
Thy Mistress or the World to hold or lose.'

23

Four are the Signs of Kingly Aptitude:
Wise Head—clean Heart—strong Arm—and open Hand.
Wise is He not—Continent cannot be—
Who binds himself to an unworthy Lust;
Nor Valiant; who submits to a weak Woman;
Nor Liberal, who cannot draw his Hand
From that in which so basely he is busied
And of these Four who misses All or One
Is not the Bridegroom of Dominion.

Ah the poor Lover!—In the changing Hands
Of Day and Night no wretcheder than He!
No Arrow from the Bow of Evil Fate
But reaches Him—one Dagger at his Throat
Another comes to wound him from behind.

* '*Shah*' and '*Sháhid*' (Mistress); a sort of Punning the Persian Poets are fond of.

Wounded by Love—then wounded by reproof
Of Loving—and, scarce stancht the Blood of Shame
By flying his Love—then, worst of all,
Love's back-blow of Revenge for having fled!
SALÁMÁN heard—he rent the Robe of Peace—
He came to Loathe his Life and long for Death,
(For better Death itself than Life in Death)—
He turn's his face with ABSÁL to the Desert—
Enter'd the deadly Plain; Branch upon Branch
Cut down and gather'd in a lofty pile
And fired. They look'd upon the Flames, those Two—
They look'd, and they rejoiced; and hand in hand
They Sprang into the Fire. THE SHAH who saw,
In secret all had ordered; and the Flame,
Directed by his Self-fulfilling WILL,
Devouring utterly ABSÁL, pass'd by
SALÁMÁN harmless—the pure Gold return'd
Entire, but all the baser metal burn'd.

24

Heaven's Dome is but a wondrous House of Sorrow,
And Happiness the rein a lying Fable.
When first He mix'd the Clay of Man, and cloth'd
His Spirit in the Robe of Perfect Beauty,
For Forty Mornings did an Evil Cloud
Rain Sorrows over him from Head to Foot;
And when the Forty Mornings pass'd to Night,
Then came one Morning-shower
Of Joy—to Forty of the Rain of Sorrow!—
And thought the better fortune came at last
To seal the Work, yet every Wise Man knows
Such Consummation never can be here!

SALÁMÁN fired the Pile; and in the Flame
That, passing him, consumed ABSÁL like Straw,
Died his Divided Self, and there survived
His individual; and like a Body
From which the Soul is Parted, all alone.
Then rose his cry to Heaven—his Eye lashes
Dropt Blood—his Sighs stood like a Smoke in Heaven,
And Morning rent her Garment at his Anguish *
He tore his Bosom with his nails—he smote
Stone on his Bosom—looking then on his hands
No longer lock't in hers, and lost their Jewel,
He tore them with his Teeth. And when came Night,
He hid him in some Corner of the House
And communed with the Phantom of His Love.
'Oh Thou whose Presence so long sooth'd my Soul
Now burnt with thy Remembrance! Oh so long
The light that fed these Eyes now dark with Tears!
Oh long, long home of Love now lost for Ever!
We were Together—that was all Enough—
We two rejoicing in each other's Eyes,
Infinitely rejoicing—All the World
Nothing to Us, nor we to All the World—
No Road to Reach us, not an Eye to watch—
All Day we whisper'd in each other's Ears
All Night we slept in one another's Arms—
All seem'd to our Desire, as if the Wand
Of unjust Fortune were for once too short
Oh would to God that when I lit that Pyre
The Flame had left Thee Living and me Dead,
Not Living worse than Dead, deprived of Thee!

* When the Cloud of Spring beheld the evil disposition of Time, Its Weeping fell upon the Jessamine and Hyacinth and Wild Rose.'—*Hafiz.*

Oh were I but with Thee!—at any Cost
Stript of this terrible self Solitude!
Oh but with Thee Annihilation—lost,
Or in Eternal Intercourse renew'd!'

Slumber drunk an Arab in the
Desert off his Camel tumbled,
Who the lighter of her Burden
Ran upon her Road rejoicing.
When the Arab woke at Morning,
Rubb'd his Eyes and look'd about him—
'Oh my Camel! Oh my Camel!'
Quoth he, 'Camel of my Soul!—
That lost with Her I lost might be,
Or found, She might be found with Me!'

25

When in the Plight THE SHAH SALÁMÁN saw,
His Soul was struck with Anguish, and the Vein
Of Life within was strangled—what to do
He knew not. Then he turned him to THE SAGE—
'Oh Altar of the World, to whom Mankind
Directs the Face of Prayer in Weal or Woe,
Nothing but Wisdom can untie the Knot;
And art thou not the Wisdom of the World,
The Master Key of all its Difficulties?
ABSÁL is perisht; and because of Her,
SALÁMÁN dedicates his Life to Sorrow;
I cannot bring back Her, nor comfort Him.
Lo, I have said! My Sorrow is before Thee;
From thy far-reaching Wisdom help Thou Me
Fast in the Hand of Sorrow! Help Thou Me,

For I am very wretched!' Then THE SAGE—
'Oh Thou that err'st not from the Road of right,
If but SALÁMÁN have not broke my Bond,
Nor lies beyond the noose of my Firmán,
He quickly shall unload his Heart to Me
And I will find a Remedy for all.'

26

Then THE SAGE counsell'd and SALÁMÁN heard,
And drew the Wisdom down into his Heart;
And, sitting in the Shadow of the Perfect.
His Soul found Quiet under; sweet it seem'd,
Sweeping the Chaff and Litter from his own,
To be the very Dust of Wisdom's Door,
Slave of the Firmán of the Lord of Life.
Then THE SAGE marvell'd at his Towardness,
And wrought in Miracle in his own behalf.
He pour'd the Wine of Wisdom in his Cup,
He laid the Dew of Peace upon his lips;
And when Love return'd to Memory,
And broke in passion from his Lips, THE SAGE,
Under whose waxing WILL Existence rose
Responsive, and relaxing waned again,
Raising a Phantom image of ABSÁL,
Set it awhile before SALÁMÁN's Eyes,
Till, having sow'd the Seed of Quiet there,
It went again down to Annihilation
But ever, for the Sum of his discourse,
THE SAGE would tell of a Celestial Love;
'ZUHRAH,' * he said, 'the Lustre of the Stars—
'Fore whom the Beauty of the Brightest wanes;

* The Planetary and Celestial Venus.

Who were she to reveal her perfect Beauty,
The Sun and Moon would craze; ZUHRAH,' he said,
The Sweetness of the Banquet—none in Song
Like Her—her Harp filling the Ear of Heaven,
That Dervish-dances to her Harmony.'

SALÁMÁN listen'd and inclin'd—again
Repeated, Inclination ever grew;
Until THE SAGE beholding in his Soul
The Spirit * quicken, so effectually
With ZUHRAH wrought, that she reveal'd herself
In her Pure Beauty to SALÁMÁN's Soul,
And washing ABSÁL's Image from his Breast,
There reign'd instead. Celestial Beauty seen,
He left the Earthly; and, one come to know
Eternal Love, he let the Mortal go.

27

The Crown of Empire how supreme a lot!
The Throne of the Sultán how high!—But not
For All—None but the Heaven-ward Foot may dare
To mount—The Head that touches Heaven to wear!
When the Belov'd of Royal Augury
Was rescued from the Bondage of ABSÁL,
Then he arose, and shaking off the Dust
Of that lost Travel, girded up his Heart,
And look'd with undefiled Robe to Heaven.
Then was his head ready to wear the Crown,
His Foot to mount the Throne. And then THE SHAH
Summon'd the Chiefs of Cities and of States,
Summon'd the absolute ones who wore the Ring,

* 'Maany.' The Mystical password of the Súfis to express the Transcendental New Birth of The Soul.

And such a Banquet order'd as is not
For Sovereign Assemblement the Like
In the Folding of the Records of the World.
Nor armed Host nor Captain of a Host,
From all the Quarter of the World, but there;
Of Whom not one but to SALÁMÁN did
Obeisance, and lifted up his Neck
To yoke it under his Supremacy.
Then THE SHAH crown'd him with the Golden Crown,
And set the Golden Throne beneath his Feet,
And over all the Heads of the Assembly,
And in the Ears of all them, his Jewels
With the Diamond of Wisdom cut, and said:—

28

'My Son * the Kingdom of the World is not
Eternal, nor the Sum of all Desire;
Make thou the Faith-preserving Intellect
Thy Counsellor; and considering TO-DAY
TO-MORROW's seed-field, ere That come to bear,
Sow with the Harvest of Eternity
All Work with Wisdom hath to do—by that
Stampt current only; what Thyself to do
Art wise that DO; what not, consult the Wise.
Turn not thy Face away from the old Ways,
That were the Canon of the Kings of Old;
Nor cloud with Tyranny the Glass of Justice;
But rather strive that all Confusion

* One sees Jámí taking Advantage of his Allegorical Shah to read a Lesson to the Real—whose Ears Advice, unlike Praise, scarce ever reached unless obliquely. The Warning (and doubtless with good Reason) is principally aimed at the Minister.

Change by thy Justice to its opposite.
In whatsoever Thou shalt Take or Give,
Look to the HOW; Giving and Taking still,
Not by the backward Counsel of the Godless,
But by the Law of FAITH increase and Give.
Drain not thy People's purse—the Tyranny
Which Thee enriches at thy Subjects' cost,
Awhile shall make Thee strong; but in the End,
Shall bow thy Neck beneath a Double Burden.
The Tyrant goes to Hell—follow not Him—
Become not Thou the Fuel of its Fires.
Thou art a Shepherd and thy Flock the People,
To save and not destroy; nor at their Loss
To lift Thyself above the Shepherd's calling—
For which is for the other, Flock or Shepherd?
And join with Thee true Men to keep the Flock—
Dogs, if you will—but Trusty—head in leash,
Whose teeth are for the Wolf, not for the Lamb,
And least of all the Wolf's Accomplices,
Their Jaws blood-dripping from the Tyrant's Shambles.
For Shahs must have Vizírs—but be the Wise
And Trusty—knowing well the Realm's Estate—
(For who eats Profit of a Fool? and least
A wise King girdled by a Foolish Council—)
Knowing how far to Shah and Subject bound
On either Hand—not by Extortion,
Nor Usury wrung from the People's purse,
Their Masters and Their own Estates (to whom
Enough is apt enough to make them Rebel)
Feeding to such a surplus as feeds Hell.
Proper in Soul and Body be They—pitiful
To Poverty—hospitable to the Saint—
Their sweet Access a Salve to wounded Hearts,

Their Vengeance terrible to the Evil Doer,
Thy Heralds through the Country, bringing Thee
Report of Good or Ill—which to confirm
By thy peculiar Eye—and least of all
Suffering Accuser also to be Judge—
By surest Steps builds up Prosperity.'

29

EPILOGUE

Under the Outward Form of any Story
An inner Meaning lies—This Story now
Completed, do Thou of its Mystery
(Whereto the Wise hath found himself a way)
Have thy Desire—No Tale of *I* and *THOU*,
Though *I* and *THOU* be its Interpreters *
What signifies THE SHAH? and what THE SAGE?
And what SALÁMÁN not of Woman born?
And what ABSÁL who drew him to Desire?
And what THE KINGDOM that waited him
When he had drawn his garment from her hand?
What means THE FIERY PILE? and what THE SEA?
And what that Heavenly ZUHRAH who at last
Clear'd ABSÁL from the Mirror of his Soul?
Learn part by part the Mystery from me;
All Ear from Head to Foot and Understanding be

30

The Incomparable Creator, when this World
He did create, created First of All
THE FIRST INTELLIGENCE †—First of a Chain

* The story is of *Generals*, though enacted by *Particulars*.

† 'These intelligences are only another form of the Neo-Platonic

Of Ten Intelligences, of which the Last
Sole Agent is in this our Universe,
ACTIVE INTELLIGENCE so call'd; The One
Distributor of Evil and of Good,
Of Joy and Sorrow. Himself apart from MATTER,
In Essence and in Energy—his Treasure
Subject to no such Talisman—He yet
Hath fashion'd all that is—Material Form,
And Spiritual, sprung from HIM—by HIM
Directed all, and in his Bounty drown'd.
Therefore is He that Firmán-issuing SHAH
To whom the World was subject. But Because
What He distributes to the Universe
Himself from still a Higher Power receives,
The Wise, and all who comprehend aright,
Will recognise the Higher in THE SAGE.

His the PRIME SPIRIT that, spontaneously
Projected by the TENTH INTELLIGENCE,

Dæmones. Neo-Platonists held that Matter and Spirit could have no intercourse—they were, as it were, *incommensurate*. How then, granting this Premise, was creation possible? Their answer was a kind of Gradual Elimination. God, The 'Ætos Purus,' created an Œon; This Œon Created a Second; and so on, until the Tenth Œon was sufficiently Material (as Ten were in a continually descending Series) to affect Matter, and so cause the Creation by giving to Matter the Spiritual Form.

Similarly we have in Súffism these Ten Intelligences in a corresponding series, and for the same End.

There are Ten Intelligences, and Nine Heavenly Spheres, of which the Ninth is the Uppermost Heaven, appropriated to the First Intelligence; the Eighth that of the Zodiac, to the Second; the Seventh, Saturn, to the Third; the Sixth, Jupiter, to the Fourth; the Fifth, Mars, to the Fifth; the Fourth, The Sun, to the Sixth; the Third, Venus, to the Seventh; the Second, Mercury, to the Eighth; the First, The Moon, to the Ninth; and THE EARTH is the peculiar sphere of the TENTH or lowest Intelligence called THE ACTIVE.

Was from no Womb of MATTER reproduced.
A Special Essence called THE SOUL—A CHILD
Fresh sprung from Heaven in Raiment undefiled
Of Sensual Taint, and therefore call'd SALÁMÁN.
And who ABSÁL?—The Lust-adoring Body,
Slave to the Blood and Sense—through whom THE SOUL,
Although the Body's very Life it be,
Does yet imbibe the Knowledge and Desire
Of Things of SENSE; and these united thus
By such a Tie God only can unloose,
BODY AND SOUL are Lovers each of other.
What is THE SEA on which He sail'd?—The Sea
Of Animal Desire—the Sensual Abyss
Under whose Water lies a World of Being
Swept far from God in that Submersion.

And wherefore was it ABSÁL in that Isle
Deceived in her Delight, and that SALÁMÁN
Fell short of his Desire?—That was to show
How Passion tires and how with Time begins
The Folding of the Carpet of DESIRE.

And what the turning of SÁLÁMÁN's Heart
Back to THE SHAH, and looking to the Throne
Of Pomp and Glory? What but the Return
Of the Lost SOUL to its true Parentage
And back from Carnal Error Looking up
Repentant to its Intellectual Throne.

What is THE FIRE?—Ascetic Discipline,
That burns away the Animal Alloy
Till all the Dross of MATTER be consumed,
And the Essential Soul, its raiment clean

Of Mortal Taint, be left. But for as much
As any Life-long Habit so consumed,
May well recur a Pang of what is lost,
Therefore THE SAGE set in SALÁMÁN's Eyes
A Soothing Phantom of the Past, but still
Told of a Better Venus, till his Soul
She fill'd, and blotted out his Mortal Love
For what is ZUHRAH?—That Divine Perfector
Wherewith the Soul inspired and all arrayed
In Intellectual Light is Royal blest,
And mounts THE THRONE, and wears THE CROWN, and Reigns,
Lord of the Empire of Humanity.

This is the Meaning of This Mystery,
Which to know wholly ponder in thy Heart,
Till all its ancient Secret be enlarged
Enough—The written Summary I close,
And set my Seal:

THE TRUTH GOD ONLY KNOWS

APPENDIX

WHAT follows concerning the Royal Game of Chúgán comes from the Appendix to Vol. I of Sir William Ouseley's Travels in the East.

Firdúsi tells of Siavesh and his Iranian (Persian) Heroes astonishing AFRASIAB of TURÁN with their Skill at this Game 600 years before Christ; and GUSHTASP (Hystaspes), to the sound of Drum and Trumpet, drives the Ball Invisible with his Blow. Nizámi sets Shírín and her Maidens playing at it, against her King, Khusrau Parviz and his Ministers:

> *'On one side was the Moon and her Stars,*
> *On the other THE SHAH and his Firmánbearers.'*

Ousely however (allowing for Poetic License) believes the Game was played 'through almost every Reign of the Sassanian Dynasty—as much esteemed by the Mohammedan Kings as by their Fire-worshipping Predecessors.'

'We find the Greek Emperor Manuel Commenus, with his Byzantine Princes and Nobles, enjoying this Amusement on Horseback in the 12th Century; the Wooden Ball having been exchanged for one more soft; form'd of stuff'd Leather; and the Stick, or Wand, instead of a Hammer-like Head, terminating in a Hoop; which, as our Battledores or Tennis-rackets, presented to the Ball a reticulated space. This Imperial sport is well described by the Historian Cinnamus, who probably was a Spectator.' It went by the slightly altered name Tsukanisterium—which word, however, since Chúgán means the Bandy-stick employed, more properly signifies, I suppose, the Ground played on; and equally related to the Persian, had they chosen to affix, as so often, the verb common to themselves, the Greeks, the Latins, and us, and called the place of Exercise Chúgán *istan;* or, Chúgán-stand.

Piétro della Valle who saw it played in Shah Abbás' time (1618), calls it 'Pallamaglio,' and found both game and Name subsisting in the Florentine 'Calcio'—only that the Florentine played a-foot, and the Persian 'piu nobilement à Cavallo.' The Spanish Jesuit Ovalle found it also (also on Foot) under the name of 'Chueca,' in South America, in 1646.

Ducange finds Name and Game also in the 'Chicane' of Languedoc, from which he naturally thinks it is borrowed; not daring to push Derivation to the English word 'Chiquen,' he says, 'qui signifie un Poullet; en sorte que "Chiquaner" serait imiter les Poullets qui ont contame de courir les ans après les autres pour arracher les morceaux du Bec,' etc.

Englishmen know the Game well (on Foot too, and with such Leather Balls as the Persians perhaps knew not how to harden), under many forms and Names—Golf, Stow-ball, Shinty, Hockey, Bandy, etc.

The Sticks or Bats were (as Chardin and others report) so short as to cause the Rider to stoop below the saddle-bow to strike; which, with the Horse going full Gallop, was Great part of the Difficulty. And Tabri describes Events in the Eighth Century (just before his own Time) when Harun Alraschid was still little so that when on Horseback, 'he could not reach to strike the Ball with a Chúgán.'

Ouseley thinks the Chúgán sticks were only *generally* or

partially semicircular at the striking End. But that they were so (varying perhaps a little Degree as our Bandy Sticks do) is proved by the Text of the Present Poem, as also by a previous line in the Original, where—

The Realm of Existence is the space of his Meidan,
The Ball of Heaven in the Crook of his Chúgán.

And passages in Hafiz speak of his Heart as being carried off by his Belovéd's Eyebrow; which no Persian Lover ever dreamt of but as arched indeed.

As the 'Fair One' of Persian Mysticism is the Deity's Self—so the Points of that Beauty (as in our Canticles) adumbrate so many of the Deity's Attributes; varying, however, with Various Poets, or their Commentators. Sir W. Jones speaks of THE HAIR as emblematic of 'The Expansion of Divine Glory.'—The Lips as of Hidden Mysteries—The Down of the Cheek as 'Spirits round the Throne,' whose central point of excessive Light is darken'd into the Mole upon the Cheek.—Tholuek, from a Turkish Commentary, interprets the Ringlets as 'The Divine Mysteries;' the Forehead their Manifestations, etc.

The Beauty of ABSÁL, though Sensual, yet seduces SALÁMÁN (The Soul) with its Likeness to The Divine; and her Tresses, as we see, play their part, involving him in their Intricacies.

Page 267, ch. II., section 2, line 5. 'The Master,' whose Verse is quoted, is Jellaladin the Great Súfí Teacher. The 'King Himself' is Yacúb Beg, whose Father's Vision appears in the next Section.

Page 277, ch. VII. 'MUSSULMAN' is very usually derived

from the same 'SALEM' element as 'SALÁMÁN.' So 'SOLOMON', etc.

Page 287, ch. XIV., line 10 and elsewhere, THE THRONE is spoken of as *under Foot*. The Persepolitan Sculpture still discovers its King keeping his Chair as Europeans do with a separate Footstool. But in Jámí's time THE THRONE was probably of the same fashion that Chardin saw Solíman twice crowned on * 200 years after—perhaps the very same 'Un petit Tabouret carré,' three feet high, Golden and Jewelled, on which the Prince gathers up his feet in Oriental fashion, so as it serves for Throne and Footstool too. 'Ce Tabouret, hors le Temps qu'il sert a cette Cérémonie se garde avec grand Soin dans le Trésor Royal qui est au Donjon de la Forteresse d'Ispahan,' where also to prove the Conservatism of Persia so far as Habits go,—'J'ai vu,' he says, 'des Habits de Tamurlan; ils sont taillés tout comme ceux qu'on fait aujourd'hui, sans aucune différence.' So the Mirrors used in Persia 200 years ago were commonly of polished Metal, just as Jámí so often describes.

Page 288, ch. XIV., section 2. 'Kai,' which almost signifies 'Gigantic King,' properly belongs to Khusrau, third king of the Kaianian Dynasty; but is here borrowed from Parviz as a more mythical Title than Shah or King.

Page 289, ch. XVI., line 4. I have proposed 'The Planets' for these mysterious 'SEVEN AND FOUR.' But there is a large Choice, especially for the ever mystical 'SEVEN'—Seven

* Solíman's Second Coronation came about because of his having fallen so ill from Debauchery, that his Astrologers said his First must have taken place under an evil conjunction of Stars—so he must be crowned again—which he was—Chardin looking on both times.

Commandments; Seven Climates; Seven Heavens, etc. The 'Four' may be the four Elements; or even the four acknowledged Mohammedan Gospels—namely, The Pentateuch, Psalms, New Testament and Kurán, for Salámán though fabled *not* of The Faith, yet allegorically represents the Mirror of all Faith, and as The original Form of The Human Soul, might be intuitively enlightened with all the Revelations that were to be—might even be in esoteric Súffism, The Come and Coming Twelfth Imám, who had *read* all the previous Eleven; it being one Doctrine in the East that it is ever the *Last* and most perfect Prophet who was *First* created and reserved in the Interior Heaven nearest to God till the Time of his Mission should come.

Sir John Chardin quotes Seven Magnificats written in gold upon azure over Shah Abbas' Tomb, in the great Mosque at Kúm—composed, he says, 'par le docte Hasan-Cazy,' mainly in glory of Ali, the Darling Imám of Persia, but of which the First Hymn 'est tout de Mahomet.' This has some passages so very parallel with the Sage's Address to Salámán, that (knowing how little worth such parallels are, especially in a country where Magnificent Titles of Honour are sterotyped ready to be lavished on Prophet or Khan) nevertheless really seem borrowed by 'le docte Hasan-Cazy,' who probably was hard set to invent any new. They show at least how Jámí saluted his *Alien* Prince with Titles due to Mahomet's self, and may perhaps light any curious Reader to a better understanding of these Seven and Four. He calls Mahomet, 'Infaillible Expositeur des Quatres Livres'—those Gospels; 'Conducteur des huits mobiles'—the Eight Heavens of the Planets, says the Editor; 'Gouverneur des Sept Parties' the Climates; 'Archetype des choses créees; Instrument de la Création du Monde: le plus relevé de la râce d'Adam. Ce Peintre incompréhensible qui a tiré tout d'un seul Coup de Pinceau "Koun Fikoun," n'a jamais fait un si beau portrait que le Globe de ton visage.'

Page 294, ch. XIX., section 2. 'Mahomet,' says Sir W. Jones,* 'in the Chapter of The Morning, towards the end of his Alcoran, mentions a Garden called "Irem," which is no less celebrated by the Asiatic Poets than that of the Hesperides by the Greeks. It was planted, as the Commentators say, by a king named Shedád,'—deep in the Sands of Arabia Felix—'and was once seen by an Arabian who wandered far into the Desert in search of a lost Camel.'

* So Sir John; but the Kurán being one, this looks rather addrest to Ali than Mahomet.

Madraztam: em 5 de Janeiro de 1705

Nicolao Manucci

MOGUL INDIA
1653—1708
OR
STORIA DO MOGOR